APERTURE

Dedicated to my darling wife Anita,
my loving son Bryn, and to
my son Gareth (1966-2009) much missed.

APERTURE

Life Through a Fleet Street Lens

John Downing MBE

with Wendy Holden

Foreword by Jeremy Bowen

Seren is the book imprint of
Poetry Wales Press Ltd.
Suite 6, 4 Derwen Road, Bridgend, Wales, CF31 1LH
www.serenbooks.com
facebook.com/SerenBooks
twitter@SerenBooks

The right of John Downing to be identified as
the author of this work has been asserted in accordance
with the Copyright, Designs and Patents Act, 1988.

© The Estate of John Downing, 2022

ISBN: 9781781726587
Ebook: 9781781726594

A CIP record for this title is available from the British Library.

The publisher acknowledges the financial assistance of the Books Council of
Wales.

Printed by Bell & Bain, Glasgow

This memoir is based on my own recollection of events, many long past.
They may not always be exactly as others recall them.
Any mistakes are my own.

Foreword

This is a brilliant book about a legendary career, a colourful tale of the great days of black and white photojournalism in Fleet Street. When John Downing first entered 'the Black Lubyanka,' the imposing Art Deco headquarters of the *Daily Express* in the 1950s, the broadsheet newspaper sold three million copies a day and employed sixty-four staff photographers and fourteen freelancers, as well as others posted around the world.

Their images were jiggled into life in trays of chemicals in darkrooms. In the newsrooms the soundtrack of the day was beaten out by chain-smoking journalists hammering away at ancient manual typewriters producing copy that fed the thundering printing presses that made the building shake. The 'street of ink' that John remembers was also known as the 'street of drink,' and he fondly identifies its many drinking establishments where reporters and photographers lubricated their days with industrial quantities of alcohol.

John worked his way from a darkroom apprenticeship to become one of the world's top news photographers. He captured some of the greatest stories of the day in an era when expenses were legendary. The crime correspondent persuaded the newspaper to pay for a flat in Park Lane while a foreign correspondent claimed the cost of a camel during an assignment in the Middle East. When he was challenged about the whereabouts of the animal, '...he replied – quick as a flash – 'Thanks for reminding me. The poor thing died and I forgot to put in a claim for its disposal.'

Aperture: Life Through a Fleet Street Lens was written with the assistance of former journalist Wendy Holden once John knew he was dying of cancer. In a life lived on deadlines, time was short and with Wendy's help he tells a compelling story, full of tales that you can imagine hearing in one of Fleet Street's many watering holes. As a student in London in the late seventies who aspired to be a journalist I sometimes used to walk down Fleet Street in the early hours as lorries loaded with newspapers or bales of newsprint manoeuvred around the narrow lanes that run off it, wondering what it would be like to be one of the people who worked there. I went into broadcasting instead and not long afterwards Fleet Street changed forever, so this book is a great record of a world of print, hot metal, booze and derring-do that no longer exists.

Beyond the high jinks John Downing took his craft very seriously. He believed, correctly, that people who have seen photographs of great events remember them long after they've forgotten the words that went with them. Even in this digital age when we have access to millions of videos on our phones, a single still image still carries immense power. For John, his best photographs were in black and white. He writes, 'Someone once said that when you take a photo in colour you see the colour of people's clothes but when you take a photo in black and white, you can see the colour of their souls.'

Even if you don't know John's name or know that he founded the Press Photographers' Association, you will recognise some of his greatest work. One was the celebrated photograph of Margaret Thatcher, her husband Denis, and her personal assistant being whisked away from the Grand Hotel in Brighton in the Prime Ministerial armoured Jaguar after the IRA attempted to assassinate her in 1984. All the tension and drama of that moment in the small hours is there in an image John was able to capture in a fraction of a second with all the skill of a lifetime as a newsman. In journalism you can get lucky by being in the right place in the right time, but more often you make your own luck through hard work and experience.

John witnessed many of the events that defined the second half of the twentieth century, from photographing The Beatles and Judy Garland to the war that erupted when East Pakistan became Bangladesh, as well as epic treks into South Sudan and Afghanistan. He was held for a time, along with other journalists and Westerners, by the brutal regime of Idi Amin in Uganda, somehow emerging from prison with his cameras, film, and another world exclusive.

I worked alongside John in Sarajevo in the 1990s, when he was part of double act with his great friend, the reporter Danny McGrory. For a while John lived round the corner from me in South London. His house was near the newsagent and I bumped into him sometimes when I was buying the papers. For me, a reporter twenty years his junior, he was always charming, friendly, and modest, never boasting about his illustrious career.

John never truly adapted to the decline of film and the new world of colour newspapers and digitally uploaded photographs. When he took redundancy from the Express it was easy to say goodbye because the newspaper was unrecognisable. It had changed from a respected Fleet Street broadsheet renowned for its photographic coverage to 'a colour tabloid full of paparazzi shots,' part of a publishing empire that included OK! magazine as well as porn mags. John hated the way that paparazzi snappers, with none of the skills he'd spent a lifetime honing, jostled their way into newspapers and private lives with long lenses and short scruples.

Like all journalists and photographers whose work takes them to the world's most terrible events, John sometimes found it difficult to slip back into normal life after weeks away covering some war or civil commotion. He's frank about that in the book. But he found renewed personal happiness towards the end of his life with his third wife Anita, his sons, and grandchildren, and believed the price his job could exact was worth paying. After John retired, he tellingly wrote, 'I didn't miss the work but I was still addicted to the news, and when a big story broke I'd wait for the phone call that never came.'

Covering the news is addictive and brings joy as well as pain; telling the world what's happening, good and bad, isn't easy but it is time well spent and a life well lived. For those who know that feeling – and for all those who don't – this book about John Downing's remarkable career is great reading.

Jeremy Bowen, 2022

Preface

IT WAS ALCHEMY. Before my very eyes, an image of a church captured through the lens of a camera and shot days earlier reappeared like magic on a blank sheet of paper immersed in a shallow chemical bath.

Slowly but surely in the crimson glow of that small, stuffy bathroom-cum-darkroom I'd been invited into as a thirteen-year-old kid, an outline appeared as if through fog before details began to emerge – the solid oak door of our local church, the rose window, the silhouettes of the trees against the pale winter light. I couldn't quite fathom that in one brief moment a camera shutter had clicked and the church had been secured for all time in a tiny square of photographic film. Its image had then been projected onto a sheet of paper via an enlarger and coaxed out with some noxious smelling fluids before being stopped and fixed. It was as if it had lain dormant until that very instant, waiting for its cue to emerge once the mix of chemicals and dim light provided the right encouragement for its shy debut. The mere sight of it took my teenage breath away.

I couldn't help but think somewhat ironically of that magical process some sixty or so years later when a doctor informed me that – just like any of the photographic images I'd been capturing my entire working life – something had been lying dormant in me too, possibly for decades, and was only now emerging to take my eighty-year-old breath away, forever.

Malignant mesothelioma is a rare cancer that develops in the linings of the lungs, heart or abdomen. It is caused by exposure to asbestos, a fibrous fire-resistant mineral widely used as insulation in schools, hospitals, offices and factories as well as in car parts, machinery, roofing, shipyards, railroads, mines, oil refineries and power plants. One only has to inhale a few of the deadly fibres for the damage to be done, but it can take a lifetime for any symptoms to emerge, usually in the lungs. Most of those who are diagnosed have little or no possibility of proving when and where they came into contact with the lethal substance. In my case this was even more so because of the huge variety of work that I did, the many strange and dangerous places I'd visited, and the remarkable era that I lived in.

Not that it would help me much to know: the outcome will be the same. The process has begun and the grainy images of my life are coming into sharper and sharper focus with every passing day. All I can do now as I wait for my future to be fixed in time is share some of my more interesting experiences and re-examine the thousands of photographs that captured them. Thanks to these often historic mementos and the stories each of them tell, I am perhaps uniquely placed to reflect back on my many blessings during an immensely rich and rewarding life and career.

None of us know how our lives will pan out in Fate's darkroom but, now that I know mine, I'm as enthralled by the magic and the mystery of life and especially of my profession as I was when I was a teenager. This is my glimpse of a life behind the lens.

This is my legacy.

John Downing
April 17, 1940 to April 8, 2020

PROLOGUE

THE BARREN Afghan landscape continued to brutalise and challenge me. After yet another long day's march across the wilderness, we finally stopped at a small fort to rest for the afternoon. The hardened Mujahideen warriors boiled up some tea and played chess on rudimentary boards they carried everywhere with them, even during a war. Reporter Ross Benson and I collapsed.

The building we were holed up in looked like a large sand castle – two stories high, its outer walls thick, windowless and made from ochre-coloured earth. The inner courtyard was lined with rooms on three sides, their entrances doorless, their windows unglazed. In the fourth wall was the only exit, a large arched double wooden door with huge bolts that were always pushed home at nightfall.

I couldn't resist taking a few photographs of these battle-hardened fighters as they lounged about in the dusty room, seemingly oblivious to the constant threat of death or injury that they – and we – faced. Suddenly, they all sat up and cocked their heads to listen, all movement frozen. They looked like startled rabbits. There was a moment's silence before the room erupted into a frenzy of activity. As one, the men leaped up, slipped their blackened feet into their cheap plastic flip flops and grabbed their Kalashnikovs before rushing out into the sandy courtyard.

Ross and I exchanged worried glances. For weeks we'd been travelling with these men across heavily mined plains and through rugged mountain passes and we thought we'd seen it all. This time we hadn't heard a thing and no one told us: 'Run! The Russians are coming!' In fact no one said anything. All we knew was that these tribespeople were far more attuned to sound than we were, so we stood up and followed them outside curiously. To our surprise, the warriors were running like hell out of the fortress and fanning out down the steep terraced valley below. Only then did our untutored ears pick up the distant warning flap, flap, flap of 'devil's wings' that indicated the imminent arrival of the feared Russian HIND helicopters with their terrifying range of firepower. As the first of the choppers opened fire, strafing the ground with 12mm bullets, we legged it.

I was about one hundred yards away from the fort when I suddenly froze and realised that, in my panic, I'd left all my cameras in the stronghold. Even more devastatingly, I'd abandoned the thirty or so rolls of film I had already shot. I was faced with an awful decision – did I keep going or run back? I knew in my heart of hearts that I had no option. A photographer without a camera isn't a photographer. After five hellish weeks I not only had some fantastic material but a world exclusive. This was the kind of assignment I had always dreamed of, as a lad growing up in the Welsh valleys. It was a no brainer. I hesitated for only a second as the two metal birds advanced almost lazily towards me, rounding the hillside in a protective pattern, one above and behind the other. The Muj were already shooting back from their positions of cover even though they knew they had nothing to match the weaponry of these deadly beasts. Even so, I hoped the pilots wouldn't waste their cannon fire on me, a lone figure without a gun. My heart was thumping crazily with fear as I turned and raced directly into their path.

Running towards the fort, I sprinted in through the half open gates and across the deserted courtyard, leaving a trail of dust in my wake. The sound of helicopter engines filled my ears as I dived back into the room we'd so casually evacuated moments before, the chess boards scattered like runes. As the cacophony of sound echoed around the room I swept up my camera bag in one fluid movement, turned on my heels and fled as fast as my boots would take me. My mouth dry and my lungs heaving from gasping dust-filled air, I sorely regretted my lack of physical training for this assignment.

As I ran from the cover of the fortress it crossed my mind that the pilots would never suspect I was British and certainly not a journalist, kitted out as I was in full Afghan dress and a large, loose turban. On and on I ran. Leaping from boulder to boulder, two at a time, I tripped and stumbled my way down the giant roughly hewn steps towards the valley bottom, my cameras crashing violently against each other as I vaulted over one low wall after another.

Way ahead of me I could see many of the 'Muj' still fleeing while the rest took cover to return fire. I was running on empty, exhausted, breathless and only faintly aware of the sound of distant shooting because the noise that filled my head and vibrated angrily in my chest was that of the rotor blades as the throbbing machines closed in fast. Sensing that I was about

to die, I half-dived, half-collapsed into a small hollow in the lee of a pathetically small tree, and lay there terrified and disorientated. Even fear could
no longer drive me on. I briefly closed my eyes, too afraid to look or lift
my camera in case a reflection on the lens gave me away.

Another burst of bullets rattled away from the Valkyries directly
overhead and I waited for the metal to rip into my body. But luck was with
me, for the Muj were now firing back from the ravine with all they had so
the HINDs turned away to focus on them and clattered ponderously past.
Somehow, I summoned up a last flicker of energy to drag a camera to my
eye and shoot off a couple of frames.

As I lay there fighting to catch my breath and relishing the euphoria of
being alive I had a sudden pang of guilt about Ross, who I'd completely
lost sight of in the confusion. We should have stuck together, as we always
did. We were a team. Hoping beyond hope that he wasn't lying in the dirt
bleeding to death somewhere, I tried to ease my conscience by telling
myself that I couldn't have expected him to further endanger his life by
running back to the fort with me.

Another angry outbreak of shooting lower down the valley finally gave
me the courage to get to my knees and look for him. Peering right and left,
there was no sign and my heart sank. Suddenly, I heard someone coughing
up dust and the dishevelled figure of my colleague staggered out from
behind a low stone wall, brushing the dirt from his Afghan garb. Still
looking like a matinee idol, he lit a cigarette, gave me a scowl and with
studied indifference said, 'Tell me, JD, what's a lounge lizard like me doing
in a place like this?'

ONE

'HIDE UNDER THAT TABLE and – whatever happens – stay there!' This strictest of orders, issued late one night by my flame-haired mother, spawned the earliest of my chaotic ragbag of memories.

As a wild four-year-old, blissfully unaware of the dangers of a German bombing raid, the idea of hiding under a table seemed like a huge adventure. And the notion of being ordered to sleep there instead of in my own bed upstairs was even more exciting. The reason this was chosen over a proper air raid shelter was that my timorous Welsh mum Glenys May Downing was so terrified of being buried alive that she rejected every plea by my grandparents (whose terraced house we now shared) to use the corrugated carbuncle in the garden – better known as the Anderson shelter. Refusing to allow me into its dark, damp interior, she hid me under the mahogany table as a compromise.

Having fled my father's flat in Plymouth where she'd lived in daily fear of the Luftwaffe, my heavily pregnant mother was eventually evacuated along with hundreds of other families. My father Kenneth insisted she move in with his parents in Llanelli, South Wales. She had little choice as her father had been killed in Palestine in the First World War and her mother died later, having moved back to her home village of Cynwyl Elfed, Carmarthen, to live with a gambling relative who then lost the family home in a card game. Widowed and homeless, my maternal grandmother had been thrown out onto the streets with her two children – my mother and her sister Vera, who went into domestic service before marrying a miner named Gwilym.

Aged nineteen, my mother trained as a nurse in Llanelli General Hospital where she met my father, a clerk in a local brewery. She first encountered him in the operating theatre in 1936 when he was about to have an appendectomy. Bored with his job, Dad enlisted into the Royal Marines and they were married in Mum's rural village in 1938, making her a Navy wife. By the time he was sent off to war as a sergeant and 'Captain of the Gun' to fire 15" shells at the 'Hun', Mum was pregnant with me. His parting words to her were his wish that she call me Elfed, a good Welsh name, and my middle name was to be Howell after a paternal great grand-father.

I was born in Llwchwr Hospital, West Glamorgan, on April 17, 1940, but Mum sneakily added John to my birth certificate so that I'd have an English first name. Although Welsh was her first language she'd been born into a time when it was thought that only peasants spoke it and that the next generation should grow up speaking English. Such was the movement against the national language back then that those caught using it in school had to wear a board around their necks publicly shaming them. Raised in this culture, Mum was also determined that we shouldn't learn any Welsh so I never knew more than a few words, sadly.

She was right to have escaped from Plymouth when she did because three months after my birth the city suffered its first 'Blitz', due to its strate-gic naval base at Devonport. It went on to become one of the most bombed cities in Britain. Some 1,200 civilians died and thousands were injured in systematic incendiary bomb raids that took place between 1940 and 1944 and destroyed more than 70,000 homes and almost every civic building. My parents' furniture, stored in a warehouse for safekeeping, was lost to a Nazi bomb when the building took a direct hit.

Even though we were safer in Llanelli, I was rarely out of harm's way thanks to my inquisitive nature. Having placed me in the highchair one morning while she prepared breakfast, Mum turned her back just long enough for me to climb out and fall head first into my grandparents' red-tiled fireplace. The flaming coals scalded my scalp, creating a patch that never again grew hair. Mum didn't tell my dad about the accident as she didn't want to worry him but whenever he received photographs of me after that, he'd write and ask, 'Why does John always have a hat on?'

Nor did she trouble him with news of the frequent air raids on nearby Swansea and Burry Port, throughout which she remained on high alert. Having deposited me under the dining table's solid Victorian girth as soon as the siren sounded, she'd stand in the garden of my grandparents' square-fronted semi-detached house at number 58 Walter's Road, waiting for the haunting wail of the 'All Clear.' God knows how her nerves would have survived had we lived in London, Coventry or Liverpool. Her anxiety about the Germans didn't abate even when there were no enemy planes flying overhead. Sitting in the living room by the flickering light of the coal fire with the blackout curtains firmly drawn every night, my mother and grand-mother would listen to the BBC Home Service on the old wireless in the corner. Whenever the snide voice of British fascist William Joyce – known as 'Lord Haw Haw' – boomed his unlawful German propaganda from his base in Hamburg, beginning with his infamous call sign, 'Germany calling! Germany calling!' these stoic women flinched along with the entire nation. His misinformation was enough to scare anyone, but my mother went into a paroxysm of fear and my grandmother's hair reportedly stood on end when one night they heard the fake nobleman add, 'Dim your lights Llanelli, we're coming over!'

That event lights up another dim memory of my being held shoulder high by my mother in the garden as she pointed me towards a red glow in the sky. My grandmother Edith, in the solemn voice she usually reserved for funerals, declared, 'Swansea is burning.' The heavily populated city was twelve miles away to the southeast and I was unwittingly witnessing the sustained firebombing of its docks and oil refinery. Like Plymouth, thousands of incendiary bombs were dropped, killing hundreds, injuring many more and making thousands homeless.

Mum's fear of being attacked proved unjustified, thank goodness, as Llanelli remained almost unscathed apart from the bombing of a fuel dump at Pembrey Burrows not far from the local RAF base. Because of this my early years were surprisingly ordinary and often quite dull; the biggest excitement being a day trip from Stebonheath Primary School to the sandy beach of the River Loughor to eat a sandwich lunch in the rain before heading home on the bus. Once I was old enough to play outside I sometimes felt to be missing the action in a war that was the most exciting thing ever to have happened in my short life. There were no bombsites to play on and no shrapnel to be hunted for. All my pals and I had was an old rubbish tip with a large brick rainwater reservoir. Bored and thirsty one summer's day, we found an old rusty can, dipped it in, and had a good drink. Within hours we were in the local hospital where we all succumbed to scarlet fever and were poorly for days, so we never tried that again.

The nearest we came to any excitement on our street was when the Lyons ice cream van made one of its rare visits to Morgan's, the corner shop – a cornucopia of a place that sold everything from my favourite pear drops and aniseed balls to shiny Izal toilet paper. Eager for one of the iced and buttery bars of delight before they ran out there would be a sudden stampede of kids. The arrival of the coal or milkman's cart also created its own melodrama. Laughing, we'd watch an army of granddads laden with buckets and shovels surge forward to scoop up every steamy dropping of whichever 'Dobbin' was pulling the cart that day. This asset-rich manure was put to good use in Llanelli's town gardens, by then wholly dedicated to vegetables in the 'Dig for Victory' campaign to supplement our wartime rations.

My grandfather Fred was often the first out with a shovel. A tall, strong, good-looking man whom I adored, he originally came from the Forest of Dean in Gloucestershire and moved to Llanelli to work in the local tinplate factory for which the town was famous. The Cambrian Works was the largest in Europe with a rolling mill that was over a mile long, or so he liked to brag. In retirement, Granddad tended his vegetable garden with the same kind of pride and also had another far more important duty. As a devoted member of that most British of institutions, the Home Guard (or Dad's Army as it was commonly known), he spent many a night guarding the town's railway sidings. Unarmed and dressed in his khaki uniform and greatcoat, tin helmet and leather puttees (bindings wound around his lower legs), he was somehow expected to fend off anything from a bailed-out German pilot to the massed onslaught of a Panzer division. It is beyond my comprehension even now how he was supposed to defend our town and when I asked him one day he replied, 'I'll throw my gas mask at them!' I had to admire him for his sense of duty, undertaken with such deep, patriotic commitment. It was this bravado and that of my absent father that I often thought of when playing at soldiers with the other boys in the street or with my tin soldiers in the privacy of my bedroom.

With so many raids on neighbouring cities, my grandfather's Home Guard responsibilities often proved exhausting and on one particular night when the sirens had dragged him from his bed for the third time he couldn't find his trousers in the dark. Half asleep, Granddad arrived downstairs in just his shirttails and long johns, much to the amusement of my mum and grandmother who teased him mercilessly. This was too much for his dignity to take. Turning on his heels, he announced, 'That's it! I'm going back to bed. Bloody Hitler can bomb me to death up there if he wants.' With such stalwart attitudes the Second World War was won.

The bombs weren't the only threat to my grandfather's sanity. The real danger lay from within – me. I was such a naughty kid at school that I was always being pulled out of class and told to stand under the clock in the assembly hall. It was a spot I came to dread, as it felt interminable to wait there for what seemed like hours until I was reprieved. I was no better behaved at home and my poor mother, who must have endured the usual conflicts of living with the in-laws, had an unruly curly-haired boy added to the equation that made for a potential time bomb quite the match of anything Germany could lob at us. And as any child instinctively knows, it's easy to play one adult off against the other so, having driven my mum to distraction (or vice versa), I could always run for protection to my Gran. Had my Marine of a father not been away fighting the Axis forces as part of the Mediterranean Fleet, he would undoubtedly have kept me under control. Sadly, I only really knew him from his letters home and as a man in uniform in the centre of a sepia photograph of their wedding day that took pride of place on top of the mantelpiece.

It was left to poor Granddad to try to exert some authority over his feral grandson as I roamed the streets with my friends, pinched the odd stick of rhubarb from a garden, sat on the steps of a Sunday church service to listen to the choir, or daydreamed in class, failing to get my grades. The moment the old man raised his hand to give me the whack I almost certainly deserved, though, the women of the house would leap to my defence, shouting, 'No, Fred! You'll hurt the boy with those big hands of yours!' They were damn right, as they were like shovels. Thwarted, Granddad would explode with frustration and either march to the South Star public house to cool off with a pint, an establishment Grandma had a strong aversion to on account of its landlady Mrs Jenkins, always described as 'very tidy'. If not there, then he would take himself off to the garage at the bottom of the garden.

This was my grandfather's oasis of sanity. After yet another skirmish between us, he retired there one day to tinker with his Flying Standard, a vehicle that received all his loving care despite the fact it could never go anywhere due to petrol rationing. Having won the first round in our ongoing war of wits, in a moment of complete madness I decided to push Granddad still further. Intoxicated by my victory and full of childish mischief, I crept up to the garage door and slipped the outside bolt as quietly as I could, locking him in.

He must have heard the sound because, in a low and distinctly menacing voice, he growled, 'Open the door, John. Now!'

Before I could stop them, the words somehow fell out of my mouth and I found myself echoing my grandmother with: 'Say please.'

His roar of anger must have been heard three miles away before he launched himself at the door with such force that I thought he was going to come clean through it. Thank God for pre-war building standards. Unfortunately for him, the impact of his assault against solid wood brought a tin of Zebo grate blacking tumbling down from an upper shelf, dislodging the lid and depositing its indelible graphite gel across the bonnet of his beloved car. The language that emitted from the other side of the woodwork – fortissimo – would have made Mussolini blanch. By this time I was in full panic mode. What the hell could I do? My first thought was to wait until Granddad cooled down. Mistake. This had quite the reverse effect and as his volume reached epic levels I realised there was only one thing for it, to slip the bolt and release the geriatric God of War.

Getting on my proverbial starting blocks, I leaned forward and in one movement unlocked the door before fleeing as fast as I could. Granddad was out of the garage like a rocket, his sixty-four-year-old legs propelled by pure rage. I still had the edge on him though, for I was fuelled by terror (with a turbo boost of lunchtime cabbage). I cornered the leeks in his vegetable garden at breakneck speed, accelerated past the carrots, straightened up between the potatoes for the home sprint down the path to the house, shrieking 'Grandmaaaaa!!' Hard on my tail and gaining fast was what sounded to this stripling of a lad like a herd of bellowing bulls. My grandmother, wondering what all the commotion was about, opened the scullery door and looked out. In the flick of an eye she realised that I was about to die so – in a heroic attempt to save me – she grabbed at the raging bovine puffing at my heels, slowing him down momentarily. It was just the break I needed.

Ducking under her arm, I raced down the hallway and straight out through the front door, not stopping until I reached the sanctuary of the public air raid shelter at the bottom of the park, a place I often ran to. It was dark before I dared return home, climbing up over the outside lavatory roof and in through my open bedroom window, famished and cold but grateful to be alive.

It wasn't just my grandfather that I irritated – there were any number of other relatives too, my uncles especially. These knobbly men with shoulders like tallboys had either failed the medical for war duty or been kept back to do vital work in the local mines and munitions factories. The noble sport of rugby was their common denominator and whenever Wales was playing a match an almost reverential silence had to be kept.

Visiting my Auntie Vera in the village of Fochriw, deep in the valleys of Caerphilly one day, I heard an unusual commotion coming from the living room, whose door was firmly closed. 'You're not to go in there,' said my auntie, in her lilting accent. 'Did you hear me, John?' she stressed, as she saw me staring longingly at the door. 'Don't go in. There's a good boy. The men are list-en-ing to the rug-by.' That was as good as an open invitation, so the moment my mother and aunt were looking the other way I slipped silently into the forbidden room. Inside, I found it full of dark-clothed men, some with faces still stained with coal dust. Tense and spellbound, they were staring intently at the high shelf in the corner or – to be more precise – in the direction of a man's feverish voice blaring from the Bakelite radio squatting there, its glowing dial blinking like a yellow eye. The rise and fall of the game's commentary seemed to have an almost mesmeric effect, like the moon upon the tides. Each time the pitch was raised this sea of men eased slowly forward in their seats as one, a couple of inches at a time – forward and forward and yet forward again. Then, with a sudden drop in cadence, the black tide would slip back into their seats, disconsolate. A minute or so later the whole performance would be repeated as the match rolled on.

Quietly as I could, I slid alongside my uncle Gwilym, a retired miner who seemed to have little understanding of children despite the fact he'd fathered one of the gentlest men I have known – my uncle Nehemiah, known as Miah. Gwilym was firm in the Victorian belief that children should be seen and not heard so I was the antithesis of everything he stood for. 'What's happening, Uncle?' I enquired in a stage whisper.

'Wales are playing Scotland!' he hissed impatiently. 'Now push off.'

I edged away a little, deep in thought. The mention of Scotland banished all thoughts of rugby and flooded my head with a guilty memory involving a pal named Phillip Swift, known as 'Swifty'. Unfortunately for him, his strict parents were deeply religious. There was even talk in the town of them having been missionaries in Africa. Just a week earlier, me and my gang had been playing one of our favourite games, which involved waiting on a pedestrian railway bridge for a steam train. As soon as it passed beneath we five young lads ran full pelt into the dense steam and coal smoke that enveloped the entire bridge and seeped up between the wooden cracks. Bumping into each other in mock blindness, arms outstretched, we'd get increasingly dirty and smelly. Without any 'Jerry' bombs falling, this was all we had.

The one major disadvantage of this game was that the bridge was at the bottom of a hill so we faced a long uphill walk home afterwards, or at least we did until we came up with what we considered to be a brilliant solution. Hiding near the bridge until a lorry came along, we'd listen out for the moment it slowed to change gear then race out and cling onto the back, cadging a free lift to the top. On this particular day we'd spotted a low, flat-backed truck approaching without a load. Perfect – or so we thought. As usual, we waited for the crunch of gears and then all five of us sprinted out and hung on to our 'taxi' ready for it to chug us to the summit. Unfortunately, as we prepared to jump off, the driver accelerated away considerably faster than we expected. As wind and panic ruffled us in equal measure, we started shouting at each other from our precarious footholds: 'What shall we do now?'

The lorry then picked up even more speed and shifted up a gear. 'We'll be late for lunch!' came a plaintive wail from a boy named Lyndon Thomas (only boys could think of their stomachs at such a time). The possibility of one or all of us dying was completely lost on us as another lad named Alan Grice shouted, 'My Mum'll kill me!' When the vehicle slipped into a still higher gear, David Protheroe uttered the clincher: 'What if it doesn't stop 'til we get to Swansea?' At that, we counted to three and let go. As bad luck would have it, we were catapulted onto a newly gravelled road. Tears trickled through the blood on our faces to create a barber pole effect as we sat on the kerb hugging our grazes and dabbing bloody noses on our shirt-sleeves. The injuries we received were nothing to the fear of facing our mothers with torn clothing – something that was expensive and only available with special coupons.

Foolishly none of us thought to get our stories straight, so each returned home with a different lie that was quickly exposed in the casual conversations of mothers over garden fences. Poor Swifty, steeped in religion, invented a biblical tale of being put against a wall by a gang and stoned. His parents were horrified. Then, a few days later, he and I had a difference of opinion over the ownership of a brass tap we'd found and – as is often the way – it broke out into fisticuffs. Somehow the tap found its way into my hand as we traded a couple of what were known as 'haymakers' punches' and it scythed into Swifty's skull. The ground rules of childhood combat were that the first to draw blood was the winner and this battle was no exception so he retreated, leaving me to my spoils. When his parents discovered that the reason for his latest bloody homecoming was a fight they jumped to the conclusion that he was turning into an uncontrollable hooligan and promptly shipped him off to a strict religious home somewhere in the wilds of Scotland. My friend was lost to me forever and the guilt lay heavy on my shoulders – it still does a bit.

Thinking of my banished pal and using the kind of logic only a child could come up with, I decided in that living room full of ardent Welsh rugby supporters that I should back the Scots as my way of showing loyalty to poor Swifty. Snapped out of my daydreaming by the sound of a high-pitched whistle, I watched every head in the room slump forward as though in prayer. When a voice crackled out of the speaker that Scotland had just scored a successful try, I leapt out of my seat and waved my hands wildly in the air shouting, 'Hurray!'

In the stultifying silence that followed every angry eye in the room seemed to bore through me. I never even saw the blow coming; I only counted the stars before my eyes. Eventually, I became aware of a woman's voice through the mist saying, 'Leave him be! He's too young to under-stand.' The next thing I knew Auntie Vera's face was peering into mine telling me to rub my head and I'd soon feel better, before she offered me one of her delicious homemade biscuits.

Goodness alone knows what my father would have made of my behaviour. Sadly, he spent almost all of my formative years away at war, manning the guns on an assortment of naval vessels and only managing to get home on leave twice during the entire six years. Due to these enforced absences he was almost a complete stranger to me but that didn't make me any less proud of him. Like every young boy of the era, I was frequently plied with tales of my father's courage and derring-do. The arrival of any new letter from Dad was heralded with such fuss and excitement that I recognised their importance from the youngest age.

The whole family would sit quietly around the breakfast table as Mum read the letter out, placing special emphasis to me on sentences like, 'Daddy says he loves you and is making you a leather rabbit.' She showed us all a photograph of him leading a parade in Greece and everyone was so chuffed that he was in front of the other men. With at least two of his letters, however, my mother was unable to hide the tension in her voice. 'Daddy had an accident but he's getting better now in hospital.' On two of the occasions when he'd been eligible for leave from Egypt he'd been injured – once very badly. An enemy shell ripped into his left arm and destroyed the muscle and sinews. Dad had to have a series of operations that scarred him for life and deprived him of full movement in his hand. He was lucky, though, for the shell took the head clean off the bloke behind him. While my father was recovering in hospital he heard that German torpedoes had attacked the vessel on which he'd been due to sail home. Three of his battleships were hit in all – *HMS Barham*, which sank with the loss of more than eight hundred lives in November 1941; and *HMS Valiant* and her sister ship *HMS Queen Elizabeth*, both seriously damaged by limpet mines in the port of Alexandria the following month.

Then out of the blue one morning in 1945 a letter arrived announcing that Dad was coming home. When my mother checked the date she realised he'd be arriving from London that night or on the milk train first thing the following morning. Nothing I had ever seen matched the excitement in the house that day. Grandma and Mum went into overdrive – dusting, polishing and washing – while Granddad was ordered to dig up the finest vegetables. A full Sunday lunch was to be prepared with a proper joint of meat, which meant that there'd be 'bread and scrape' (dripping) for tea the next day. There would also be rice pudding (with its coveted skin), a dish that was always referred to as 'paddy fields' in our house and as infinitely better than the lumpy tapioca that looked like congealed frog spawn which we were forced to eat at school. There would undoubtedly be a sing-along around my grandmother's piano, which meant that I could march around the living room to my favourite hymn, 'Onward Christian Soldiers', as my father looked on and joined the cheers. Thinking of all the gastronomic and other delights to come, I was carried along with the general frenzy and raced around getting under everyone's feet.

The adults were mightily relieved when our neighbour Owen Thomas, a soldier who'd also just returned from war, called round to announce that he was taking his son Lyndon and some other kids from our street to play cricket and would I like to go? I didn't need to be asked twice. Owen was a lovely man who, when he was posted to Africa, sent me a postcard of an elephant that astonished me as I'd never seen one before. Having heard how fascinated I was by it, my father sent home a leather elephant he'd made in hospital as part of his therapy, one of my most precious toys that I kept for years.

The day Dad was due to come home was especially hot so I went to the park dressed only in khaki shorts and sandals. The cricket match was good fun but I couldn't stop thinking about his homecoming, so as soon as the sun began to dip I announced that I was leaving. 'Where are you going, lad?' someone asked.

'To meet my Daddy,' I replied, uttering a sentence I never expected to say. Instead of going straight home though, I made my way to the nearest bus stop and hung about trying to look innocent. When the single decker pulled up, the waiting passengers boarded, the conductor rang the bell and the driver pulled away from the kerb. This was my signal: ducking low, I sprinted to the door that was always left open and jumped onto the lowest step where I tucked myself neatly out of sight. This was a tried and tested practice by our little gang every time we wanted to go into town. The only irritation was that, to avoid the conductor, I had to hop off at every stop and repeat the risky manoeuvre each time the bus collected more passengers.

It was dusk by the time I finally arrived at Llanelli's mainline station to the far west of the town. Everything seemed terribly chaotic and I had to fight my way into the noisy booking hall. There were people struggling to get this way and that, some with cases, others with kit bags. I saw couples kissing and soldiers and sailors in uniforms shouting to each other and laughing loudly. The whole place was harum-scarum and made ten times worse with the arrival of each new train with its attendant steam, smoke and slamming doors. It was two hours before a porter noticed me, a dirty, curly-haired (shirtless) ragamuffin tucked into a corner.

'What are you doing here at this time of night, sonny?' he asked.

'Waiting for my dad to come home.'

'Where's he coming from?'

'From the war,' I announced, puffing up my five-year-old chest like a pigeon.

The man smiled gently. 'Yes, but do you know where his train is coming from?'

'Yes, London.'

To my disappointment, the porter informed me that the last train from London had arrived and there'd be no more until the milk train early in the morning. He added that as it was well past nine o'clock, I should: 'Get on home now before your mother starts worrying.' This turned out to be something of an understatement as at that very moment Mum, close to hysterics, was searching the neighbourhood for me with friends and neighbours. In blissful ignorance, I wandered to the bus stop by the Railway Hotel. Being a lovely balmy evening, many of the regulars were sitting outside, which meant that jumping on without paying was out of the question. A long uphill walk home didn't appeal so I decided to cadge the fare home instead.

Picking my target carefully, I approached three old chaps chatting over their pints and selected the one with a watch chain looped across the front of his waistcoat. 'Could you lend me a penny for my bus fare, mister?' I pleaded. The old boys were kind enough but they were clearly going to get their penn'th of fun first. With mock seriousness, they openly discussed the implications of loaning money to a stranger while I stood there abashed. Finally, pulling a coin from his pocket, the man held it out to me. As I reached for it he held on tight and asked with a wry smile, 'But when will you pay me back?'

With something approaching genuine conviction I assured him that I'd repay him the very next day. Eventually, the bus came along and I boarded wearily to find that it had come directly from the steelworks at the end of a shift for it was packed with dirty-faced workers with red-rimmed eyes staring out from under flat caps. On their laps rested empty sandwich tins and blue enamel tea flasks with wire handles and rounded lids that doubled as cups. Everything rattled together as the bus jostled us along. There was only one spare seat, next to a young woman. With no other option I joined her, my gaze fixed firmly on my grubby knees in an effort to hide my embarrassment as the workers teased me for being bare-chested in front of a lady.

Tired and disappointed, I finally sloped into our house at around ten o'clock. Grandma met me at the back door with the fiercest of scowls. 'Just wait till your mother gets hold of you! She's been searching everywhere. Where have you been 'til now?'

'I went to meet Daddy off the train,' I replied, dismay etched across my grubby face. My lovely Grandma softened immediately and – after a brisk wash with a wet flannel – she bundled off me to bed before my mother got home.

The next morning I woke late after a deep rest and tottered sleepily into Mum's bedroom. To my shock and surprise, I found a stranger in bed with her. 'Who's that?' I demanded, pointing incredulously at the man I had no recollection of at all.

Mummy smiled broadly. 'This is your Daddy.'

Crossly, I climbed up into bed – forcing my way between them. Daddy or not, no man was going to sleep next to my mother.

TWO

MY CHILDHOOD in Wales was extremely happy but having my father home after the war meant that discipline was quickly restored. Not that he was a hard man in any way, but I'd been allowed to run wild for years and I resented the hand of authority.

His return meant something else too, for within three years of the war ending my younger brother Ronald arrived on the scene. It also meant the biggest upheaval of my young life – being uprooted and moved to London the same year. After leaving the Royal Navy and to avoid having to go back to work as a clerk, Dad had decided to put his grammar school education to better use, along with the little Greek he'd picked up in the war. He went to London to train as a teacher under a post-war emergency teacher-training scheme designed to fill empty staff rooms. Once he'd qualified he found a job in a school in Hoxton, East London. My mother followed him in 1948 with me and my baby brother Ronald and then remained at home to raise the two of us as well as our youngest brothers Andrew and David, born in 1950 and 1951. She was the perfect stay-at-home Mum, wonderful at cooking simple country fare and always great with kids: the kind of mother who baked fairy cakes and wasn't afraid to make a fool of herself singing and dancing. We adored her.

Life in London was very different from all that I'd known in Llanelli. I suddenly found myself thrust into a dangerous city in which I wasn't allowed to venture out on my own or run wild like I had back home. Our new address was 40 Stockwell Park Road in Stockwell, south London, the lower half of a rented three-storey Victorian house. I missed my friends and the freedom of my hometown and I'm sure Mum missed a lot too, although I remember how astonished she was by the arrival of white bread in the shops, as up until then our bread had always been grey.

On my first day at the local Reay Primary School aged eight my first question was, 'Where is the clock?' as I wanted to eyeball the offending item I expected to spend much of my time standing beneath. To my surprise, the school didn't have one. My parents enrolled me in the cub scouts, which I learned to love eventually, but I didn't find it very easy to make new friends at first. The other boys pestered me about my thick accent and the ubiquitous Welsh lace-up boots I wore instead of their southern shoes. Needless to say, I got into a lot of fights. The best part of my day was going home for lunch as we had a large garden that backed onto a bombsite and was adjacent to another pile of rubble and an empty orphanage where I could play in relative safety within calling distance. Our few holidays were spent visiting relatives in Wales or caravanning in Porthcawl, but then my auntie Vera and uncle Gwilym moved to London after he'd retired, taking over the top half of our house so that we had family close by.

At the age of eleven I was enrolled at the pretentiously named Aristotle Secondary Central School in Clapham, but I didn't enjoy my school days there much either. I was not at all academic and somewhat lazy so my weeks were marred by homework, detentions, algebra, fistfights and canings. As a teacher on his way to becoming a deputy head, my father was disappointed that I hadn't made the grade for the local Henry Thornton Grammar, a rival boys' school to ours and a place towards which we had a certain amount of hostility on account of them being cleverer than us. Our only consolation was that we had a better uniform – a fetching shade of deep maroon – and a far superior badge that featured a macho gold Viking helmet embroidered in vivid relief against the deep red cloth. On such trivia, a boy's pride is balanced.

Abutting the grammar school gates and separated from it by an eight-foot wall was the entrance to the Batger & Company sweet factory, one of the largest makers of confectionery and jam in the twentieth century. The factory had relocated here during the war when its enormous premises in East London was bombed. The company had secured the contract to supply jam to the Army in the war and it specialised in making toffee, Chinese figs, Jersey Caramels, and fruit drops known as Silmos Lollies. Even though the war had been over for several years, there was still a great deal of post-war austerity and sweets were among the many items that remained on ration. We were allowed just one quarter of a pound per person, per week. I have such fond memories of Sunday afternoons when my parents would persuade me to take my younger brothers to Sunday school and then onto the park while they had a 'little rest,' something my mother surely deserved (although with hindsight 'rest' may have been a euphemism for something else).

In normal circumstances there was no way that I'd be seen dead in public with my siblings, the youngest of whom was still in a pushchair, except for the promise of some sweet coupons, smaller than a postage stamp with the number of the week and the all important identifying letter 'E' that translated to sweets, stamped on the cheap buff-coloured paper. The going rate at my senior school for these little treasures was 6d (in old pence) each or they could be swapped for a multitude of goodies. I can certainly vouch for one such transaction when – after considerable haggling – I secured the highly prized *Health & Efficiency* magazine, the organ (if you'll excuse the pun) of the Naturist Society. At the time it was the only magazine in Britain that published pictures of naked men and women, so I discovered for the first time that breasts weren't sharp and pointed as the brassieres of the time seemed to indicate. Male members' members were strictly forbidden to be shown but women could be photographed full frontal as long as their pubic hair was retouched out. This led me to some surprisingly hirsute revelations during tentative research with girls later.

Fearful of being caught at home with such a wicked journal, I hid it between the pillars of a gate in Groveway, a street conveniently on my route to and from our school. Each day a large group of giggling boys could be found crowding around me as I surreptitiously fingered its tattered pages, until that black day when the magazine simply disappeared, my first hard knock of life. Its hiding place was adjacent to the home of a boy named Michael who was bright but not physically strong so he soon became the victim of the school bullies. This was something I had some sympathy for as I had also been bullied – a natural target with my accent and bald patch. Fortunately for me, I was much stronger than Michael and after a number of bloody playground encounters in my first year in London I developed into the kind of tough kid no one dared to bother. Well, that is, nobody except the Reay School headmaster Mr Walls, the first to introduce me to that old chestnut, 'This is going to hurt me more than it does you, boy,' as he lashed my palms with a bamboo cane. Returning to the classroom after that punishment was surely the ultimate test of toughness, for every eye would be upon you searching for telltale tears. Misplaced bravado would push them back behind a forced grin and a swagger to my desk, where some relief could be gained by sitting on throbbing fingers.

Having known of the misery bullying can bring, I decreed that Michael should be left alone, 'Or else!' That's how he came to be in our gang as we made our way home for lunch one day. Suddenly two fire engines, bells clattering, came tearing past us on their way to a call-out. With a great whoop we boys took up the chase, yelling and shouting as we ran pell-mell after those scarlet vehicles of virility. We arrived breathlessly at the scene just in time to witness a woman leaning out of a billowing top-storey window, smashing the glass and screaming for help. As the firemen unravelled hosepipes to snake between their ladders we kids ran around, excitedly shouting, 'Can we help, mister?' only to receive the odd cuff across the ear for getting in the way. Blissfully unaware of the seriousness of the situation, we encouraged Michael, who'd fallen behind, with shouts of, 'Come on, a house is on fire and a woman is trapped!' I still remember his ashen face at the realisation that it was his house and his mother. Fortunately it all ended well, if not exactly happily, with his mum rescued and their home mainly damaged by smoke and water.

Even though he attended the posh grammar school my inseparable pal was Bob Hay – who has remained a true and loyal friend of over seventy years. It was he who reminded me of a date stamped on the memory of many wartime children – February 5, 1953 – the day sweet rationing ended. As he and his fellow students spilled out into the playground for their lunch break they were amazed to see employees of Batger's factory standing on the dividing wall throwing armfuls of sweets high into the air, showering them with a cornucopia of treats. The ensuing riot was apparently a sight to behold. As pupils on all fours grabbed, shoved and fought for the treasures raining down upon them, hard-boiled masters cut swathes through them, dragging students to their feet and shouting for restraint – a lost battle for sure.

It wasn't sweets that were uppermost in our grubby little minds most days, however. Other more earthly things held sway in our pubescent heads. Once a week we were marched to Clapham Common for sports lessons that included repeated and hopeless attempts at football – in driving winter rain – and equally abysmal endeavours at cricket on summer days – in driving rain – on the same cinder pitch. Our only light relief was to search for a used condom, which flourished competitively with the daisies. The twist came when one of us would enquire in a loud voice: 'Sir, Sir, what's this?' It may not sound much now but it was pretty daring for those pre-contraceptive pill days when sex education was never even discussed. We could always be sure of catching out one of the newer teachers, who'd go puce with embarrassment after coming to investigate. The old hands were far too shrewd and would merely bark, 'Get a move on, boy. No time for messing about', accompanied by a smack across the head or a summons to the headmaster's office. This almost always prompted the age old cry of innocence, 'Oh Sir, it wasn't me!'

Despite the constant risk of another caning we boys savoured every diversion from schoolwork and games. In a vindictively childish sort of way, we even derived pleasure from a fellow pupil squirming on the skewer of the humour of Mr Earle, the headmaster of my secondary school. Not that this was surprising, as we were actively encouraged to ridicule the luckless victim while the 'Head' poured scorn on him. I had experienced that miserable position myself more than once. His cutting wit was something we all came to fear, although in later life I often dined out on a caustic comment he attached to my end of term report: 'John is thoroughly idle, the only thing in which he is thorough.'

Despite the terror he struck in all of us, Mr Earle had one saving grace for me – he loved music and took all the school's music lessons personally. It was he who taught us how to read sheet music using a system of musical notation called 'tonic solfa' that employed letters instead of dots and squiggles. With his persistence, our school earned a justifiably high reputation for its singing, always executed in three-part harmony. Though even with this (his first and probably only love), we didn't escape his tongue-lashing with comments like, 'You sound like sparrows with influenza!' delivered with a smile like a razor. Despite these constant jibes, I loved my music lessons most of all and several difficult lines from Gilbert and Sullivan still live with me to this day, the last two lines sung very fast were hell to manage on a single breath:

We will dance a cachucha, fandango, bolero,
Old Xeres we'll drink Manzanilla, Montero;
For wine, when it runs in abundance, enhances
The reckless delights of that wildest of dances.

Music had been a mainstay of the Downing household since as long as I could recall. My mother had a fine voice and my parents had a deep affection for Welsh male voice choirs. In Stockwell, my parents threw frequent parties that usually ended in singing. There was a good bass baritone next door named Winford Morse, a proud Welshman who'd sung with Paul Robeson and who did a wonderful duet of the well-known Welsh song 'Blodwen' with Mum. And there was Mr Fava, a Spanish emigré from the Civil War, who was a chess master and played mandolin – when he wasn't earnestly discussing politics over wine with Dad. My father usually sang comical songs and my brothers and I would join in or just run around.

If not for my music lessons, singing in the choir of the local St Michael's Church, and my scouting chums, my time in school would have been marked by boredom and frustration. Never more so than with that absolution of schoolboy wrongs – the one hundred lines – a punishment for such heinous crimes as sniggering or running on the stairs. I still remember those repetitive declarations of intent, never to be fulfilled: I will not…followed by any number of sins: talk in class, chew gum, be cheeky, flick ink… written out one hundred times. Hoping to bypass the tedium, we invented a system in which we taped three pens divided by pennies stuck to a wooden ruler so that when we wrote out I will not with one, the other two pens wrote it out twice more. This trick very often failed, however, and I could never get it working with all three. So the lines had to be written the long, hard way and handed in before the morning's humiliation when the master who set them maliciously tore them up and dropped the fragments into the waste paper basket.

This felt like mental torture and I found the physical punishments rather easier to bear, executed as they were with an astonishing assortment of implements – plimsolls, books, rulers, canes and cricket bats. Our inventive maths teacher Mr Copley brought into play the wooden handle of the blackboard duster. Well, at least until it mysteriously disappeared. Chalk was also thrown at fidgety or inattentive boys regularly with the impressive accuracy that only comes with years of practice. Our science master Mr Branch preferred a wooden ruler, a good eighth of an inch thick and a yard long, which he foolishly left in the lab one morning. Folly upon folly, he also left the key to the poison cupboard. By the time he returned, the school aquarium would have been a credit to the witches from Macbeth for its greeny-black bubbling water. It didn't take long for him to twig what had happened, and he angrily called for the perpetrators to step forward.

Receiving no volunteers and unable to root out the culprits, he beat every boy in the class with his weapon of choice, applied with such force that it broke halfway through his marathon. Not that this saved us, for our enraged master simply continued his retribution with a replacement. Having got the measure of the man we never played him up again.

One scorching hot day in 1953 also remains embedded in my memory, as the sun blistered down on our crocodile of teenage boys making our way towards Clapham Common. We were on a 'special outing,' but we cared not, for anything that gave us an opportunity to escape the interminable lessons in our dusty, old-fashioned school was welcome.

Queen Elizabeth II had recently been crowned, for which Dad bought us our first television and Mum and Vera worked their fingers to the bone to create pies, cakes and sandwiches to enjoy with all our neighbours. As part of the nationwide celebrations, Her Majesty was to tour the country, starting in London. Our school, along with many others, was invited to line her route and cheer her on her way, a sort of instant 'rent-a-crowd' without the rent. In preparation for the parade we each received two rather useless teaspoons, one made of steel and presented by the Borough of Wandsworth with a coin-like roundel of the Queen at the tip of the handle, and the other minted by the government for every schoolchild in the country and embla-zoned with the letters ER. It was the joke of the school that day that as the headmaster thrust a spoon into each hand in assembly he might use the Cockney way of saying, 'Here you are,' by saying, 'ER you are.' (You probably had to be there.)

Having been lined up on the edge of the Common, we waited and waited for the Queen. I'd just turned thirteen and was of the firm belief that I had far better things to do with my time. Our chief excitement was the rumour that we'd be joining up with a girls' school, one we wrongly assumed to be a sort of sister college due to its identically-coloured uniform. Ludicrously, we presumed that this minor coincidence would give us an instant entrée to their inner circle and lead us to untold joys. Oh, the welcoming grass beneath us, the hot sun on our backs, and our genes flexing their muscles. Who knew what might transpire? If only we'd realised how ludicrous we must have all looked in the long shorts that only just covered our knees, faces full of pimples inelegantly framed by a healthy growth of 'bum fluff,' topped by an ill-fitting school cap (which I still have to this day). The girls in question were, we were told, genteel young ladies of the Catholic faith while we were the savages of the Acne tribe. Still, that didn't stop our imaginations running wild as we told each other boastful lies of sexual conquests, the details of which had been garnered from smutty books and forbidden Brigitte Bardot films. All seemed so hopeful until we arrived at our allocated rendezvous to be joined by a school of... five-year-old girls. Oh, the disappointment.

Finally, our boredom was broken by the distant sound of children cheering wildly. As we craned our necks, the vehicle at the centre of all this attention hove into view – a dustcart. No one enjoyed the joke better than the dustmen who got into the spirit of things by casting regal waves in all directions and doffing their caps. The next highlight of that long, hot afternoon was the stately drive past of the Walls' ice cream van. We cheered to the treetops, but the free samples we hoped for were sadly not forthcoming.

Finally, what seemed like several dehydrating hours later a gleaming Rolls Royce swished into view and the general excitement grew to fever pitch. We waved madly and cheered our hearts out for – oh, at least the three seconds it took the polished beast to cruise past. The Queen looked radiant as she and Prince Phillip acknowledged everyone who'd been waiting. Well, I'm sure she would have looked radiant had I seen her, but unfortunately she and the Prince were facing the other direction as they passed by. Loyally, I waved at the bald spot on Phillip's head – for which I had some sympathy. Needless to say, the anti-climax was overwhelming as we kicked and scuffed our way sweatily back to school.

Little could I have known then how much I was to see of this Royal family in the future, or that one fine day I would be invited to Buckingham Palace to receive a medal from the Queen.

My life's great epiphany happened around this time on an otherwise unremarkable day. I watched as David, the older brother of a fellow cub scout called Morris, developed some of his amateur photographs in his darkened South London bathroom. A sheet of white paper was dipped into a stinky tray of chemicals and – before my eyes – a black and white photograph of a church suddenly appeared as part of a project he was doing for the parish magazine. I thought the whole process was nothing short of magical. That was it for me then, I was hooked.

As was my way whenever I became obsessed about something, I kept talking and talking about it until Morris's brother let me take and develop some of my own photos for the magazine. Then, not that long after I went into long trousers at the age of thirteen, Mum and Dad bought me a little Agfa Billy folding viewfinder camera one Christmas, a treasured possession that I still have. From that day on, I took photographs of everything I could see and spent all my pocket money on film. Everything else in my life became secondary.

I was never especially clever or sporty and all my toys, books, clothes and games had to be shared with my younger brothers so – apart from my growing record collection that featured everything from Peer Gynt and Lonnie Donegan to the pop classics – this was the first time in my life that I had something that was just for me. Nothing had ever excited me as much as photography, not even music, and I was sorry that there was no outlet for it at school other than possibly science. Instead I took photographs of everything I could at home – my brothers dressed up as cowboys and Indians with a wigwam in the garden, my mother stirring the Christmas cake or making Welsh cawl (a delicious broth with leeks and cheap cuts of lamb), or the tin soldiers we used to play with when I was younger. I even took photos of my brother Ron when he was hospitalised with polio, an event that led to my father being kept out of school for several months in case he accidentally infected his pupils. I loved skiffle music and created a five-member group called The Renegades with my pal Bob Hay. I was the drummer and he played the tea chest bass, and I also took photographs at all our gigs.

Then our headmaster decided to launch a school magazine so I immediately volunteered to take all the pictures for it. I even did the layout and design. Best of all, at our school prize-giving ceremonies I was allowed to wander around and take photographs with my Agfa. I especially loved being able to break ranks when everyone else had to sit quietly and do as they were told. The idea of being an observer rather than a participant appealed to me immensely and I really got the bug for it. In fact, I never lost that enthusiasm for the whole of my career. When a professional photographer who worked for the *Clapham Observer* encouraged me further, I couldn't wait to leave school and look for a job.

I knew it was possible to work in newspapers because my father's brother Ron was a journalist who'd worked on the *Brighton Argus* and then moved to the *Daily Mail*. He later wrote a bestseller called *The Long Walk – A True Story of a Trek to Freedom* about a Polish cavalry officer he'd met who claimed to have walked 1,500 miles across mountains and deserts after escaping from the Russian gulags. Tall or not, it was quite a story and my uncle seemed fascinating and exotic to me.

Then, one Sunday in November 1955, something really important happened. We were waiting at home in Stockwell for my uncle Miah to visit from Wales when the news came on the radio that his train had been involved in a serious accident. The brand new 08:30 train from Treherbert in South Wales had derailed at Milton, near Didcot in Berkshire after the driver missed spotting a signal due to the updated design of the locomotive, rolling several of its carriages down an embankment. Eleven people died and more than one hundred and fifty were injured. Uncle Miah was thankfully unscathed and later that evening I went with my father to collect him from Paddington Station after he and the rest of the survivors were ferried there on another train. Standing on the platform were dozens of press photographers in trilby hats waiting to take pictures of those disembarking. It was night-time, everything was illuminated by TV lights, and all the cameras were flashing. There was an unholy scrum of similarly behatted reporters jostling for the best quote and it all seemed unbelievably exciting to this teenage boy. I was so fired up by the whole bustling atmosphere that it made a lasting impression. From that day on I resolved to become a newspaperman.

Having never been in love with academia, I rejected all suggestions of continuing with my education, especially once I'd learned about an apprenticeship scheme on the *Daily Mail* from Uncle Ron. At the age of fifteen, I applied for it and was fortunate enough to be offered a job as a darkroom apprentice in the newspaper's offices at Northcliffe House in Tudor Street, just off Fleet Street. Mine was to be a five-year apprenticeship starting on my sixteenth birthday in April 1956. This meant I'd have to leave school and miss all my GCEs, something I wasn't too unhappy about as nobody thought I had much chance of passing them anyway. I have to give full credit to my father, who supported my decision and told me that although exams were important, he understood that this was a golden opportunity that only came up every five years.

I was taken on by the *Mail* on a three-month trial which gave both sides the chance to opt out at the end. By the time it was over, however, I signed my indentures in such eager haste that I put my name where my father's signature should have been and, shamefully, had to do it again. Once my embarrassment passed, I was filled with a surge of excitement and hope. I had made it into Fleet Street at last.

THREE

WORKING IN 'The Street' wasn't nearly as glamorous as I'd imagined it to be to begin with. Newsprint rationing during and immediately after the war had reduced the *Mail* to only four pages, although this was slowly built up again in the following years. So was its circulation, which was around two million copies a day when I first worked there – less than half of the bestselling newspapers the *Mirror* and *Express*.

Not that I was aware of circulation figures as I spent the majority of my time on the fourth floor doing cheap labour in an airless room with blacked out windows. My job was to make up all kinds of toxic chemical compounds like sodium hyposulphite crystals, in between brewing up endless cups of tea. We cleaned the huge drying drums with hydrochloric acid, something health and safety would never allow today. Dense clouds of stinky vaporised fumes would rise up from the drums, enveloping us completely to make us cough and give us runny noses, sore throats and streaming eyes. We thought it was terribly exciting but, in retrospect, we were probably receiving a near-lethal dose.

Whenever I could I'd offer to help develop and print the pictures of the staff photographers who were out doing the kind of jobs I longed to do. These included photos for an exhibition the newspaper was promoting of the Kon-Tiki expedition, a legendary raft journey across the Pacific by Norwegian explorer Thor Heyerdahl. It was an interesting time news wise with the resignation of Anthony Eden as Prime Minister after the Suez crisis, the creation of the Common Market, the tragedy of the Munich air crash which killed so many of the Manchester United players, and the launch of the Mini car. The Clean Air Act was brought in to reduce the deadly London smogs that my family and I lived through (I remember being unable to see my hand in front of my face at Admiralty Arch once as Dad and I tried to cross to Trafalgar Square).

Still very green, I spent all my spare time shooting pictures and doing on spec jobs overnight for the three evening newspapers whose names were cried out by the newsboys on every London street corner – 'Star, News, Standard!' I covered a few weekend football matches too and eventually had a few photos published. Whenever I was sent on a sports job, my immediate hope was for leather on willow, freshly mown grass and tea in the pavilion, but it was never quite like that. One job, to cover the Arsenal team's victory bus ride to Islington Town Hall, was a nightmare. A huge crowd of 250,000 people had blocked the streets for hours and those photographers who'd been sent much earlier in the day had already requisitioned every balcony within sight of the Town Hall. As the 10:30 deadline crept depressingly close and I still wasn't in position, I caught sight of a group of pretty girls hanging out of a window. It took a long time to catch their attention but eventually one spotted me and after a shouted exchange, agreed to share their window. No Romeo could be more ardent in his pursuit of a balcony.

Once inside the flat, one of the girls suggested I'd get a better view from the roof. A ladder was produced and we clambered out onto the tiles and edged our way on to the balustrade. She was right and I was all set up when a swarthy old lady dressed in black suddenly appeared and shouted at me to get down. I assured her with a smile that I had permission to be there but she assured me that I hadn't. She was the landlady and my prime position would cost me £200. When I offered her £50, she insisted that two nearby policemen should arrest me. Reluctantly, they told me to get down. Hearing the roar of the crowd and seeing the victory bus approaching, I couldn't leave without taking at least one shot so I swung my long lens around and squeezed off a burst. As the old woman screamed her indignation inspiration hit me. Spotting a dividing wall, I quickly scaled it and dropped onto a small gulley on the adjacent roof that was no longer part of her domain. Smug with satisfaction as she glared at me in anger, I could take as many pictures as I liked there until I realised that to return to street level, I'd still have to go back down through her building and face her wrath. Aided by the girls who warned me she was waiting furiously for me downstairs, I eventually leapt back onto their roof, picked my way across the tiles, down a gutter, onto a fire escape and out into one of Islington's back lanes, my camera and film intact. I always joke that was the day I joined the 'gutter press'.

Every photographer has their own similar tales of triumphs and disappointments and I was lucky enough to meet some very famous Fleet Street names back in the day, most of whom told wonderful stories that influenced me enormously. These included men like Dickie Warhurst, Frank Hudson and James Jarché (the grandfather of the actor David Suchet). By watching them and studying their work I was able to learn so much and develop my own style based on what I saw. One of the basic rules that every amateur photographer is told, for example, is to keep the sun over your shoulder so that the subject is in light but by watching how others did it and especially from my experience of printing pictures, I began to realise that a flash wasn't a requirement at all but an additional option. Shadows and natural light could make a picture far more interesting and authentic.

Once a week I attended the London College of Printing and Graphic Arts in Elephant and Castle on day release. I was the top student for practical assignments but among the worst at theory. The tutors were far more focused on studio work and print criticism, which didn't appeal to me so much although it did help to build up my knowledge. Much more valuable for me was learning the technical side of things in the darkroom and talking to some of the young photographers who were working with Nikon 35mm cameras, still quite an innovation in Fleet Street back then when all the other photographers were still using 'Rollies' – Rolleiflex cameras – with 120 film. I was always excited to see what the new boys produced.

After three of my five years of apprenticeship I was desperate to get out and get on with the job. So was my friend Bob Hay, who'd also signed up for five year indentures as a compositor. We were deeply envious of all our friends who seemed to be moving on with their lives, getting married, and starting to earn good money. Sensing my restlessness, my father offered me some of the best advice I ever had: 'Keep at it, John,' he told me. 'Finish this, keep taking your pictures, and be sure to make them the best quality you can. Quality always shows out.'

With his words ringing in my ears, I finished my apprenticeship in 1961 at the age of twenty-one and hoped to walk straight into a job. Surprisingly, I'd learned that the newspaper that trained me wouldn't take me on. Instead, I was expected to leave and become a 'journeyman,' working for other papers. I was immediately offered a job as a printer in the *Evening News* darkroom but that still wasn't what I wanted. It was my father who wisely suggested that I take it, especially as I now had someone other than just me to consider. At a relatively tender age, I'd married a teacher named Barbara Gregory in the Stockwell church where I used to sing and was living with her in a small rented flat in Peckham. Barbara and I were so poor that our honeymoon was a couple of nights in a pub in Gloucester owned by one of my uncles.

'Do a full year as a printer and then see how things shape up,' Dad advised. I enjoyed my time at the *News* and made several good friends, including a photographer called Steve Davis who liked what I did with his prints. By the end of that year, though, I was desperate to break out and I tried to get back in with the *Mail*. I pleaded with them to give me some photographic shifts, even one day a week, but they turned me down as all I had going for me at that point was my enthusiasm. Going freelance, I was helped by Steve Davis who introduced me to his son Tony who worked on the night picture desk at the *Express* – the biggest and most important photographic newspaper in Britain. Thanks to Steve in early 1963 Tony offered me a trial.

At the age of twenty-two, I found myself in the famous Art Deco 'Black Lubyanka' building working one day a week, on nights from either 5pm to midnight or 8pm until 3am – surely the longest, loneliest shift. Staff photographers never had to do nights, so the freelances drew the short straw. As I was eager to work at such an esteemed broadsheet I accepted the job gladly, only to discover that the competitive ethos amongst my fellow photographers was disappointingly intense. Not only did the established staffers guard their hallowed positions most jealously, they all dressed impeccably in suits – always with a tie or bowtie – while I preferred a far more casual look. Imagine their shock when I walked into the office one day wearing a denim suit, proudly purchased from a shop in the King's Road.

When I first joined, the *Express* was selling three million copies a day and had the largest picture team in the world. There were no less than sixty-four staff photographers and fourteen freelances, plus others posted all around the world. The paper was extremely proud of its picture coverage and especially its double-page Photonews spread that was the envy of the profession. Sadly, its bragging ultimately led to the department's downfall when the newspaper published a team picture of its photographers across a full page. When Lord Beaverbrook, the proprietor, saw this in his morning edition he demanded: 'Why do we need so many bloody photographers?' From that day on the decline set in, and – astonishingly – the paper is now reduced to two staffers in London.

As the newest and youngest recruit consigned to 'the graveyard shift' (and a freelance at that), I was placed somewhere beneath the bottom rung of the ladder but, God, I loved that place and can still vividly recall the sights, sounds and smells of Fleet Street in those days. My first impression was one of industry, chaos and irreverence. From the ceiling above the news desk hung a sign: Make It Early, Make It Accurate, to which some wag had added, Make It Up. Later the sign was changed to the more prosaic Get it Straight and – to everyone's delight – it was hung crookedly. By contrast, above the foreign desk were four huge clocks reminding us of the time in Moscow, New York, Sydney and London. The most manic period was late afternoon when the first edition deadline was looming. By this point, every chipped green metal desk was piled high with paper, newspaper cuttings and reference books amid teetering files, overflowing ashtrays and dirty coffee cups, while phones rang off the hook and there was a constant staccato of clacking typewriter keys.

Chain-smoking journalists and sub-editors, their shirtsleeves rolled up to the elbows, tapped furiously on ancient machines with their two best fingers to a backdrop of shouting, cussing, and hacking coughs. Then as the night wore on, the huge printing presses would thunder into life, shaking the entire building. In the background, the all-pervasive noise from the tape room chattered out its ticker tape messages from around the world adding to the general disharmony from this ant's nest of activity. It was a cacophony of endeavour, served up with unspeakably bad tea.

By the time the first edition deadline had passed, the office was awash with a sea of typing paper – on spikes, in trays, on desks, in hands and creating trains of frothy white petticoats across the floor. Every story required five or six carbon copies – one for the news desk, one for the sub-editor, one for the file and so on. The last two were scrunched up and thrown on the floor, all but illegible. Years later, when we were graced with a visit from the then Prime Minister Margaret Thatcher, she was so appalled at all the discarded paper that she picked up a bin and started clearing it up, much to the chagrin of the executives proudly showing her around (it was thanks to this fawning crowd pressing around her that I never got a decent shot of her as our char lady).

Better still than all the noise and the mess and the hubbub of the office was my fervent hope that one of my photos would make it into the newspaper the following day. More than that, I wanted to be offered a staff job, but purely on my merits and not by stealth. The unions ruled Fleet Street in those days and there was a rule that if the paper employed anyone for five days or more for a week for a period of six weeks then they had to offer them a job. I knew the rule but never pushed for it because I wanted to earn it. Keen to make a name for myself, I'd pick up any reject jobs that the staff photographers thought were beneath them or were too busy to take on. The desk wasn't much interested in these secondhand no-hope assignments but it was all good experience for me. One was 'door-stepping' Judy Garland at her Kensington house the day after she'd spent a few days in a Harley Street clinic. She claimed to have had a stomach upset but I suspect it was more to do with her liver. To our surprise, she came out and invited us in for photographs but only if the article mentioned her daughter Liza Minnelli.

Another job was photographing prima ballerina Margot Fonteyn and the newly defected Russian star Rudolf Nureyev at the Theatre Royal, Drury Lane in 1962. It was for his first ever performance in Britain and their first time dancing together. The surly Russian, was probably the nastiest and most foul-mouthed person I ever photographed. I expect he was nervous but when something went wrong during his set, he'd blame everyone but himself, screaming: 'That fucking photographer put me off!' when all I was doing was sitting quietly at the back of the room. I had the last laugh because my pictures not only made the paper but were later syndicated around the world when they became more famous as a duo.

By contrast to Nureyev, the Queen Mother was the easiest to deal with – always gracious and kind. She seemed to know just how we worked and exactly what we needed and I am very fond of the many photos I took of her over the years. I won an award for one picture of her with an entire platoon of Irish Guards lined up for a regimental picture after their traditional St Patrick's Day Parade. I was shooting through the railings of the old Chelsea Barracks and, after presenting the men with shamrocks, the Queen Mum came out, sat down and just for a moment looked to the right, towards me, which made the picture. She had a proud smile on her face and the caption when published read: 'My boys'.

One of the more exciting nightshift jobs I had to do in 1963 was babysit a prostitute named Ronna Ricardo, a key witness in the Profumo affair. This was a huge political scandal involving a woman called Christine Keeler that led to the resignation of a Cabinet Minister and ultimately to the defeat of the Conservative government. Ronna had agreed to sell her story to the *Express* so I was tasked with picking her up each morning from her hotel and delivering her to the Old Bailey where reporter Tom Mangold was covering the trial of Stephen Ward, a central character. Then I had to double back to the hotel to check Ronna out of her room and book her into a different hotel in case the opposition discovered where she was staying.

Once the court proceedings were over each day, it fell to me to stick around and amuse her for the evening. I was young and naïve and she was exactly the opposite. My instructions were to 'give her what she wanted,' so I did. Bored one night, Ronna insisted that she wanted to go swimming but I couldn't imagine where or how. Then I discovered that there was a swimming pool in nearby Holborn that closed at 8pm. Hurrying over there, I bunged the security guard £50 and he opened it up just for her. I then took a series of photographs as she swam, hoping it might make a feature for the paper, but the legal department went mad saying that I had effectively paid for a witness during a trial, so my pictures were never used.

Whenever any were, though, it was the greatest thrill. No matter how tired I was after a shift ended early in the morning, I'd emerge blinking from our building and walk down Fleet Street just to watch the *Express* vans speeding out from the basement in convoy and roaring off down the street. It was so exciting knowing they were taking the news to the world and I often thought with pride, 'One of my pictures is in that edition!'

Fleet Street was known as 'the Street of Ink' for many years but it was also justifiably known as 'the Street of Drink'. Alcohol was a huge part of the culture and reporters and photographers alike seemed to consume industrial quantities of it all the time, starting astonishingly early in the morning. Many thought nothing of downing a bottle of wine as an aperitif before moving on to the hard stuff.

It was truly a time of excess – drinking, smoking, and eating. The old adage 'work hard, play hard' had long been adopted and helped enormously by the fact that there were at least thirty drinking establishments within short walking distance of heart of Fleet Street. Each of the watering holes has gone down in social history as the venue of some of the greatest stories ever told. They included Ye Olde Cock Tavern, The Old King Lud and – confusingly – The New King Lud, The Old Bell Tavern, The Punch, The Falstaff, Codgers, The Hoop & Grapes, The Punch, The Three Tuns, The Printers' Devil, two Rose & Crowns, The Coach & Horses, The Welsh Harp, Mother Bunches, The Poppinjay, Ye Olde Cheshire Cheese, The King & Keys, The Feathers, The White Swan (or 'Mucky Duck'), The Harrow, The White Hart (known as 'The Stab in the Back' because it was only frequented by treacherous *Mirror* men), The Wig and Pen, The Cartoonist, Vagabond's Wine Bar, The Colony, The Red Lion and El Vino's.

On the corner of Ludgate Circus and Fleet Street stood The Albion pub, one of the *Express* photographers' favourite lunch haunts at least for most of my early years there. The menu was limited mainly to steaks, grilled to perfection behind the bar by two hard-working stalwarts who were low on charm but generous on helpings. Olive was the taller of the two, with a penchant for foundation that looked as if it had been applied with a palette knife. When the full heat of the lunchtime battle was raging, her face oozed beads of sweat like rainspots on a greasy window. This inevitably earned her the affectionate sobriquet of 'Greasy Olive'. Lil didn't seem to suffer as much from the furnace-heat of their workspace, which was surprising as she was not only very short but was as wide as she was tall – a veritable Mrs Tiggywinkle.

Olive and Lil might have been rough diamonds, but they were kindness itself to us young freelancers and presided over their domain with the fortitude of rugby props. Their paraphernalia included a grill and a hopelessly inadequate extractor fan; all squeezed into a dangerously small working area behind the bar. The hazard was only increased when they came to serve us, for they had to negotiate a narrow chicane at the far end created by a wall and a small thigh-high fridge, well, buttock-high to Lil. She'd approach this obstacle at speed, plates held high, then at the last moment swivel her body sideways as she sucked in a mighty breath and – against all known laws of gravity – drew up her backside just far enough to ski over the lip of the fridge and explode out the other side. This manoeuvre completed seventy or eighty times a day had worn down the edge of the appliance to raw metal.

In my earliest times at the *Express* I'd hang around The Albion at lunchtimes sipping a light ale and hoping that I might be invited to join the large table where the deputy picture editor Frank Spooner held court. He usually sat with half a dozen or more staff photographers, all laughing, joking, and telling tales, including the legendary Terry Fincher – an early exponent of using 35mm film and a hero of mine for his coverage of the Suez Crisis and the Vietnam War. Frank didn't treat us freelancers particularly well but he was allegedly responsible for boosting the careers of photographers like David Bailey, Antony Armstrong-Jones (later Earl of Snowdon), and Norman Parkinson.

I deeply envied the skill, confidence and international experience of these top-flight photographers who traversed the world. They travelled business class on all trains and planes but first class if crossing continents (until the bean-counters came in). Because it was so expensive, you had to be experienced enough to justify the cost. If you did a good job, the world was your oyster. One photographer was famously sent to Paris to cover an event and didn't return for eight years. Listening in to their conversations, I picked up all kinds of tips and one was to keep my immunisations up-to-date so that I could travel anywhere at short notice so I turned myself into a human pincushion on the (unlikely) off chance of a sudden foreign. Until that day, I was fit only for trivial stories and the hated night duty – which I served for seven long and lonely years.

Even after I had been there for a while, most of the staff photographers remained less than friendly to the likes of me. Many of them had served in the RAF or the Army during the war and regarded us as young upstarts as usurpers to the thrones that had taken them years to reach. This often made for an miserable working environment, such as when I was sent to Downing Street on my very first job and my colleagues completely ignored me. I vowed there and then that if I ever made the grade, I'd try to give something back and pass on my love of photography to younger committed professionals. All it takes is a friendly word of encouragement, a smile, a few tips or the loan of a lens. It was youthful altruism, but a promise I have adhered to ever since.

Then one day, quite unexpectedly, I was invited to the sacred Albion table to join 'the stars.' Revelling in the joy of being accepted I hardly said a word as I soaked up every word of their banter while the landlord, a huge boxing fan called Mickey Barnett, ensured our glasses were never empty. I managed to make it unscathed almost to the end of the lunch when Mike McKeown, renowned for his exotic bow ties and his likeness to Mr Pickwick, turned on me and said, 'How can you *possibly* wear a striped tie with a check shirt, Downing?' It was a throwaway line for him as his cronies laughed, but utter humiliation for me.

With Fleet Street awash with alcohol, the idea of a new drinking den may have seemed ludicrous but not to one clever landlord named Robin Arbuthnot. He realised that the only way he was going to break into this lucrative but overly subscribed market was to offer something unique, which he did with the City Golf Club. When every other pub had to close at 3pm due to the strict licensing laws, he planned to stay open all day. He achieved this via a loophole in the City regulations that a sporting club with suitable facilities would be treated differently. So he rented a large underground premises in an ancient lane leading to St Bride's Church just off Fleet Street, tarted it up, installed three bars, a steam room with an ice-cold plunge pool, and – most importantly to clinch the approval of the authorities – two mock golf courses. These consisted of small imitation greens with artificial grass leading to large screens on which images of a virtual course were projected. By using the clubs supplied and striking a golf ball at the screen, the picture would change, giving details of the length and distance that had been played. His ploy worked.

Armed with its generous new alcohol licence, the City Golf Club was a roaring success. On my first night there I ambled in and, following an old Fleet Street tradition that demanded no newcomer should buy their own first drink, I plonked myself down on a stool in a corner and was given a large G&T. It was a position – and a drink – that served me well for many years. The place was packed from dawn 'til 9pm but the few punters who came in to play golf soon became an irritant to the hardened drinkers, chiefly because every time a ball struck the screen of the virtual golf course it let out a noisy 'thwack'. The complaints of the high-spending imbibers were heeded and within days the club was down to a single screen. Next to go was the plunge pool, followed by the steam room – after it was discovered full of semi-naked men and women enjoying a Bacchanalian style party.

The long suffering Arbuthnot probably thought that he had seen it all, only to arrive unexpectedly one evening in time to catch the end of a human wheelbarrow race. Secretaries obligingly did handstands, legs and skirts akimbo, before us eager chaps grabbed their ankles and ran along behind them, screaming encouragement. I won that race by 'wheeling' Lyn Hargreaves, our picture desk secretary, at full tilt. She was a bundle of fun, loved by all, and everyone was bitterly disappointed when we were denied our prize of a bottle of bubbly due to the governor's unreasonable fit of pique who then banned us all for a week.

The City Golf Club (which was also known as the Snooker Club) was the place we went to celebrate special occasions – a scoop here, a brilliant picture there, a competition won, a daring foreign assignment completed or a promotion earned. These were the parties when the losers would graciously band together to offer plaudits and buckets of champagne to the winners and the victor would return the compliment. The evening would occasionally end in a good fight with a soda syphon or two to cool us down. Friday nights there were sacred and Robin would often go home and leave us the keys. Good humour and intemperate drinking would fritter away the time as hours sped by and wives, girlfriends and families forgotten. We'd buy in a few kebabs, drink several bottles of wine, play snooker until one in the morning and then drive home smashed. The congeniality of that club was responsible for many a: 'Gone to bed. Dinner in oven' note left on kitchen tables across the Home Counties. One photographer's wife offered her counterparts the advice: 'Don't cook until you see the whites of their eyes!' Turning to her husband, she added pointedly, 'Or should I say red?'

The banter in any crowd of photographers was all about the job and some of it was worthy of a TV comedy sketch. *Express* staffer Mike Dunlea, known for being 'stabbed in the Gorbals' on a job (which always raised a laugh), was an especially good raconteur. One of his best stories was when he was a young photographer in a group waiting at Glasgow airport for Billy Connolly. Some of the other lads began to wind him up with exaggerated tales of the comic's hatred of photographers, telling him that – given half a chance – Billy would lash out. After the flight was delayed, the tension rose and the stories became even more exaggerated. Finally the doors flew open and out strode Billy, arms thrown wide in a gesture of welcome, whereupon Dunlea let him have a right hook to the chest. 'I don't know what came over me. Billy looked genuinely hurt, and asked me, 'What the fuck was that for?'

'Just in case,' I mumbled and slunk away, hoping he wouldn't remember my face.'

This was the stuff of Golf Club gold.

As time and the nights of drinking rolled on, I gradually became accepted and was given more responsibility. One of these was to photograph Louis Armstrong at a party the *Express* threw for his birthday at the Savoy, at which he got up and played with Humphrey Lyttelton. I also did photo calls with people like Raquel Welch, the Rolling Stones and Peter Cook in which we were allowed just a few minutes each before the next reporter and photographer was rolled in.

I remember photographing Benny Goodman, the American bandleader and 'King of Swing,' who arrived late with a glass of wine after a good lunch and asked if he could lie on the settee during the interview. Within minutes he'd fallen asleep so I took some pictures and then did some judicious coughing to gently wake him. I also photographed Cassius Clay (who later became Muhammad Ali) but being around him was always unbelievably chaotic, surrounded as he was by heavies who promised the earth but made everything difficult and late. Bizarrely, one of Clay's PR guys turned out to be an Asian teacher who'd once worked with my Dad, and who recognised me straight away. He was almost unrecognisable from the gentle colleague my father had known, behaving in a completely over the top way, but our connection at least guaranteed me access.

Another photo call I was sent on in 1967 was to photograph The Beatles for the launch of their album *Sgt. Pepper's Lonely Hearts Club Band*. It was at Brian Epstein's house at Chapel Street in Belgravia. One of the pictures I took there was of an American photographer named Linda Eastman kneeling on the floor in front of a seated Paul McCartney. It was four days after they'd first met, briefly, at a Georgie Fame concert. Linda was there to take photos of 'Swinging Sixties' London for a book, and Paul was going out with the model Jane Asher at the time. Within two years Linda became Mrs McCartney in 1969, so I was able to catch that early moment in their relationship.

It wasn't all film stars and glamour, though. There was a great deal of sitting around the smoky office waiting for the next job and a lot of long, boring assignments as well as the dreaded door-stepping in all weathers before sending our film back to the office in the panniers of Patrick, our busy 'DR' or dispatch rider. Any journalist will tell you that Downing Street is one of the worst doorsteps, a wind tunnel and completely sunless. Bitter. Talking of the cold, another job I was sent on around this time was to Dover to try to find anyone who was leaving 'Broken Britain' for a new life on the Continent. Unusually, I came across two Irish tinkers walking along the road in snow and hail with a two-wheeled cart bearing all their worldly goods. It was pulled along by two donkeys and shepherded by their collie dog Anne. The couple told me they'd been walking for a year since leaving Connemara and were on their way to make a fresh start in Europe. Their picture was published in the *Photonews* section, looking for all the world as if it had been taken in Eastern Europe, not the Garden of England.

I thought nothing more of it until years later when we had another change of Editor (I survived thirteen of them) and his secretary asked me if I wanted a picture that was hanging in the former Editor's office. When I went to have a look I was astonished. A lady reader had so liked my photograph that she'd recreated it exactly in embroidery with stitching so fine that it looked just like a photo. Along the bottom she'd embroidered: *The Emigrants. Photo John Downing for Daily Express. Embroidered by O Pearce.* Nobody had ever told me about it and I'd never had the chance to thank Mrs Pearce, whose accompanying letter had been lost. Her masterpiece still hangs on my wall at home next to the original picture and gives me a thrill each time I pass by.

It seems funny to me now that some of the least glamorous or dangerous of my assignments have produced some of my finest work. In the summer of 1968, having been sent to cover the so-called 'Great Flood' after weeks of torrential rain across Surrey and the Home Counties, I took the photograph I still consider to be one of the best at telling a story. It was at Molesey Cottage Hospital near Hampton Court where police and soldiers were rescuing patients in a DUKW amphibious vehicle as the waters rose to hip height. Jumping onto the front of the vessel, the shutter on my camera clicked away as I captured the moment when an old lady, draped in a blanket with her handbag on her knee, reached over to light a cigarette for a similarly festooned patient as they sat alongside two others. There's such a lot happening in it: every part of it tells a story and you don't need any words to know what's going on. It captured a defining moment for me. Sadly, the paper didn't use it and I didn't find it until sifting through my photos many years later but I'm still proud of the work I did that day.

By then I had come to appreciate that press photography was living history, especially at a time when newspapers were the chief source of information for millions. Photographers had to be the eyes of the reader and try to catch a defining moment. Occasionally that defining moment meant taking one of the last ever photographs of someone before they died. That happened to me in quick succession in the Sixties, starting with a photo call for a French actress named Françoise Dorléac, the elder sister of actress Catherine Deneuve. She was a lovely young woman in her twenties and we got on very well as she posed for pictures in her hotel room. Opening up, she suddenly told me that she was terrified of fire which was uncanny because the following day, her hotel's fire alarm went off in the middle of the night. I was on the dog watch and was sent to see if there was a story and I found her standing outside in the street with all the other guests. Pulling her fur coat around her shoulders, she was wide-eyed as she said, 'I told you! I'm terrified of fire!' A few weeks later, she was back in the south of France and hurrying to Nice airport to catch a flight when her car flipped and burst into flames. Tragically, she was burned alive whilst trying to escape. The photos I took of her in London were among the last taken.

The following year, I was sent to Eaton Square to get a photograph of bride-to-be American actress Sharon Tate before her wedding that day to Hollywood film director Roman Polanski. I knocked on the front door and, to my surprise, was invited in. Sharon was gorgeous, and very sweet. She wore a pretty white mini-dress and had flowers interlaced through her hair. At just twenty-four years old she was so happy to be getting married to the man she loved that she posed quite readily in the hallway before heading to the Chelsea Registry Office and the waiting crowds. The shots I took of her that day would come to haunt me a year later when I heard that she'd been brutally stabbed to death by members of the crazed 'Manson Family' in Los Angeles. She was almost nine months pregnant with her first child, who was also killed.

Rightly or wrongly, few people remember in detail the graphic words written about events like the Kennedy assassination or the evacuation of Dunkirk, but the photographs are often indelibly printed on their minds, as those of Françoise and Sharon were with me. These kinds of pictures are important records of a time and a person gone by yet their negatives (if they even still exist) are rarely preserved and at constant risk of being destroyed.

After each long shift, I'd retire to The Albion with my fellow freelancers Ian 'Soapy' Watson, 'Buddy' Powell and Clive Limpkin. Many nights we would stay on longer than we had to, chatting or playing cards just to be company for whoever was on the dreaded dogwatch until its lonely finish. If not for the refuge of the pub, we'd be sent on menial tasks for the night editor such as getting his car serviced, collecting his takeaway, or picking up the Piccadilly untipped cigarettes that he was too lazy to go and get himself.

Soapy, a cheery, easygoing Liverpudlian and former Royal Navy photographer, was a terrible spendthrift and at one time was the proud owner of no less than three Jaguars, none of which were paid for. His wife was losing patience with all his late nights and it finally came to a head when Soapy found out his old ship was due to dock at Portsmouth. Mrs Watson warned him of dire consequences if he went to see his mates but he couldn't help himself. As soon as his shift ended he launched his Jaguar down the A3 for the highly anticipated reunion. He returned home four sheets to the wind as dawn was breaking to find that he'd lost his front door key. Putting his mouth to the letterbox he called out, 'Yoo-hoo! Darling?' but his words came echoing back at him and he peered into the darkened hallway through the gap. 'Do you know what I saw?' he gasped later. 'Nothing, absolutely nothing.' His wife had stripped the house and cleared out. 'She even took the bloody lino!'

Buddy was another remarkable character who'd trained with the Royal Marines in his native Bristol and was an exceptionally good diver. Once he was more established, the *Express* would send him away for weeks on end covering treasure hunt stories around the world allowing him to dive on old wrecks. Tragically, Buddy died whilst on holiday with his family in Spain. Ironically for a man proficient at diving, he drowned in the sea whilst trying to save a swimmer who'd got himself into difficulties.

Clive Limpkin was by far the most intelligent of us all. He could not only take great photographs but was a very competent writer. As keen as mustard, he had a habit of running everywhere, something of a disadvantage when he was carrying his kit around in a large, old-fashioned, plate camera case. It was so heavy that we could comfortably pop in an odd block of printer's lead without him noticing, just for fun, a trick I often fell prey to myself. Some years later, Clive produced a book of iconic photographs entitled *The Battle of Bogside*, after a series of assignments in Derry, Northern Ireland for the *Daily Sketch*. It won the prestigious Robert Capa Gold Medal from *Life* magazine and is still one of the best photographic books of its kind. He went on to enjoy a successful career as a travel photojournalist.

Many of the Fleet Street reporters I came across in those early days were legends in their own lifetimes and their stories live on to this day. A high proportion of these involved expenses, such as the foreign correspondent who put in a claim for the purchase of a camel on some job in the Middle East and when the accounts manager challenged him regarding the whereabouts of the '*Express* camel', he replied – quick as a flash – 'Thanks for reminding me. The poor thing died and I forgot to put in a claim for its disposal.'

Or the crime correspondent who, when told that the Detective Chief Inspector he'd been entertaining at enormous expense every week for years had actually died two years earlier, jumped up, picked up the phone and cried, 'Get me The Yard! I've been entertaining an imposter!'

To anyone outside Fleet Street it is difficult to convey the horseplay and banter that were the constant companions to every working day as light-hearted ways to relieve the tedium of jobs that were less than exciting. One of the characters I knew well in London was an *Express* writer named Michael O'Flaherty, affectionately known as 'Oafers,' who had a great talent for descriptive writing but a problem taking his drink. Well, not so much taking it (that he could do all night long) but with the mischief and noise it created in him. Famously, during one of his nightly drinking sessions he was seen propping up the bar wearing only his underpants.

On another infamous occasion, the *Express* threw a party for the advertising sales staff at their hotel of preference – the Savoy – to which they invited the great and the good as well as a few politicians and all the top executives. TV personality David Jacobs was the presenter and Norman Tebbit, then Secretary of State for Employment and much in the public eye due to the mass unemployment of the time, was making the keynote speech. For reasons lost to time, some bright spark in the office decided to send our man O'Flaherty to write it up and they teamed him up with Tom Smith, one of our top photographers, also renowned for his ability to hold prodigious amounts of drink. As they left the office together, a colleague commented wryly, 'There goes matches and petrol!' And so it proved.

Our dynamic duo began their assignment in the VIP lounge where Tom took a few pictures of those assembled, thereby fulfilling his brief. After a couple of interviews and several shots not of the photographic kind, O'Flaherty tripped over and tottered backwards, scattering guests before crashing into a table laden with drink. The legs of this gave way quicker than his and collapsed with an almighty crash to cries of 'What a waste!' Once dresses were sponged down, suits brushed, and a modicum of decorum returned, luncheon was announced.

Our two heroes joined their table where it didn't take long for them to tuck into their first course – a nice little Bordeaux – swiftly followed by another before moving on to a more substantial main course Medoc. After a bread roll fight they were enjoying their port and brandy when silence was called for and Tebbit rose to speak. It was then that O'Flaherty really came into his own. Just as Tebbit began, he shouted, 'Gizza job!' – citing the mantra for the unemployed popularised by playwright Alan Bleasdale. The future Chairman of the Conservative Party hesitated only to be met by more of the same as O'Flaherty got into his stride. Tebbit struggled on for a bit but finally broke when O'Flaherty yelled, 'Gizza job, Norm!' The casual abbreviation of his name was too much for him. Beside himself with anger, he issued an ultimatum: 'I will not continue until those men are removed!' Security was called and the two reprobates were unceremoniously ejected onto Embankment Gardens via the back door.

As they tottered out onto the street 'Smiff' (whom Oafers referred to only as 'double ff') sobered up a little and, realising that they'd be in a sea of trouble on their return, did a runner. He wisely disappeared for two days in the hope that things would calm down. O'Flaherty was taken in a cab to the station by colleagues, put on a train (probably with a placard round his neck) and sent home to sleep things off. No sooner had they returned to the office then O'Flaherty stumbled back into the newsroom to be warned that Struan Coupar, the managing editor, was on the warpath. With the logic of the inebriated, he crawled under his desk. We were well accustomed to hiding 'tired and emotional' colleagues in the darkroom or elsewhere, but this was trickier.

Minutes later Struan marched back in, beard bristling with hostility, and demanded, 'Has anyone seen O'Flaherty?' The few of us who were there mumbled a collective 'No', while trying to keep our eyes from drifting towards Oafers' feet.

'Tell him I want to see him in my office *immediately*!' Turning sharply to leave, Coupar almost got away but the thought of him departing was too much for O'Flaherty, who launched himself from under the desk and grabbed the poor man's ankles, pinning him to the spot. It took us some time to persuade him to release his grip and when he finally did, Coupar was incandescent with rage. His parting words were, 'In my office – NOW!' before he stalked off, no doubt to issue a P45.

Reporter Danny McGrory, the union FOC (father of the chapel), bravely offered to accompany Oafers to this crunch meeting. Before entering Coupar's office, Danny told his swaying colleague, 'Whatever you do, don't say a word. You'll only make things worse.' O'Flaherty nodded and when Danny finished talking on his behalf he pleaded with Coupar to defer all punishment until O'Flaherty was in a fit state to understand the gravity of his situation. Coupar eventually agreed but just as Danny was escorting the miscreant out he turned around and said, 'You stupid Scottish c***!'

Incredibly, he lived to fight another day and when he wasn't sacked the joke went round Fleet Street that you'd have to commit murder to be kicked off the *Express*. To everyone's huge surprise O'Flaherty eventually gave up the demon drink, married an African princess, and moved to a deprived black township on the Eastern Cape to teach children. Such is the mystery of life. Tom, too, got away lightly although when he discovered that the new Editor had no idea of his name he told Coupar, 'Tell him it was John Downing.' Cheeky sod.

*

My own long journey to the *Express* took a dramatic upturn in February 1970 when I was finally offered a staff job a few months before my thirtieth birthday. It marked the end of night shifts and the start of something rather wonderful.

To my delight, the new Assistant Editor of Features and Pictures, a man named Robin Esser, invited me to formally join the paper's remarkable team on a starting salary of £57 a week or £2,964 a year. This seemed like a small fortune to me at the time, when the average price of a London house was just under £5,000 and the average salary £1,664. The job offer came as a welcome surprise, but after seven years of freelancing for the newspaper I'd gained experience and confidence, and more and more of my pictures had made the grade. One of the most memorable was a random shot I took of a dairy farmer who'd abandoned his tractor and cows to witness the launch of the first Concorde prototype at the Filton airfield near Bristol in 1969, a photograph that won me an award.

I was grateful for the stability a staff job gave me because I now had more than just my own mouth to feed. It is a cause of regret and guilt to me that my marriage to Barbara failed in 1967, but we'd married far too young and chiefly because all our friends were getting hitched. Then because of my job (especially the night shifts), we were like ships in the night, meeting only occasionally at the kitchen table for a meal. Our son Gareth was born in the summer of 1966 and, although I loved him dearly and did all the fatherly stuff whenever I was there, I'd never forgo a job for his sake, which meant that I missed a lot of the things I could never get back. With hindsight, I probably wasn't a particularly good husband or father and Barbara and I separated when Gareth was just over a year old, which – coupled with her resistance to me seeing him – effectively meant that for the next two decades I was no longer a part of his life.

In 1969 I had married again, this time to Jeanette Claes, a model I'd photographed on a job for a Scottish magazine but who, after we met, had a career in newspapers. Hers was one of the most successful stories of any woman in Fleet Street, in fact. She joined as the lowest of the low, answering telephone calls in the classified ads department and within a few years was made a director of the *Evening Standard* – at that time the only woman director in the Street. I was the one who brought her in but she surpassed me in no time at all, becoming a national picture editor and far more important to the newspapers than I ever was. The best part was that her company car was a Triumph TR6, which I not only borrowed for jobs every now and again (while she took my company Vauxhall Cavalier), but I was able to use her dedicated parking space – a privilege set aside only for directors.

Our wedding took place in Finsbury Park Town Hall before a small reception on a rickety boat out on the Thames. We didn't have much money to begin with and couldn't afford a honeymoon so we just went back to our flat in Tottenham instead. Although we didn't know it yet – when I was offered a staff job she was a few weeks pregnant with my second son Bryn, born in September 1970. Before too long, though, Jeanette and I bought our first house together, a semi-detached property in Beech Close, Walton-on-Thames, where we did all the things that newly married couples do, including stripping wallpaper and painting partly rotten banisters. I had most Saturdays off so we usually went to the pub with a bunch of mates before heading back for a good lunch.

Life was good and I loved every minute of being a dad again, having a new wife and pursuing my chosen career, but I was also painfully aware that I had a mortgage for the first time in my life and not one but two children to pay for. It was time for me to knuckle down.

FOUR

EVERY JOURNALIST and photographer remembers their first foreign assignment, known universally in Fleet Street as 'a foreign.' This was the real badge of success and what we had all been waiting for. So when an assistant picture editor barked the order, 'Downing, go and see the foreign desk', my inexperienced heart soared. I knew what this had to mean.

'What's it all about?' I ventured nervously.

'Don't ask me,' the world-weary deskman replied. 'They never tell us anything.' It was a complaint I was to hear numerous times in my career.

Intrigued and excited, I made my way across the busy newsroom, which was in its usual meltdown that February afternoon in 1971. What could it be, I wondered, knowing that anything was possible. There had been so many dramatic events around the world in the previous year, including the hijacking of three airliners by Palestinian terrorists, a tidal wave that killed 150,000 in East Pakistan, and rioting in Poland. General de Gaulle had died, and Charles Manson and his followers had been jailed in Los Angeles for the murder of actress Sharon Tate and four others.

When I reached the foreign desk a man with a phone pressed to each ear saw me waiting, pointed across the room and mouthed, 'Editor's office.' An invisible hand gripped my stomach and gave it a good twist. This was the holy of holies. In my thirty-eight years at the *Express* I was only ever in the Editor's office three or four times, and in those early days never at all. Gingerly, I knocked and entered. Derek Marks, the Editor, was sitting behind his desk and our foreign editor Stewart Steven (later to become editor of the *Mail on Sunday* and the *Evening Standard*) was in conversation with our most experienced reporter, George Hunter, a man ten years my senior who'd cut his journalistic teeth in his native Scotland before being lured to Fleet Street.

Stewart Steven peered at me through intimidating horn-rimmed glasses and, waving me towards a chair, said, 'I want you and George to go on a secret assignment to the Sudan.' The word *secret* flashed in my mind like a neon sign. This was a proper mission then, something important, not just a job. It was *real* journalism and, best of all, *secret*. Adrenalin flooded through me like mercury racing up a thermometer and burst out in a spray of over-enthusiastic thanks.

Trying to rein in my euphoria, I told myself crossly, '*Concentrate, John! Think. He may ask questions.*' My mind raced back over long forgotten geography lessons at my reviled secondary school. All I could recall was that the name Sudan means the lands of the blacks, that it's the largest country in Africa and the Nile runs through it. Oh, and there was a Gordon of Khartoum who fought the 'Mad Mahdi' played by Laurence Olivier in a bad movie. That was it – a startling display of ignorance for a budding newspaperman.

I was brought back to earth with the sudden realisation that our venerable foreign editor had asked me a question, for he and George were staring at me and his hand was outstretched. My first reaction was to kiss it, my second to shake it, but ultimately all I could manage was a rather pathetic, 'Pardon?'

'Give me your visiting card!' he repeated, with evident irritation. I fumbled in my pocket and produced the little white card with the famous *Express* Crusader logo that I'd finally earned three years earlier and was still so terribly proud of. It read: *Daily Express. John Downing. Staff Photographer.*

Taking it, he carried on talking as I listened far more attentively. 'There's a civil war going on in Sudan. Has been for almost twenty years. The northern Sudanese, predominantly Arab and Muslim, are waging genocide against the Christian and Dinka population of the south. The southerners go under the name of 'Anya-Nya and are fighting a guerrilla war in the bush. We need you to go and bring us back a full report.' What our esteemed leader didn't tell us was that an estimated half a million people had died in the conflict that began in 1956 when the British and the Egyptians arbitrarily merged North and South Sudan without consulting the southern leaders. Or that Anya-Nya means snake venom in the Madi language.

Steven's excellent contacts had arranged for us to fly to Kampala, capital of neighbouring Uganda, where we would be clandestinely contacted by members of the guerrilla army. They would then take us up country and illegally smuggle us across the border for exclusive firsthand coverage of the war. Before we set off he gave us our final instructions: 'Book into the Grand Hotel. Act like tourists. Do not make any contact with the office, and keep a low profile. The next time you see these,' he added, holding up our cards, 'they'll be in the hands of your contacts with this mark.' He pointed to a small cross he'd made in the top left hand corner of each card alongside his initials. 'Don't say anything until he shows them to you to identify himself. To confirm that they're legitimate look for this.'

I felt like a latter-day James Bond.

To begin with, we did exactly as we were told, checking into the local tourist office and provisionally booking an evening trip on Lake Victoria in the boat *The African Queen*, as featured in the eponymous film starring Humphrey Bogart and Katherine Hepburn. The trouble was we had no idea when the guerrillas might turn up, so we kept postponing our ride until one weekend when we thought we'd be safe and joined a group of American psychiatrists, enjoying the boat trip as much as they did.

Eventually the rebels made contact although it took them a while to remember to show us our business cards so we chattered on mindlessly, stalling for time until one of them finally produced them. Talking freely from then on, they explained the arrangements to get us into Sudan. And so it was that I found myself on a dusty unmade road in the middle of the Ugandan bush a few nights later peering into the darkness ahead as a torch was waved from side to side to slow down our vehicle. Our driver tensed visibly, sitting ramrod straight as he cut the headlights and brought our Peugeot to a standstill at the isolated military checkpoint. There was an almost indiscernible click of the keys as he switched off the ignition before the stifling heat closed in on our oven of a car and the last of the deep red dust settled on us like a ruddy shroud. There was silence – or what passes for silence in an African night, with its leg-rubbing crickets and garrulous tree frogs.

One of our guides squeezed into the front seat leaned forward and flicked on the wan interior light. This simple life-saving procedure was the first of many I was to witness in my career – seemingly insignificant actions that can have life or death consequences. Night sentries, who are notoriously nervous especially in times of trouble, often shoot first and ask questions later, especially if they're unable to quickly identify the occupants of an approaching vehicle. Nervously, I traded glances with my colleague George, whose rugged looks were hidden beneath his Army jungle hat and a bandana facemask, our only defence against the choking dust. I was similarly attired as we sat astride our rucksacks. We looked to all intents and purposes like two desperados about to hold up the Deadwood stage.

Slowly we became conscious of unshod feet kicking up the dust around our vehicle. Without warning a Kalashnikov rifle was thrust through the open back window, its barrel clipping the doorframe with a noise that made me jump. A second weapon was thrust into George's face. Angry questions in Swahili were barked at the driver and his passengers. '*Wewe ni nani? Usenda wapi?*'

We understood the unease of the soldiers – the whole country was jittery. Only a few weeks before the Ugandan Army Commander Idi Amin had led a successful *coup d'etat* before declaring himself President and throwing his country into turmoil. Our position was even more dangerous as we were travelling without permission during curfew. This had never been the plan but our windscreen had shattered after a couple of hours' driving, forcing a return to Kampala for a replacement and delaying us by over four hours.

Unbeknown to us, we were in a strategically sensitive spot on the border of Amin's tribal homeland, adding to the soldiers' anxiety. The chief inter-rogator eventually lost interest in those in the front and turned his attention to George and me. 'Identification!' he shouted, holding out his hand. I handed over my crisp new passport and, in a sudden rush of madness, considered drawing his attention to the wording inside: '*Her Britannic Majesty.... requests and requires.... to allow the bearer to pass freely without let or hindrance and to afford the bearer such assistance and protection as may be necessary.*' Thankfully, my common sense prevailed, encouraged by George who flicked me a warning look.

We then witnessed a classic piece of pantomime as the interrogator and a colleague, trying to be as officious, carefully examined my little blue passport in the torchlight even though they were couldn't read a word of English and the document was upside down. It wasn't until they reached my photograph that they realised their mistake and, to cover their embar-rassment, quickly waved us through with their AK47s.

Less than a mile further along from the bridge the driver brought the car to another unexpected halt. Nervous, I leaned forward and asked what the problem was. He put his finger to his lips and pointed. For a moment there was silence, then we became aware of a rustling sound that built in intensity like wind in reeds. Suddenly a huge grey ghost rumbled into the headlights kicking up clouds of dust; then another, and another. We had driven into the path of a herd of elephants. These gentle giants, all shapes and sizes with their small but penetrating eyes reflected in our headlights, lumbered across the track in front of us seemingly unperturbed by our presence. It was a marvellous sight that sticks in my memory still.

What felt like hours later we stopped in a one-goat village for what our driver quaintly referred to as 'refreshments'. There was no moon and all we could see was the shadowy outline of wattle buildings. I stepped out of the car and straight into someone, giving them a blow to the shins that elicited a wince of pain. My victim turned out to be the owner of the only bar in town, who graciously accepted my apology and escorted us inside. With every pore seeping in claustrophobic darkness we waited until a match flared in the corner and a hurricane lamp was turned up high. The room was bare save for a small plastic bar at one end topped with a few chipped glasses, a wooden bench and a six-foot fridge.

The 'landlord' told us to sit and, with a big grin, produced an ancient wind-up gramophone from beneath the bar. Giving the handle a couple of cranks, he gently lowered the needle onto an old '78. As the scratchy music filled the room, he opened the door to the fridge, exposing several rows of bottled King beer before handing one to each of us. Thirstily, I took a long draught but was disappointed to discover it was warm – the fridge was purely decorative, as the village had no electricity.

We didn't stay long. It was too risky. There were spies everywhere, we were told. When the Anya-Nya catch a traitor, they make him dig his own grave before dispatching him into it with a single shot through the head. There is no time or inclination for any other kind of justice in the bush. An hour or so further along the road we stopped again, this time at a cluster of straw-roofed mud huts, just outside the border town of Arua. After inspecting our accommodation we opted to sleep in the car. Early the following morning we breakfasted on black tea and a boiled egg (a luxury), before making our way towards the Sudanese border. We drove through Arua without stopping, registering only that it was teeming with slovenly looking Ugandan troops, and negotiated roads that were little more than rough goat tracks. After bumping and bouncing our way along a dried-up riverbed we were finally brought to a halt by impassable boulders and had to continue on foot, our passengers acting as our guides. This was, as George described it, 'the land that God forgot', a barren lump of territory that felt to us like Hell on earth.

Several sweaty hours later they informed us that we'd crossed the border into Sudan and would wait here for the Anya-Nya guerillas. Hoping for a better viewpoint from which to take photographs, I climbed up into a huge mahogany tree and settled myself into a forked branch amongst insects that made a high-pitched sound like a kettle at the point of boil. The heat was rising fast and after two hours in the midday sun I was parched so I took a swig from a plastic bottle of sickly sweet orange drink we'd bartered from our guides, immediately regretting. I was musing how much I'd have appreciated even a warm beer when a rustling in the bushes snapped me out of my daydream. We had company.

George and I were suddenly acutely aware of automatic weapons and arrows pointing directly at us from the bush. We didn't dare move. Into our clearing strode some heavily armed guerrillas with unblinking eyes dressed in what I can only describe as rags. Ignoring us completely, they fanned out and disappeared into the bush on the other side just as quickly as they'd arrived. More fierce-looking ragamuffins appeared and simultaneously arched their bows at us. Minutes passed, nothing was said, and no one moved. I felt especially vulnerable and more than a little foolish stuck up the tree. Terrified, we remained stock still until I hissed, 'For God's sake, someone say something!'

Someone did. 'Welcome to Southern Sudan!' cried a boyish soldier we later found out was Lieutenant-Colonel James Loro, the twenty-eight-year-old commander of the Second Battalion of the Anya-Nya. Looking more like a skinny teenager than a leader of men, he rose from the bush, hand extended, grinning through broken teeth. 'We've been expecting you, but we have to be careful. We never announce our arrival. Surprise is one of our best weapons.' From that moment on we realised that, whatever their apparent inadequacies, this was still a force to be reckoned with.

As I climbed down from the tree and shook hands with Loro, I noticed he was the only one dressed in a proper military uniform. Despite that anomaly, I was amused to note that his belt buckle read: *James Bond, 007*. That made two of us then. Having told us that their camp wasn't far, he cradled his Sten gun in his string bean of an arm and led the way. Hours later, having tramped through murderous bush with the heat topping one hundred degrees, we finally approached the little encampment of straw-roofed huts. As we got near, a disembodied voice from a nearby bush unexpectedly demanded, 'Password!'

'I'm the commander!' Loro announced imperiously.

'Password!' the guard repeated, followed by the sound of a weapon being cocked. This time the code word was promptly given. The owner of the voice emerged from the darkness. A huge man who handled a Bren machine gun with the ease of a child's toy pistol and had bandoliers of bullets crisscrossing his chest, he lumbered along at the head of our patrols ever solid and reliable. We gave him the nickname Goliath. Later that night I became aware of the stupidity of the password that had been chosen. Everyone had bedded down for the night around the fire when I felt the call of nature. I stumbled off into the bush and when I felt I was sufficiently alone and far enough away from the camp, undid my zip. Suddenly I froze for I heard ahead of me, in the darkness, the unmistakable sound of a person moving towards me. Then a low whisper came out of the night: 'Password?' I took my first breath in a while and sighed with relief. Then with blinding clarity I realised that I could still be about to die as I inwardly cursed the imbecile who thought up the password. Tensing myself for the shot I felt sure would follow, I called out 'Fire!' Needless to say, I wasn't shot on the spot as I feared but it did occur to me afterwards that my obituary might have made amusing reading – 'He died with his boots on, weapon in hand.'

Two others characters from that patrol stick firmly in my memory. One was 'Mr Beer,' Kenyi Athanasio, who wore a large-rimmed Australian-style hat with a feather thrust jauntily into the headband; a prize he assured us he'd taken from a dead Sudanese officer. His nickname came not from his hat, but his favourite pastime. 'Mr Beer' was the sort of soldier you could find in any barracks the world over – a little devious but extremely knowledgeable. Fuelled by his love of beer, he was always trying to persuade us to buy some for the troops, insisting it was good nourishment. In the absence of food, it was hard to disagree. We suspected he kept ordering it anyway, wherever we were, as it always arrived in a gourd, balanced on a woman's head soon after we settled anywhere. Pretending to be outraged, he would cry accusingly, 'That woman! – She has brought beer!' and then set about sharing it out, saving the lion's share for himself.

We christened one other member of our patrol 'Sheepdog.' An unassuming man with a meagre frame and bare feet, he had the stamina of a marathon runner. When, after hours of footslogging our patrol collapsed to the ground for a rest, he'd carry on for another half hour or so, ranging out around our temporary camp to assure our safety and bring in any stragglers. At one such stop, some two weeks later, a conversation sprung up about how unfit George and I were by comparison. Goodness knows how it came about, but somehow I was set up to race against Sheepdog. The hundred-yard course was to involve a sprint across a burnt-out clearing before touching the tree on the far side and returning. At the age of thirty, I was considerably fitter and leaner than I was in later years, and – as an added incentive – I was carrying not only the honour of the *Daily Express* but of Britain itself (or so they had me foolishly believe).

The race was started with a gunshot and I managed to keep stride with Sheepdog, pulling on his shirt at one point (only in retaliation for a blatant dig in the ribs at the start). Modesty prevents me from revealing the winner – by a gnat's whisker – as the race finished with a volley of gunfire. Afterwards, we fell to the ground, rolling around in the dust, laughing our heads off. The teasing went on well into the night as we sat around the campfire and I still have the sneaky feeling that Sheepdog let me win.

For the next few weeks we lived the life of a Sudanese fighter, going on feet-blistering daytime patrols and long night marches, sleeping where we could – which often meant out in the open – and helping the many refugees we met along the way. These often older men, women and children epitomised the ravages of war on a civilian population, as they staggered beneath heavy bundles of possessions, seeking safety, food and water. Their experiences were typical of others in South Sudan and, as the trust between us and the men we travelled with grew, we learned even more.

Lt-Col Loro, we discovered, could never return home because the Arabs had already killed his brother and tortured his father for information about him. Refugees told us that their villages had been burned out and their women and children taken hostage. Even in the midst of such desperation, most of them backed the rebels and resisted the threats of the Arabs to report any they'd seen. Even so, the men with us had to be careful not to be spotted in any large towns and it was essential that we all kept moving.

The kit we'd brought with us from London consisted of a lightweight sleeping bag, a sturdy pair of boots, a toilet roll, a few basic medicines, some food, and water purification tablets. These tablets were an absolute necessity, even though they gave the tepid drinking water more than passing likeness to a gulp from a swimming pool. Dehydrating fast, we drank it in great draughts nevertheless. The only luxury we'd packed was a small packet of coffee beans, some of which we'd foolishly swapped for the disgusting orange drink. To add to the daily burden of the kit I had to carry everywhere, I had stupidly bought three arrows as a souvenir from one of the warriors on day one and then had to hump them everywhere I went. Beautifully crafted, very old and bound with cord to a fine wooden shaft, I had visions of them adorning my walls back home.

There was little or nothing to eat and whatever food was available was shared. Sitting on our haunches around a chipped communal bowl our main diet consisted of a starchy root vegetable known as cassava, baked in the fire like potato but dry as dust. The alternative was the Sudanese staple diet of boiled millet, a congealed mess of porridge eaten with our hands, and we might get an occasional egg or a little pawpaw. One day we straggled into a village to be met by the ancient chief and his elders. There were official speeches of welcome for the 'honoured guests from England' before a fine looking goat was produced and formally presented to us.

With some embarrassment George and I turned to our guardians for guidance, explaining we couldn't possibly accept such a gift from these poverty-stricken people. 'If you don't, they'll be offended,' Goliath told us, although I suspect he had his own belly in mind. Cannily, he added, 'If we cook it, the villagers can share it.' This appeared to be an admirable solution and we parted happily with our cloven-hoofed dinner as they pored over what they considered the treasures we'd given them in return – a throwaway lighter and a ballpoint pen inscribed with the words London Airport.

To my nervous query as to how the unfortunate creature would be slaughtered, Goliath unsheathed a wicked looking knife, grabbed the animal's horns and – jerking the head backwards – went to cut its throat. When George and I shrieked, 'No!' Goliath's face was a picture of surprise at our reaction so, in a far more measured tone, we suggested, 'Please. Do it over there somewhere,' waving him away from where we were about to take our afternoon nap. I was shaken awake from my sleep an hour later by one of the soldiers standing over me with a smile and holding out a tin bowl. 'Mister John! It very good. You feel?' In my sleepy state I foolishly allowed him to plunge my hand into the bowl. Feeling the goat's slippery liver beneath my fingers wasn't so bad but holding its still warm heart gave my squeamish stomach a nasty turn, particularly as I could have sworn it was still pumping. After I wiped the blood on my trousers, I watched George set about preparing dinner. The wafting aroma of roasting goat – indistinguishable from beef – got the better of me. Using the meat, a little of the liver and a few extra ingredients, including some tiny onions he'd acquired, he produced a most presentable, if watery, soup. In salute to his Celtic heritage he insisted on calling it Scotch broth.

Finding enough water to drink each day was one of our major concerns so each day's march started and ended at some kind of watering hole, many of them terrifyingly dirty. We soon learned the rituals involved in collecting it. First, we had to post sentries before driving away wild goats, and waving our arms to try to disperse the swarms of flies. We then had to drag our hands across the slimy green film that always formed on top before immersing our water bottles, remembering to drop in a sterilising tablet before we drank anything. During one afternoon foray we arrived at a small river and threw ourselves in with utter abandonment, splashing each other like children in a paddling pool. We were completely oblivious to the dangers of any number of life threatening waterborne diseases including *bilharzia*, known as 'snail fever,' in which tiny worms burrow into the skin, swim through the bloodstream, and colonise in the liver and bowel.

As the long days wore on and George and I lost weight and stamina, we often wondered how much more we could endure. Our war-hardened companions gave us Western 'townies' no quarter, however, and continued to take us on arduous patrols, often marching through the heat of midday claiming, 'It's safer then; the enemy are resting.' Or, if in a particularly dangerous area, waking us all for a 4am start with the warning: 'This is when the enemy is most likely to attack,' before sitting up until dawn, their loaded guns across their knees.

'Do not have fear,' they'd tell us as our hearts hammered against our ribcages. 'We sleep with our eyes open. You will be safe.'

On one blindingly hot day as we struggled along another dried up wadi, George collapsed. The guerrillas, who never suffered from sunstroke, stood around staring down at my colleague, seemingly unmoved by his plight. I was all but done in myself and, angered by their lack of sympathy, I ordered them to build a small shelter from branches and brush wood so that he could be laid in its shade. Rather unreasonably, I then demanded that someone go and find water – 'Lots of it! Immediately.'

Amazingly, one of the men returned quite quickly with two native women balancing large water gourds on their heads. He wouldn't have been seen dead carrying it himself, of course, as this was considered-women's work. Stripping George of all but his underpants, I washed him down from head to toe. It seemed to do the trick, for he soon professed to feeling better than at any time since we'd arrived in this 'fly-blown' country. A while later, when he felt well enough to sit up, he asked me, 'I don't suppose you'd consider a full-time appointment as my butler?'

Evening was our favourite time of day when the blood red sun dipped over the horizon, its savage heat drawn and dissipated. That's when we'd take turns to stand stark naked in a bowl just big enough for our feet and pour a jug of water over our heads, enjoying the cool liquid running down in rivulets to wash away the sweat and grime. After slipping into a spare set of clothing we'd sit by a dying fire and drink a tiny cup of our treasured black sugarless coffee. It was our one civilising moment of the day – a time for reflection not conversation. Staring into the embers we allowed nostalgic thoughts of home and the families left behind to pick at the selfish, guilty corners of our mind.

Mornings were the worst. Not, as you may imagine, for the slow awareness of painful, blistered feet, or a body aching from the unforgiving ground. No, it was something worse and it began on the very first morning. As I blearily opened my eyes, I was shocked to find an old man sitting on his heels at the side of my head, staring quietly down at me. Startled, I jerked upright. Behind him a small line of assorted refugees, equally silent, had formed a queue. I summoned Goliath and asked what was going on. 'Well, Mr John, they think all white men are doctors. I've told them that you're journalists but they do not believe me. They ask, 'Why would they leave a good country to come here?' The same question had crossed my mind more than once.

Naively, I suggested that they needed to seek out a local doctor, but Goliath smiled benignly. 'Mr John, there is no doctor in the whole of Southern Sudan; only a few small clinics.'

The enormity of his statement struck home as the region he was talking about was well over twice the size of Britain. Looking at the pathetic line of people waiting for treatment, I protested, 'I can't help them, Goliath. I'm not a doctor!'

He wasn't taking no for an answer. 'But Mr John, that woman has walked all night to get here. You have medicine. Please.'

George and I looked helplessly at each other. Aside from the fact that we felt morally bound to help, Goliath was right – we did carry a few rudimentary meds such as painkillers, antiseptic, eye drops and sticking plasters. Knowing that I had some basic knowledge of First Aid from my scouting days, George gave me an encouraging nod. With rising panic, I reluctantly accepted the responsibility being forced on me and prepared to act out the role of physician in what he dubbed 'Dr Downing's Dispensary'. I hoped that minor injuries such as burns and cuts could be treated relatively easily and prayed I wouldn't be presented with any suppurating sores – to which I had a particular aversion.

My first 'patient' was the woman who'd walked all night to see me. She was virtually carrying her teenage son who'd fallen from a tree. After a cursory examination I suspected he had a fractured skull, something that was way beyond my expertise. Wondering what I could offer him until he found proper medical aid, I borrowed the woven ring his mother used to cushion the water containers carried on her head, and adapted it as makeshift bandage. Then I urged her to take him to the nearest hospital, which turned out to be a three-day walk back into Uganda. Having tended to him, I was then asked by his mother to examine what appeared to be a small open sore on her stomach. Fetching some cotton wool and Dettol I proceeded to clean it but, to my horror, as I dabbed at it the skin started peeling away until what had begun as a patch the size of my fingernail was an open wound as big as the palm of my hand. All I could do was continually douse my folded handkerchief in antiseptic and cover the wound with a large plaster in the hope that it wouldn't go septic. As I watched the mother lead the boy away I wondered if either would survive the journey.

Once I was established as the local 'medicine man,' I'd awaken every morning to ever more patients whose healthcare I supervised with frighteningly little knowledge and even fewer resources. My inadequacies tormented me, and I dearly wished I'd had a magic Mary Poppins bag of everything I needed to tend to these people. What I was doing may have been deeply questionable medically but to have done nothing was unthinkable. Psychologically, I was performing wonders for those who had suffered so much and they went away with a renewed sense of hope and gratitude for the 'doctor' who'd come to help them. I did make one really useful discovery – if I filled my empty but watertight Ilford HP5 film canisters with antiseptic and a small wad of cotton wool, I could hand them out to the injured with a few basic guidelines on how to clean wounds so that they could minister to themselves. It was yet another salutary lesson in what it was like to be born, through an accident of geography, into a country that had none of the facilities I had always taken for granted.

By living and breathing the world of these guerilla fighters and their families in South Sudan, sharing their scant rations, constant discomfort, and the ever-present threat of injury or death, a bond built slowly between us. We had nothing in common with these men and knew very little about them at first but, after a scary and mistrustful start, friendships developed and even flourished until we had a mutual respect and a strong sense of loyalty. It was going to be strange to finally leave them and go home, and – although George and I were more than ready – we couldn't help but feel tinges of sadness at our parting.

So it was that on our last night we staggered, exhausted, into another small encampment, close to the border. 'Mr Beer' had promised us a farewell party. From early evening there had been a constant stream of women arriving with large gourds of a liquid that had all the consistency and colour of runny porridge. This passed muster as beer – at least as far as our fighters were concerned.

As the last red daubs of evening sky slipped below the tree line, the campfire was sparked into life by something I'd never believed possible until Africa – rubbing two sticks together. A small group of local musicians settled themselves down and, to the background chorus of the insect population of an African night, plucked the first notes of a rather repetitive tune from drums and instruments made from thin strips of metal nailed onto blocks of wood and arched to resemble the palm of a skeletal hand. The music was nonetheless haunting for all of that.

As the sludgy ale took hold (noticeably fast in the case of our soldiers), Mr Beer announced that it was time for dancing. The start to each dance was very stylized – the guerrillas would form a line facing an equal number of village 'maidens.' I use that word in the loosest possible sense, for although the underage girls fitted this description, the ages and provocativeness of many of the others would suggest the title was somewhat questionable (not to mention the sprightly and entirely toothless seventy-year-old). The young woman at the end of the line would dance across to a man of her choice, touch him lightly on the wrist and then, turning her back on him, dance away. This was his cue to follow and partner her. The next girl would repeat the process and so on until everyone was dancing.

It didn't take long for me to be inveigled into the line. Immediately the music struck up, I was buttonholed by a seductive and particularly well-endowed young woman, much to the amusement of the guerrillas and the giggles of the other girls. I had not the slightest idea of how I should dance so, not wishing to be a wallflower, gave them my best Elvis Presley imitation with some jazzy footwork thrown in for good measure. 'Not a pretty sight,' was the only comment from George, who wisely sat this one out. Surrounded by the singing, swaying crowd, I noticed that the alcohol-fuelled musicians were playing faster and faster, on and on and bloody well on. In a desperate bid to save my aching legs and bursting lungs, I threw myself to the ground in an exaggerated collapse. While this played well with the crowd it was definitely a mistake, for I hadn't noticed that all the stamping about had created a foot-high dust cloud around our ankles, which I was now blindly crawling around in, coughing my lungs out. The dancers, meanwhile, assumed that this was all part of my act.

With the party still in full swing, George and I eventually retired to our appointed hut to find two beds created for us by weaving bits of old string and rope together across wooden struts. It was hardly a Slumberland but it definitely had the edge over sleeping on the ground. We lay there for a while listening to the music and watching the giant shadows of the dancers flickering across the wall in the firelight. Just as I was drifting off to sleep George said softly, 'What an amazing experience! This is something we will never forget.'

He was right.

At dawn the following day we handed over parting gifts of spare notebooks (used for rolling cigarettes), shirts and socks to our raggle-taggle army, said our goodbyes, packed our kit – including my precious arrows – and headed back to the Ugandan border, a journey of some four hundred miles – this time in a car. Arriving deadbeat at our hotel in Kampala – bearded, caked in dust and several pounds lighter – we took showers, ate some real food and got a little rest. Wandering past a row of tourist shops on the way to a local bar for our first decent beer, I stopped dead in my tracks. Almost every stall was selling the very same arrows that I'd purchased from the Anya-Nya and carried for hundreds of miles of bush – for even less than I had paid.

Once refreshed, George and I reported in to the office to let them know that not only were we still alive but that we had all the words and pictures they had hoped for. His hand over the mouthpiece, George repeated the praise being shouted long distance from our foreign editor and then mouthed, 'The Editor wants to speak to us!'

Standing to attention instinctively, I leaned into the telephone as we waited for the compliments that would surely follow. 'Have you finished your little trip?' Derek Marks asked, somewhat sarcastically, down the crackling line.

George answered in the affirmative.

'Well, get off your fat arses and get back here with the story as soon as possible!'

That's journalism for you, although I did think it a bit rich from a man who was chiefly renowned for his pudding-like figure and his love of port.

Thankfully, when we got home the *Express* gave George's story and my photographs the space they deserved. Beneath the banner headlines: '*The Forgotten War. A Nation Fights for Its Life*' and '*These are the venom fighters hitting back as their homes are razed*', George's story described what we had witnessed as 'a cry for help in a land of despair.'

It was a proper old-fashioned scoop, earned the hard way, and I am not only very proud of the work we did there, but I will never forget my time with those brave men in that deeply troubled country.

FIVE

NOT LONG AFTER our return to London, triumphant in spite of the Editor's lack of praise, I was sent on my second foreign. It was June 1971 and I was called out of the City Golf Club where I was drinking with Micky Brennan of *The Sun* and instructed to see the foreign editor.

My mission, I learned, was to cover the consequences of the bloody civil war in East Pakistan in what became known as Bangladesh Liberation War. The sole reason I was chosen to hook up with the *Express*'s Far East reporter Ian Brodie was because I was the only photographer in the office who had an up-to-date vaccination against cholera, an antidote that took five days to come into effect. My pincushion gamble had finally paid off.

The war had started earlier that year when the authorities in West Pakistan, supported by Islamist groups, launched a brutal military crackdown on the Bengali population that were seeking self-determination. In the genocide that followed up to three million people were killed and almost half a million women raped in a systematic campaign that declared all Bengali women 'public property'. As a result millions fled, including many Hindus, seeking refuge in neighbouring India.

When I got to Calcutta, the first person I came across in the hotel bar was Micky Brennan who I'd just been drinking with in the Golf Club. 'Gin and tonic, John?' he said. Delighted as I was to see a friendly face, I wasn't there to socialise. Naïve and over-confident I hoped to cross the border to try to find some fighting, but the veteran Ian Brodie wisely explained that I would most likely get shot. Instead, he suggested that a story about the refugees in a camp outside Calcutta would have far more human impact. He was right. It was a shock to experience the bitter reality of life in such a place, where death and disaster unfolded before my very eyes. In my inexperience, I photographed everything I saw and it was nearly always the children that made the most haunting pictures, leaving an indelible stain on my memory. Like faded flowers, they'd been cut down and cast to the wind.

Many were poor and hungry, most were dirty, and the majority the victims of the ravages of war. A surprising number made the best of their circumstances, focusing all their efforts on begging, borrowing or foraging for their family's daily needs. Similarly, the brave nurses from the War on Want charity did incredible work in dire circumstances. In a place with no buildings to speak of, they set up a makeshift hospital in nothing more than a chicken hut with no electricity and canvas walls.

One day a father, haggard with hunger and worry, brought in his tiny son who was clearly very seriously ill. I looked at this horribly emaciated child with the staring eyes and swallowed hard against the thought of my own two boys back home. In the dark interior of their clinic, a nurse had to fetch an oil lamp in order to examine him, placing a hand gently on his feverish brow. This scene I captured in black and white, using only natural light. As the shutter clicked I thought, 'This is like something from the Crimean War with a modern day Florence Nightingale'. I watched in tears when the little lad died soon after and had to step away from his father as he broke down. I was grateful at least that the photo I took of his son was used widely later, and helped to sum up the dire conditions these people and their nurses were facing.

One other event that remains embedded in my mind from that filthy camp with all its mud, open sewage and disease is the attempts to inoculate children against cholera using a new type of compressed air syringe that looked a bit like a gun. One naked little Pakistani refugee who can't have been more than four years old was so scared of this 'weapon' that he took off barefoot and screaming when a twenty-six year old volunteer nurse named Carol tried to minister to him. Wearing a T-shirt, trousers, and flip-flops she chased after him and managed to grab hold of his arm as he tried to leap across a water-filled ditch. I captured just one shot of the moment when she grabbed his emaciated left arm and, with a pleading expression called out, 'Don't run! Don't run! I'm not going to hurt you.' She was trying to calm him down as he glared at her in abject horror. That one frame is brutal in its honesty and said so much about what they were both going through that day.

Later, I was walking through one of the camps when I saw a boy aged about eight squatting on his haunches on the edge of a dirt track and clinging to the emaciated hand of a dead woman. Her body was covered in a piece of old cloth for a shroud and she lay next to a second body, similarly draped. Through a translator I was told that these were the boy's parents.

They had walked all the way to Calcutta with their only surviving child before dying in front of him.

As the boy sat there in stunned silence and I stood beside him wondering what I could do to help, a flat-backed lorry came to a dusty halt and two men jumped off. Without saying a word, they grabbed the bodies of his parents by the arms and legs and chucked them unceremoniously into the back of their vehicle, which was laden with other corpses. Then they drove off, no doubt to a ghastly mass grave I'd already spotted in the distance, leaving the orphaned boy without a soul to comfort him. Appalled, I didn't know what to do and, as I was already late for a rendezvous, I did the only thing I could think of, which was to stuff a wad of money in his pocket. I suppose this lasted about five minutes in that camp until someone stole it from him, but I hoped he realised that someone at least cared. I then escorted him to one of the aid tents and left him in the care of a nurse. For the rest of my life I have often wondered if that little orphan boy survived.

My time in the refugee camps was cut short, as it didn't take long for the office to get a more senior photographer jabbed up and sent out in my place. Four days after I arrived I was pulled back but it was tremendously exciting to have my pictures published with a byline. This was all part of being accepted as people started congratulating me. I began to think, 'Maybe I can do this.' Some of the pictures I took there were entered in the prestigious World Press Photo Competition, earning me a place as a runner-up. That tragic assignment that marked me for life finally established me as a photographer in the making.

Coming home to 'Civvy Street' after something like this is always difficult and the adjustment back to a normal life is a fine balance. Having just left people desperate for clean water, it is hard to listen to colleagues complaining about the quality of their coffee. Or having watched starving orphans stagger into a refugee camp weak from hunger after days under fire, it's difficult to see Fleet Street's finest order up enormous steaks in The Albion.

Strangely, when you're out there taking photographs the camera acts as a great defence, somehow standing between you and the horror. Plus, you're concentrating on the technical side of the job, harnessing whatever light is available, finding the best angle, and deciding which type of lens to use. It is always worse later when you come to developing the film and exposing the pictures you've taken. Suddenly you see the dead child or the grieving father as if for the first time, and feel all the incumbent shock and abhorrence at the tragedy of war and the waste of innocent life. That's when the tears fall, and the enormity of what you've witnessed really hits home.

Afterwards you emerge bleary-eyed from the darkroom to find a world that goes on regardless of that tragedy. Everyone is behaving as normal and you're expected to join them in the pub, eat your lunch, go on a mundane photo call, or return home to your family and pretend that nothing's changed. I've met many a journalist who longed to go to war but found that when they got there it was far too grim or frightening. Many turned tail and headed straight home. No one ever forced the rest of us to go but if we did and could push on past the fear, we reminded ourselves that we were doing something truly worthwhile and then we went again and again.

I never had a lust for the dangerous, difficult stuff as some of my colleagues did, but – to my surprise – I found that, even though I was often very frightened, I seemed to be able to handle it. I probably would have made a good soldier for that reason alone. Although, as I kept reminding myself, the difference between being in the Army and being a journalist is that when it got too dangerous we could pull out whereas the soldiers couldn't. In dangerous situations you run on adrenalin and even though you see some terrible things, you look back at some of the more famous pictures of war and think, 'This isn't as bad as that', so you just get on with it. What I didn't have was a true appreciation of how hard it must have been for the people back home who loved me and worried for my safety.

My Mum and Dad had been moved from Stockwell to a council house in Tooting by then (which they later bought, thanks to Maggie Thatcher) and would have gone through all sorts of agonies over my foreign assignments, Mum especially. I say would have because I never asked and they didn't say. What I do know is that they were secretly very proud of me. Dad would clip all my cuttings from the paper and paste them into huge scrapbooks that he pored over and showed off to his friends. I guess the scruffy rebellious kid who'd been all but feral in Llanelli and hadn't even sat his GCEs had finally proved himself to the former Royal Marine and deputy headmaster of St Andrew's and St Michael's School in Waterloo.

My grandparents had retired to their family home in Lydney in Gloucestershire where my dear old Grandad died, followed soon after by my Gran, who spent her final months in a hospice. Sadly, because of my job and the distance, I didn't get to see her as much as I would have liked. My kid brothers were all doing well, too. Ron and David had both gone to work for Thames Television as post boys but were destined for greater things. Ron became a props master on a few famous films and ended up working on Spaghetti Westerns in Mexico, where he met his future wife and had two children. Sadly their son Kenneth was murdered and Ron never really recovered. He died of heart failure in 2018. Andrew followed Dad into teaching and never married or had children but David became a floor manager for Thames, married and has two children, Paul and Hannah.

My son Bryn was a babe in arms just as my career really started to take off and, although it was wonderful and exciting to be father again, I regret to say that it still didn't stop me doing all the things I wanted to do. Years later one of my protégées, Ian Jones, rather tellingly summed up what he thought my priorities in life were and he was probably right – 'Work first, friends second, relationships last'. The truth was, I had this fantastic new job and was climbing the ladder, being offered better and better work and more exciting assignments. After all my years of hard slog, my dreams were finally coming true. Nothing was going to stand in my way.

From my first ever days in Fleet Street I'd watched the tanned foreign correspondents in their pale colonial suits wander through the office and was filled with envy. They were usually en route to the Editor's office before being wined and dined, only to return to their exotic postings with their ears full of praise and their wallets freshly replenished. One of them was Réne MacColl who'd been with the *Express* since just after the war and covered the Spanish Civil War before heading up the Paris and Washington bureaus. Another, Robin Stafford based in Rome, was a witness to Richard Burton and Elizabeth Taylor's wedding, and the chief crime correspondent had an apartment in Park Lane paid for by the newspaper.

The kind of life he and the other senior correspondents led was exactly what I wanted. It was what we all secretly wanted, but the truth was that this kind of world didn't always fit well with family life.

The next big international news story I was sent on was back to Uganda in September 1972, following the announcement by Idi Amin that he was going to throw out the Asian minority, including some 50,000 who were British passport holders. The man who would later become known as 'the Butcher of Uganda' gave them just ninety days to leave the country before their homes and property would be 'reallocated.' It was an ethnic purging that created a tremendous problem for those who were trying to get them all out safely and in time.

I was flown out to cover the story and told to hook up with reporter Gareth Parry, a fellow Welshman. The job initially went quite well as we covered the fleeing Asians, but then we heard an announcement on the radio that Amin had further denounced all Europeans as spies. We immediately suspected that this would cause us some problems and I, for one, was nervous. There were already stories leaking out of how Amin treated those he considered his enemy. Taking them to his summerhouse on Lake Victoria, he'd have prisoners beaten almost to death and then thrown into the water to feed the crocodiles.

The police were tapping the telephones and as soon as a journalist started filing their copy, they'd be cut off. They were also marked. In such a hostile climate, Gareth was to be flown out with his story instead but before he left I asked him to help me make a coded call to my parents to reassure them that I was all right. I dialled the number and said hello, chatting to them idly without saying anything controversial, and then I said, 'Mum and Dad, I have a Welsh-speaking friend here called Gareth.'

'Oh, there's lovely,' said my Mum.

'And he's a poet, actually (he really was). He wants you to hear some of his poetry, so listen well, okay?'

'That's nice,' Mum said, always happy to hear her native tongue.

Gareth, a fluent Welsh speaker, took the phone, said hello and – in a lilting cadence that would sound to anyone listening in as if it *was* poetry even if they didn't understand the language – he told them that the authorities were closing in, and listening in, that we could be arrested and imprisoned at any minute and could they please alert our newspaper as to what was happening. As my parents stood side by side, their ears pressed to the receiver, my father immediately understood his secret message and told Gareth at the end, 'Thank you. Lovely poem. Take care.' But when the call ended I heard my mother turn to Dad and say, 'Oh, I didn't think much of his poetry, did you?'

Reporter John Harrison replaced Gareth but within days, as we were lounging by the pool of Kampala's Hotel International with a few of the local Brits who came regularly to swim, we heard the sound of tracked vehicles and Ferret armoured cars. Within minutes there were soldiers dressed in khaki carrying rifles and machine guns in the lobby. They escorted nearly all the journalists to their rooms and ordered them to pack. John's room was opposite mine so I followed him up and kept my door open a crack so I could watch what was going on. Once he'd gathered up his things, the soldiers marched him away and put him into a campervan, which I later found out was driven straight to an Army prison. Apart from John, the others arrested included John Fairhall from the *Guardian*, Chris Munnion from the *Telegraph* and Don McCullin, then a freelance, who had all his camera equipment taken from him. For some reason, they left me alone.

Convinced I'd be next, I contacted the desk and they arranged for a freelance writer named Simon Dring to meet me in my room. When he arrived, very late, I briefed him on what had happened so Simon took a risk and quickly filed his copy from my room before going to his to freshen up. Within the hour, our hotel was surrounded again and I sensed that our time was running out. Nervously, I dialled the number of the *Express* copytakers and filed my final report, which appeared verbatim in the newspaper the following day: '*I'm having to keep my voice down in case anyone hears me. They tell me that anyone caught making an international call will be in trouble, whatever that means. There are troops all around the hotel, in the bushes. I can see them. In fact they are everywhere.... You better let my wife know I am alright. Tell her I'm great. But I'm afraid that's all for the moment. They're coming to cut me off....*'

Within a short time of being cut off – and after secreting rolls of film – four plainclothes policemen wearing dark glasses burst into my room and started searching everything. They were looking for news reports or photos, which I had already discarded. It was almost midnight when they arrested me and placed me in handcuffs. I managed to sling my camera bag over my shoulder before they took me down to reception and demanded that I check out and pay my bill. From there it was out to the car park where they pushed me against a vehicle. One of the policemen kept harassing me, shouting, 'You think because you are white, you are gods. I'm black and we are going to die for our country.' A couple of passing Africans came up and asked the policemen what was going on. They answered in Swahili and I had no idea what they said but the taller of the two men hit me hard across the face as the policemen pinned my arms.

Simon Dring and I were handcuffed together before being bundled into the back of the vehicle and made to lie on the floor. There was an almost farcical moment then because the police had left a loaded machine gun on the front seat and a rifle in the back. If I'd been the kind of James Bond figure they imagined me to be I'd have made a dramatic escape. However since I was just a well-brought up lad from the Valleys, I politely passed the weapons to them before they drove off. Lying on the floor of that car, I was really scared. Where were they taking us? Were we about to become dinner for the Lake Victoria crocodiles?

Instead, we were taken to Kampala Central Police Station where we were separated and my interrogation began, conducted by police officers trained by the British who seemed relatively controlled. I was answering their questions as best I could seated at a table when there was suddenly some shooting outside. When the gunfire stopped, Army soldiers burst in yelling and started to randomly beat up an African. A police sergeant was also dragged in off the street whereupon the Army major laid into him with his fists and a nightstick. When the man fell to the ground other soldiers started kicking him.

I suddenly knew what real fear felt like. These men were out of control and could do what the hell they liked. In such a volatile crowd, events got out of hand very quickly. One of the soldiers sauntered over to where I was sitting and glared at me. 'What are you doing here?'

Trying to speak in as measured a voice as I could, I shrugged and told him, 'I'm just a British journalist doing my job.'

'Okay,' he replied with a toothy smile. 'I'll have a word with the major. He'll sort things out for you.'

The last thing I wanted was to draw the Army major's attention to me. I'd much rather have taken my chances with the Ugandan police as it was clear that he was on something. His eyes were bloodshot and he was slurring his words as he tripped one of the policemen up, helped himself to their belongings, and was nasty to everyone. I suspect the young soldier was only trying to be helpful, but I replied quickly, 'Oh, no, thanks but don't worry. I'm sure it'll be all right.'

Ignoring me, the eager young officer went over and spoke to the major who looked as if he was about to leave. Instead, he turned slowly as if noticing me for the first time. This was one of those moments in my life when I knew that I could die. Without a word, the major pulled his pistol out of his holster, slammed my head down onto the table and – with the barrel of his weapon pressed painfully into my temple and his face inches from mine – shouted, 'We admire England. Why do you want our country?'

It occurred to me that if I moved or sneezed that would be the end of me, but I tried – quite literally – to keep my head. I can't say that my life flashed before my eyes, but for a second or more I did have images of my boys and of my poor old Mum and Dad. Sweating profusely and with my mind spinning with a hundred grim possibilities, I knew that there was no way to reason with the major but I was nevertheless determined not to let him see how frightened I was. 'I don't want your country,' I replied, surprisingly steadily and with one hundred per cent honesty. 'I'm a British journalist. I'm just here to take photographs.' This seemed to stop him for a moment and, to my enormous relief, he put his gun away, growled at his soldiers to follow him, and marched out.

The policeman who'd been interrogating me was clearly ruffled by what had happened and, pulling on his uniform and righting a chair, he sat down and resumed my questioning. Tediously, they went through everything I had on me and made me explain every slip of paper and negative I possessed. They even went through my diary. It seemed crazy sitting there explaining the notes for pictures I had taken earlier in the year of a minor TV star or the first man to win half a million pounds on the Pools.

Eventually, at goodness alone knows what time in the night, the commander gruffly his men: 'Take him down.' When I realised with disappointment that he meant me, I asked, 'Can't I go back to my hotel now? I'm terribly tired.' His expression told me that the answer was a definite No. That was the crucial moment for me as I had to take my cameras with me or I'd lose them forever. I knew there was no point in asking for permission so I just threw my case over my shoulder and followed the sergeant. Amazingly, no one stopped me.

Downstairs I was pushed into a long, dark corridor stinking of human waste, which turned put to be a basic prison with a few cells off to each side. At the far end was the only toilet – doorless and crude – from which an 18-inch open gutter ran down the middle of the corridor. The stench was unbearable and there were already people bedded down on the floor, right next to the sewage, as there was nowhere else to sleep.

The first thing I did when the guards locked me in was open the back of my camera and expose my film to the light to 'fog' the images and deliberately ruin them. I'd taken several images of tanks on the streets earlier that day and I knew they would have got me into serious trouble. Then I began to investigate my surroundings. There were ten men, several women and three children in that stinking jail crawling with cockroaches. Several of them were British and European citizens working in Uganda. Suspecting that nothing further was likely to happen to me that night, I decided it was worth the gamble of trying to take some pictures. I felt I had to show what these people were going through. But because of the poor light – there was only a single light bulb – each exposure had to be unusually long. And to capture the whole scene, I knew that the best angle would mean standing the camera on the filthy floor of the toilet and putting my face to the wet ground to focus it.

Among those being held with me were two boys named Andrew and Robert Stanley, aged four and two, who'd been arrested with their twenty-six-year-old mother Jean, the only white woman in the jail. Their father Richard, an engineer who lived and worked in Uganda, was imprisoned up country and his wife had no idea what had become of him. Nor did she know what would happen to their Kampala home and all their belongings. Her two boys were adorable and had no idea of the gravity of their situation. Jean had told them they were staying in a hotel, which must have stretched even their fertile imaginations. She also kept promising them that they'd be home soon eating fish and chips.

They reminded me of my own boys, Gareth – six years old by then – and Bryn who would, the very next day, be trying to blow out the candles on his second birthday cake. It was yet another major family milestone I was destined to miss. Perversely, one of the best photographs I took in that jail was of the two blonde boys climbing the bars of the prison as if they were playing happily on a frame in a school gym. It was a touching picture.

After a tough night with very little sleep on uncomfortable camp beds as the cockroaches ran over me, the following morning we were all ordered to line up to get some breakfast from the women – large greasy fried egg sandwiches. Hoping for a shot of the three armed guards standing at the head of the queue supervising the serving of food, I hid my camera under a towel and asked my fellow prisoners to bunch around me to hide it. When I was ready to shoot, a couple of them conveniently had a coughing fit so that the guards didn't hear the shutter.

The rest of the day I spent trying to cheer everyone up. To give their mother a break I played with the Stanley boys and another kid named Peter – whose only crime was to have come from the Seychelles. To keep them occupied for a while longer I made them a ball out of an old orange skin stuffed with newspaper and bound with Sellotape to keep it together.

Some time later a plainclothes policeman came in and called my name. I was told they were going to deport me, which filled my heart with glee, not least because I had my exclusive pictures and the best thing that could happen was if they put me on a fast plane back to London. When I looked out of a window and saw another campervan full of journalists, I knew I would quickly have to hide my film in plain sight. I opened up about two dozen new boxes of 35mm film to make it look as if they'd all been used and – having discreetly marked my two viable ones – I threw them into the jumble of my case. There was a tearful farewell then – handshakes from the men and kisses and tears from the women and children before I grabbed my things and was marched out. It was a Wednesday.

As I left, I turned back to the Stanley boys and their anxious mother and called cheerily, 'See you in London at the weekend!' It was more of an attempt to lift their spirits than a genuine hope.

'Goodbye, Uncle John!' the children chorused from that stinking hole of a prison as I left, almost breaking my heart.

Stepping inside the waiting vehicle I was reunited with reporter John Harrison and the other newspapermen, the first time I had seen them for four days. We were driven at speed to Entebbe airport, but my deportation wasn't to be as simple as that. Faced with yet another group of angry policemen who were convinced that I was a spy, I was searched yet again. The contents of my case were thrown out onto a table – lenses, cameras and boxes of film. All the while they kept asking me, 'Where are your weapons?' They didn't seem to believe me when I repeatedly told them that I didn't have any.

Finally they seemed to get bored and put me in a room with some of the other journalists including John Harrison who'd been locked up in a different prison. We waited and waited until nearly midnight when men came to escort the others across the runway to the aeroplane to be boarded. For some reason, though, the police held me back again and refused to hand over my passport, which had already been stamped with the word '*Deported*'.

'Where are your guns?' they asked.

I couldn't help but sigh. 'I've told you, I don't have any.'

'We want your film.'

They insisted that I empty the films loaded in each of my three cameras. In my attempt to fool them I'd deliberately left one blank film in my camera so I quickly opened the back to expose it, whereupon the officer in charge went potty.

'I'm a photographer and I know what you've done!' he yelled. 'You've ruined the film!' He grabbed my other camera and tried to open it but the technology was too advanced for him and he couldn't find a way to get into the back. Frustrated, he tried with his teeth. Thankfully, it didn't seem to occur to him to simply keep the camera. Embarrassed when he still couldn't get it open, he eventually gave up but he took all the films he thought had been exposed and all my negatives of the earlier pictures I'd taken and a few random boxes from the unexposed batch. Everything else was tossed back into my bag.

To my relief, he then ordered two armed soldiers to escort me to the plane. As we crossed the runway I looked up and marvelled at the millions of flying insects swarming around the runway lights. I've never been more relieved to feel an aeroplane lift off the tarmac. Soon after we'd reached the safety of a certain altitude, I went through all of my films, my hands shaking. To my amazement and relief, the two vital films I had shot were there, untouched. A few minutes after take off the captain came back to see us and congratulate us for escaping from Idi Amin's clutches.

'I can send a very short message through our office to someone to let them know you are safe,' he said. This was kind, as no one knew what had happened to us or if we were dead or alive. Everyone duly passed on their messages, mostly to their loved ones, but mine was to my picture editor. It said simply: 'I've done my job.'

Relieved to be free, I nevertheless felt a strange mix of elation and depression. I could finally show the world what was happening in that hellhole but I feared for those left behind and sat throughout that 4,000-mile journey home praying that the Stanley family especially would be okay. After all we had been through those of us on that plane couldn't wait to get home so it was with frustration that we were told that our flight was being diverted to Manchester Airport because of fog.

We arrived at some ungodly hour and I made my way to the Manchester office of the *Express* to develop and wire my films. Exhausted, I took a train to London and a taxi to Fleet Street. There had been dozens of journalists in Uganda, but I was the only photographer with the pictures. As this was a big exclusive I suddenly found myself lionized by the desk who promised me a front-page 'splash' plus several inside pages. The Editor even took me to a victory lunch at The Press Club, somewhere only the executives normally dined. I returned to the office triumphant afterwards to receive the devastating news that the printers were going on immediate strike over an ongoing pay dispute. This meant that my world exclusive pictures had no paper to run them in.

Managing the Fleet Street print unions was a notoriously tricky affair, even for their members. The sad truth was that the majority of the printers I came to know were one hundred per cent decent and devoted to the newspaper that employed them, often for their entire working lives. The unions often tied their hands, however. Cannily, my picture editors knew this and they had an idea. Waiting until just before edition time, they said, 'Come with us,' before escorting me to the compositors' room, a dark and forbidding place. All the men were sitting around, smoking, drinking tea and doing nothing, as instructed. My bosses walked me through the room to show me the hot metal pages that were ready to go to print. These were the glorious five half-pages and when I saw the photo of the boys at the bars of the jail I simply couldn't help myself, I broke down. I can still get emotional when I think about that moment.

The compositors watched in silence as this hopeful young photographer, fresh from hell, was staring at the prospect that the work I'd risked my life for wasn't going to be published. Still emotional, I was led back upstairs in time to hear the powers-that-be take a phone call. It was the compositors: 'We're running the edition – just one.' With this news, I hurried home to my family, only to stand protectively over Bryn asleep in his cot and pray to God he never came to any harm.

My article and its accompanying pictures appeared on Friday September-ber 22, 1972 with the headline, *Babes in Hell: World Exclusive from Inside Amin's Terror Jail. John Downing presents his incredible file of pictures taken inside Amin's prison.* The front-page image used around the world was of the two boys in the police station's 'Black Hole of Kampala,' climbing the bars of the window. The caption read: '*Two little boys look through prison bars at a world gone mad. Andrew Stanley is four, brother Robert two. I took the picture in Kampala Central Police Station at the height of the purge in Uganda...and thought of my own son at home. But children are wonderfully tough and adaptable. And boys will be boys, Amin or not. So Andrew and Robert climb the prison bars as if in a gym. They have now been released with other Britons. My picture is a tribute to their courage.*'

The printers' strike didn't last and soon afterwards I had another front page splash in which I was featured being reunited with Robert and Andrew Stanley and their mother Jean, who'd been allowed home a few days after me. This time I was in the eye of the lens, sitting with the boys on my knee as their relieved mother looked on. The two boys had recognised me instantly and threw their arms around my neck. Their mother kissed me on the cheek and said, 'Good to see you, my old cell mate.'

The article, which carried my byline, carried the headline: '*Hell-hole babies home from nightmare.*' It said: '*Behind their mother's smile there is continuing anxiety. Her husband Richard was released from jail, but in the Amin reign of terror, he is still in danger.*'

The situation in Kampala only worsened after we left, as an erratic and unpredictable Idi Amin came to be known as one of the cruellest dictators in African history. Under his brutal eight-year regime, as many as half a million political dissidents and others from various ethnic groups were murdered. Thousands more were exiled. As well as those countless unnamed souls who were fed to the crocodiles of Lake Victoria, others were tortured and dismembered and the human heads of his political opponents were found in his fridge. It was a very dark time for the region and for all those forced to start new lives as refugees elsewhere.

SIX

THE VIETNAM WAR had been raging for nearly two decades and was in its death throes by the time I was sent there in January 1973. Officially started between North and South Vietnam, it became a proxy Cold War between China and America, between Communism and Capitalism. As many as two million civilians and hundreds of thousands of soldiers from all sides died in the process.

So it was that I found myself standing with a group of hacks including my colleague John Harrison in the middle of Highway 13, on the outskirts of Saigon, as an American air strike went into an area up ahead called Trang Bang where the Americans were attempting to clear a Communist stronghold of Vietcong (or 'VC' as they were universally known). I was already nervous after witnessing several US fighter-bombers known as Starfighters drop from the sky above us. Using our road as a guide they flew directly over us, firing their 6,000-rounds a minute Gatling guns before arcing hard skywards to dispatch deadly Sidewinder missiles.

What unnerved me the most was that, for the pilots to get the right trajectory, they had to start firing from just behind us. It was terrifying to watch them bear down on us before releasing their weapons with a deadly racket. The epitaph: '*John Downing: Killed by friendly fire*' flashed through my mind, but no one else seemed as frightened as me so I was forced to apply my British 'stiff upper lip' and pretended that being under effective fire in the middle of a foreign war was an everyday occurrence.

Daft as brushes, our little group stood our ground even though we were close enough to the action to hear shrapnel fizzing around in our general direction. No one was prepared to be the first to break and take cover. Our bravado only cracked when a South Vietnamese soldier clambered down from one of the tanks waiting to lead the ground attack and, using a piece of old newspaper, picked up a smouldering fragment of jagged shrapnel about the size of a saucer. Holding it out to us, his eyes wide, he said. 'You take cover! Velly dangerous!'

'I think he's probably right,' someone calmly suggested.

'Yes, yes,' we all agreed, secretly relieved. 'May as well.'

As casually as we could manage (although I'm sure none of us felt remotely at ease), we sauntered over to the cover of the tanks where I continued to photograph what I could.

Due to the seven-hour time difference with the UK, plus the age it took to process our film and wire our pictures to London, it meant that, along with the only other photographer – Peter Stone of the *Daily Mirror* – I had to return to Saigon ahead of the 'scribes' to meet our deadline. Among the pictures I had in my bag were images of happy young children splashing naked in a ditch filled with water from an irrigation pump, a stark contrast to the war raging all around them that was all they had ever known. To get these images wired to London in time we had to drive like the clappers to the offices of the Reuters news agency then race back to our hotel before the 10pm curfew. It was exciting but the queues at Reuters were so long that you often risked breaking the curfew. This was policed by American and South Vietnamese troops who drove around in Jeeps picking up any stragglers. They threatened us with jail every time but for a few hundred dollars they'd usually drive us back to our hotel. Someone gave me some very good advice on Day One there – if you're out after curfew be sure to walk in plain sight down the middle of the road and never in the shadows, as you might be tempted to. Only the guilty do that.

The day of the air strike and not long after we had we left our colleagues for Saigon, the very tanks we'd been cowering beside came under direct attack, putting the remaining journalists in imminent danger. There was no more *sang-froid* then as everyone scattered and men threw themselves into a ditch. In the scramble for cover, Brian Freemantle of the *Daily Mail* slipped and sustained a minor injury to his arm. This news somehow got back to his London office, suitably embellished, which ran a lead story in their early editions with the headline, '*Mailman wounded!*' After getting the full, unblemished facts from Freemantle himself (sporting a sticking plaster on his arm), this sensational story had to be downplayed for the later editions. With typical Fleet Street humour, David Eliades, the *Express* night foreign editor and an old friend and colleague of Brian's, sent a telex to him that read: '*First edition has you wounded. Last edition has you unwounded. Congratulations on miracle cure. Presume next dateline Lourdes?*'

Despite the dangerous predicament the journalists found themselves in when the tanks were targeted, there was one moment of hilarity when Don Wise, the Far East correspondent for the *Daily Mirror*, spotted a man of diminutive stature trying to flee the area on his 50cc motorbike. Wise, who stood at 6ft 3ins, grabbed hold of the handlebars as he passed, jumped onto the poor man's pillion seat and, with an Imperial flourish of his lanky arm, ordered him to, 'Take me to Saigon!' The rear view of Don disappearing in a cloud of dust, heels almost scraping the ground and knees stuck out sideways like the wings of Concorde was a sight to behold.

Don was an elegant man with a ramrod spine and a crisp moustache, hallmarks of the British Army officer he had once been. He swore he was so tall for his Hong Kong flat that he could stretch out from his bed and fill the kettle for his morning cup of tea. He was by far the most experienced journalist of us all, and a willing helper to anyone who needed it, as I most certainly did. Like me, he'd been jailed in Kampala under Idi Amin but that was nothing to this old hand, who'd been imprisoned by the Japanese when Singapore fell in 1942 and was lucky to survive the experience. In Kampala's Central Prison, the BBC reporter Keith Graves found himself standing next to Wise as they were ordered by the guards to strip to their underwear.

'How long do you think we're going to be here?' whispered Graves.

Wise, laconic as ever, his trousers and jacket neatly folded over his arm, replied, 'Well, the last time it was three-and-a-half years in Changi.'

When he finally emerged from the notorious Japanese prison where he and some 50,000 other POWs had been held, he weighed just seven stone or 42 kilos, a weight that uniquely qualified him to test experimental parachutes for the Paras. Later, he helped lead an irregular unit known as Ferret Force, fighting Communist Party guerrillas during the Malayan Emergency, before becoming a foreign correspondent.

Don had a pathological hatred of the Japanese and, during a lull in the Vietnamese air strike earlier that day he had spotted three immaculate limousines sporting Japanese flags cruising into view. It was an opportunity he couldn't resist. Stepping into the road and raising his arms like a traffic cop, he waved the cars forward – directly towards the enemy. It didn't take long. There was a crump of a mortar and the limos came speeding back in full flight, pursued by machine gun fire. Don gave a vindictive smile and said something under his breath which I believe referred to their parentage.

Don was a wonderful raconteur and confided in me that he'd rather tell stories than write them. Many a night he'd have us in fits of laughter as he held court in his favourite French restaurant just off the flower market in the heart of Saigon. It was a scruffy little place with no discernible name that had chicken wire over the windows to discourage any *further* throwing in of hand grenades. The patron, an ex-legionnaire who'd stayed on after the 1954 French defeat at Dien Bien, refused point blank to speak any language except French and – according to Don – was on twelve opium pipes a day. No surprise then that the service was a tad uneven.

Saigon was a crazy but wonderful city and a place I have fond memories of, especially one little chap I called 'Bootsy' who set himself up as a shoeshine boy on the corner of one of its busiest streets. Most afternoons on the way to the so-called 'Four o'clock Follies' – the name we gave to the daily US Forces press briefing – I would call on his services, although the first time was almost the last. Sitting in the chair he'd provided, I was reading a telex from London when I glanced down to see my shoes on fire. Leaping into the air I did a passable copy of a moonwalk as I tried to stamp out the flames. It took some time for Bootsy to stop laughing and assure me that he'd discovered that melting the polish with a naked flame and then dripping it onto shoes, still flaming, gave them the best possible shine. He was right; it was the best shoeshine I have ever had.

After that we became good friends and I would often stop and chat with him. Like the orphaned boy in the refugee camp in East Pakistan, I often wonder what happened to Bootsy when Saigon eventually fell just two years later in 1975.

Back home, I moved up in the world when Jeanette and I bought the larger portion of a house called Tudor Lodge in Oatlands Drive, Weybridge in Surrey. Our new home was three quarters of a country mansion with a big garden – the perfect place to bring up our son Bryn.

Life was still good and I was able to take a few family holidays that were more exotic than any I had ever known as a child. Instead of caravanning or visiting relatives in Wales, we frequently went to Spain with friends and I was sometimes able to extend a foreign assignment in order to fly those I loved out for a family break. After a Royal tour of Canada with the legendary columnist Jean Rook (whose desk aptly sported a block of wood with a nail sticking out of it above the caption 'Hard as Nails'), I then flew to New York and did a few jobs for the *Express* team based there, including a piece on the Rikers Island jail. Once I was finished, I flew Jeanette, Bryn and Gareth to New York for a few days, before we all went to Disneyworld in Florida. Gareth's mum Barbara had continued to make it very hard for me to see him, so this was a real treat. Other than that, he and I could only reconnect on the few occasions that I was allowed access and could take him to museums or the zoo, to lunch or to the park. Those were the days that only served to remind me what I was missing with my first born.

Work-wise, I was on a roll with the newspaper and continually sent to cover events, big and small, doing exactly what I wanted to do – well, that is, apart from being at the top of Nelson's Column to photograph it being repaired and cleaned (I longed for a fortifying pint before I went up). One day I might be dispatched to cover 'the Troubles' in Northern Ireland, and on another I might witness teenage girls screaming themselves into a faint over the arrival of The Osmonds in London. The next I could be in war-torn Beirut trying to sneak a photograph of PLO soldiers lobbing hand grenades into the sea to catch fish, or at Waterloo station photographing pop sensation Abba.

Any regular weekday could find me photographing rebels crossing the border from Mozambique to Rhodesia, or in Paris to photograph Sophia Loren, who was gorgeous and asked me why I was breathing so heavily. For that job I was accompanied by the formidable columnist Jean Rook, who insisted on loading up my already overweight luggage with her favourite Dijon mustard after every French trip. I was also sent to the Golden Gate Bridge in San Francisco with a team to capture the world's first ever bungee jump and, on my return, snapped the likes of the Monty Python team, Peter O'Toole and Alfred Hitchcock. I was also in the press pack outside the Sussex farmhouse where Rolling Stone Brian Jones drowned in a swimming pool at the age of twenty-seven.

Like everyone else who lived in the UK, I also witnessed the effects of a fourteen-month campaign of terror attacks by the Provisional IRA during which some forty bombs exploded, killing thirty-five and injuring many more. Those were dangerous times especially with the random car bombs as you never knew what you were walking past. In December 1975, I happened to be in the right place at the right time when the Balcombe Street siege ended in London. This had lasted six days after four members of the IRA gang responsible for several of these attacks were hunted down. They holed up in a block of council flats in Marylebone, taking a hapless middle-aged couple as hostage.

For those six days we reporters and photographers worked our entire shifts at the scene, only changing over when someone was sent to relieve us for the next shift, handing on the baton. It was a 24-hour operation during the bitter days and nights of winter. The Metropolitan Police Bomb Squad officers, who were involved in very delicate negotiations, blocked off the road and erected huge screens to shield the property from view, raising them higher and higher to try to foil us. We photographers simply went higher and higher too, using longer ladders or hiring neighbouring apartments for exorbitant fees.

The police had been using deprivation tactics with the terrorists and they also 'leaked' a story to the press that the SAS were being brought in imminently to storm the building. The four suspects heard this on the radio in their besieged flat and panicked. I had just come on duty on the night of December 12, 1975, when – realising the hopelessness of their situation – the terrorists finally agreed to surrender. From a distance of about one hundred yards, using a 600mm f/6.3 Novoflex lens with an exposure of a quarter of a second, I managed to capture the moment an armed officer, standing on the floodlit balcony of the flat, pointed a gun directly at a hooded terrorist, whose arms were raised above his head. This picture was later selected by the judges for the top award in the prestigious Ilford Print Contest but, annoyingly, was later disqualified because the office lost the negative, which meant I couldn't prove it was mine. The terrorists were later convicted of seven murders, conspiring to cause explosions, and false imprisonment, each receiving twelve life sentences.

Every day through the lens of my camera I was lucky enough to witness the very best – and sadly the very worst – of human behaviour. It was a privilege I never took for granted, even more so when I started to receive awards for my work along with the printer I most favoured, a young man by the name of Larry Bartlett who was as passionate about black and white photography as I was. He was a master in his craft and an artist in the darkroom. He even wrote a book on the subject. When his union tried to stop him working exclusively for me, Larry set up a home darkroom just so he could develop my photographs. In 1977, when I won the British Press Photographer of the Year for a portfolio of photos, including those taken in Kampala, Larry deservedly won Photographic Printer of the Year. Annoyingly for him, the union declared that he had to share his prize money with the rest of the *Express* printers. Little did Larry and I know that, together, we would go on to win those two awards an unprecedented six more times, until the judges decided I'd taken enough glory and asked me to join them. Tragically Larry killed himself years later after leaving

Fleet Street and falling out of love with his work following the career-changing advent of colour photography in the mid-80s.

Each time I won an award, by the way, the first person I would call was my mother Glenys, who was by then running infants' play centres for the Inner London Education Authority and still living in south London with Dad. She was so excited and proud, and we'd all celebrate together the next weekend I was around with one of her traditional family Sunday lunches. If I was lucky she'd make me rice pudding and her famous 'paddy fields' made it all worthwhile on its own.

In a newspaper office that was so highly competitive there was, of course, a lot of rivalry and good humoured banter when anyone won an award or received any kind of praise and there was no one more acerbic or hilarious than the photographer Tom Smith, who'd been famously involved in the Michael O'Flaherty 'Gizza job!' debacle. The two of us had worked together often over the years, latterly becoming very close. To everyone in the office he was Smiff and I was JD or we were 'Starsky & Hutch,' and quite a double act. Completely coincidentally, he also happened to be one of our neighbours so our friendship extended into our private lives.

Living so close to each other in the Surrey hinterland enabled our two families to spend time together. Although I was in my rather grand house, I much preferred Tom's cosy cottage – one of a pair that had been variously a blacksmith's, a gardener's cottage and a pub. On discovering this latter fact, Smiff had a ceramic pub plaque made to hang outside featuring a horse's head which read: The Nag's Head. He always claimed it was a reference to his wife Brenda. Nobody escaped his tongue-lashing and many was the time he welcomed me at his front door with a caustic, 'I don't think we can get your ego into a house this small, John!' I always laughed, even though I was always secretly a little hurt. Tom also loved to remind me that, although his cottage was small it was at least detached, while I lived in 'a semi.'

There are two people in my life who have been very important photo-graphically – Larry Bartlett, of course, and Tom Smith. Having come from the prestigious *Camera Press* and *Observer* magazines, there were few others as knowledgeable about our craft as Tom, who possessed an impres-sive library of books on some of the world's greatest photographers, most of whom I was shamefully ignorant about. He was particularly generous to me with his time and support and it was he who educated me about the eye-catching portraits of Arnold Newman, the brilliant war photographs of

David Douglas Duncan and Don McCullin, the marvellous humour of Elliot Erwin, the sheer beauty of Heather Angels' nature pictures, and the night steam trains of O. Winston Link. He probably paid me the greatest compliment ever when he announced that my work reminded him of that by W. Eugene Smith, a renowned American photojournalist for *Life* magazine and the Magnum photographic agency.

'Who?' I asked.

Tom shook his head in exasperation. 'You ignorant bastard!' he replied, and – after fetching me a book of photographs called *Miasmata* – I realised that W. Eugene Smith was my hero. That changed my life because it introduced me to the true value of the photo essay and the use of natural light.

Smiff's wife Brenda, who was Welsh, had a real talent for combining soft lights and Victoriana, and many a cold winter's evening we'd sit around a log fire after dinner, Brenda and Jeanette deep in conversation (no doubt complaining about how little we were both home), while Tom and I righted the newspaper world, photographically. They were such joyous evenings – all small talk and large brandies.

Tom always joked that I worked too hard while he was the master of doing the minimum. On our regular assignments to the Epsom Derby, for example, he'd set himself up at Tattenham Corner and wait there comfortably before taking a couple of frames of horses coming round the bend at full pelt. I, meanwhile, would be running around the rest of the vast site taking pictures of everything else from the weighing in and the Royals to the ladies' hats.

Back in those days Smiff and I also seemed to be involved in a lot of car chases in which we were hunting down those making headline news. Invariably, he'd offer to drive, claiming that I drove like an old man so we'd never catch anyone. This allowed me to take the photograph, although his driving was usually so fast and so dangerous that there was always a chance I wouldn't make it back with the film.

One case we covered in 1978 involved the story of Michelle Booth, a fifteen-year-old girl who'd been savagely attacked on a Reading to Waterloo train. Her attacker threw her out of the moving carriage onto the busy track. The poor girl lay unconscious in a siding all night in the bitter cold, her jaw and wrist broken until a train driver reported what he thought was a tailor's dummy and rail workers discovered her near-lifeless body. Michelle eventually made a recovery after being kept in a coma for eight weeks while her family kept vigil at her bedside.

Several witnesses saw the suspected attacker and said he had a peculiar shape and a pronounced walk, which resembled that of a penguin. An artist's impression was circulated and 'The Penguin' quickly became the suspect's sobriquet. Police picked him up within weeks and his first appearance was to be at Brentford Magistrates Court in West London. That morning he arrived in the back of an unmarked blue Ford Cortina covered in a blanket, denying us a picture. Smiff and I decided that he'd be similarly covered when they left and guessed that he'd only remove the blanket as soon as they were clear of the court. With the Cortina's registration number jotted down on my chequebook, we took a calculated guess and drove back in the direction the car had come until we found what we thought was a perfect spot – a place where the traffic was restricted because of roadworks. Best of all, there was a bus stop where we could hang about without being too obvious. This was going to be a one shot chance so it was vital we get it right first time.

Having parked our Ford Escort around a corner we took our place in the bus queue, cameras kept out of sight, hoping that we'd picked the right route. We needn't have worried; the vehicle hove into view, headlights full on. 'I'll take the far side,' Smiff whispered. Neither knew who'd get the shot but it didn't matter as long as one of us did; we were the *Express* team.

Squinting through the reflective windscreen we couldn't tell if the Penguin's face was hidden or not. All we could see was a silhouette slumped between two burly officers. Suddenly Lady Luck smiled upon us because we saw a pair of handcuffed hands come up and pull the blanket from his head. Focusing intently on that one side window, I rehearsed my steps in my mind – four brisk strides, raise camera, lens to glass, trigger, explosion of flash, job done.

The car was almost on top of us when with a last glance at each other, we mouthed 'Go!' and ran towards our quarry in unison, at the very moment one of the guards in the back leaned forward to talk to the driver, completely obstructing my view. As he did so the traffic lights changed and the Cortina accelerated off. By the time we'd got back into traffic our quarry was long gone, so we headed for Brixton Prison in the hope that was their likely destination. Waiting as a line of nose-to-tail traffic moved slowly in front of us, we couldn't believe our luck as the Cortina rolled into view.

Trying to keep calm, Smiff forced his way into the traffic, putting just one car between the target and us. As we crept slowly forwards and I ran through a quick check on our two old Nikons – both long overdue for replacement – I accepted the unwritten rule that I'd be the 'hit man'. When the Penguin's car came to a brief halt I flung the door open and, half-crouching, sprinted through the traffic, oblivious to everything. The lights changed and the Cortina started forward but I was almost there. Breathlessly I reached the side window, drew up the camera, leaned in and – as my shadow fell across him – the Penguin turned, looked straight into my face and immediately cowered. In that briefest of seconds all thoughts of an exclusive vaporised. Just one thought filled my mind – that's exactly the expression Michelle must have had on her face when you attacked her. My bile rising, I thought, '*Retribution*'. I hit the button, expecting the flash to light up his bloated face, but instead of a paralysing explosion of light all I got was the click of the shutter and the whirr of the winding mechanism. I hit the button again and again with increasing panic – still no flash – as the occupants of the car jolted to action. The Penguin went for his blanket and his vanguards while the officer in the front seat leapt from the car in an effort to grab me. Giving my camera an almighty shake, I gave it one last shot. Nothing.

Sprinting back, I threw open the door of our now moving car and jumped in. Smiff roared off down a side street throwing lefts and rights until it felt safe to stop. We were devastated. Incredibly, the next time the Penguin appeared in court we did get one last crack at it and this time his face momentarily bleached out snow-white as the flash reflected his expression. We scored what seemed like a great victory that day, but the irony of this tale is that the Penguin was acquitted at the Old Bailey on the grounds that his police statements were inadmissible because of his mental immaturity. My hard-won photograph was never published.

In July 1980, I found myself on an assignment in Romania with reporter Liz Gill – who later became the wife of fellow staffer Danny McGrory. I travelled all over the UK with Liz, and Danny often joked that when he started on the *Express* he was little more than our chauffeur as he was forever either dropping us off or picking us up from a job.

No-one knew that she and Danny were an item for years but when they eventually decided to confess up and get married, he asked me to take their wedding photos. The reception was at Highgate Town Hall which, bizarrely, was decked out with posters in support of the Solidarity trade union in Poland but Danny and Liz were so much in love that I don't think they even noticed.

The Romanian assignment that took me to Bucharest with her was the wedding of Swedish tennis star Bjorn Borg to his fellow tennis player and countrywoman Mariana Simionescu. Unusually, journalists were invited into this forbidding Eastern Bloc country during Nicolae Ceausescu's rapacious, avaricious reign. While he siphoned off millions into his personal coffers and lived in extraordinary grandeur with his wife Elena, his country was disintegrating into financial ruin.

Liz and I pushed our way through the glass doors of the Intercontinental Hotel and entered the gloomy reception area, thick with the aroma of stale sausage and strong cigarettes. The place was full of people including a few devious looking men in ill-fitting suits reading newspapers that were never read. As with all Communist countries at that time, the service was rude and perfunctory. The other thing they had in common – despite their ubiquitous and highly ostentatious chandeliers – was abysmal lighting, due in part to a shortage of electrical power which usually meant that they were powered by a couple of low wattage bulbs. There was no such thing as porters, only the occasional doorman with an eager hand for collecting tips or for cuffing young beggars who encroached too far onto the hotel's forecourt. But one had to admire the Communist lifts and the fact that the (tapped) telephones at least worked, albeit intermittently.

Seeking out any fellow journalists, we made our way to the upstairs bar which was a joy of Stalinist veneer. While the mirrored shelves held every bottle known to imbibers the world over, they were all empty. The choice was simple, beer or whisky. These were the real McCoy, all imported, but at astronomically over-inflated prices and to be paid for only in US dollars or the universal currency of American cigarettes.

The burgeoning relationship of Borg and his co-star had been followed eagerly the world over by those far more interest in their off-court activities so the announcement of their wedding guaranteed mass interest. This created a major communications problem, though, for although the phones worked well enough for reporters to file their copy, the transmission of photographs was strictly monitored and only permitted through the Romanian Press Agency, which was government-controlled. To add to our misery, the wedding itself was to prove considerably more complex than we'd expected, for the nuptials were to be divided into three distinct sections. The first was the official town hall ceremony demanded by socialist diktat, and then the happy couple would be driven out into the countryside for a religious service in an ancient and beautiful monastery, before heading to Marianna's rural birthplace where the bride and groom would ride through the small hamlet on a traditional flower-decked horse and cart. In a Western country these arrangements would prove enough of a challenge, but behind the Iron Curtain it would be a logistical nightmare.

Liz and I made a quick recce of the town hall and ran through all the usual concerns – timings, routes, access to telephones, film processing, car hire, drivers and translators. Then we visited the government agency to oil the wheels of officialdom (with that well-known lubricant Bell's whisky) and were shocked to find there was only one photo wire machine available, to be shared by at least two dozen photographers. I realised then that if the *Express* were to get pictures in time for the first edition everything hinged on us being the first back to that lone machine. The trouble was, I suspected others had figured that out too.

The morning of the wedding found us milling about in the company of our peers and a surprisingly small crowd of inquisitive well-wishers at the base of the grand steps which swept up to the old town hall. We were all closely watched by the omnipresent police. A little earlier we had found a friendly officer (no mean feat) who'd agreed to us tucking our car and driver just around the corner of the building. This officer was smartly turned out in dark blue uniform, the lines of which were now misshapen by a bulging carton of Kent cigarettes.

The happy couple finally appeared, posed for a kiss at the top of the steps, then descended through an arch of tennis rackets held aloft by their friends. That was good enough for me, so we made the dash to our car. As we piled into our revving vehicle our delighted policeman stepped author-itatively into the road on our behalf, stopped any imaginary traffic with his raised left hand and waved us out with the other. Our car roared around the corner and only just avoided ploughing into the last of the official wedding limousines waiting to leave. This raised the eyebrows of the police motor-cycle outriders, but before anything could be said, the line of black limos started to pull away so we simply gave a Queen Motherly wave and tucked ourselves onto the end of the procession.

This turned out to be our next lucky break, for not only were most of the roads blocked off for the easy passage of the bridal cavalcade but the route took us right past the news agency, where we quickly peeled off. But Lady Luck hadn't quite finished toying with me yet because as I sprinted eagerly up the steps and along an endless passageway before finally swing-ing into the darkroom, my hand caught on something sharp, cutting it open

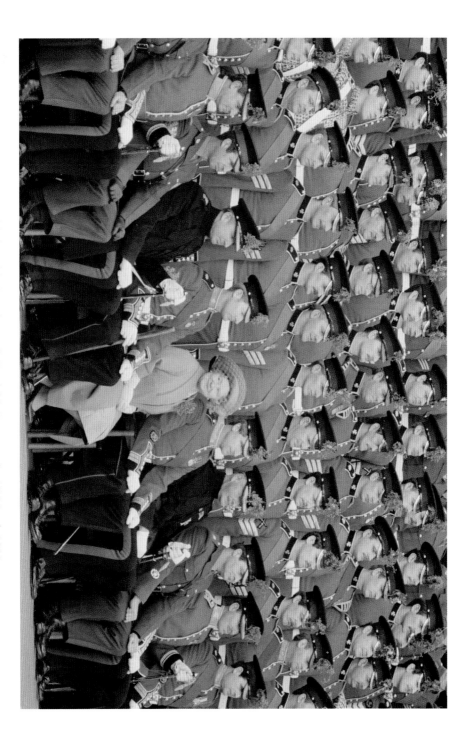

'My Boys' – the Queen Mother with the Irish Guards at a St Patrick's Day parade, 17 March 1981

(Credit: John Downing/Getty Images)

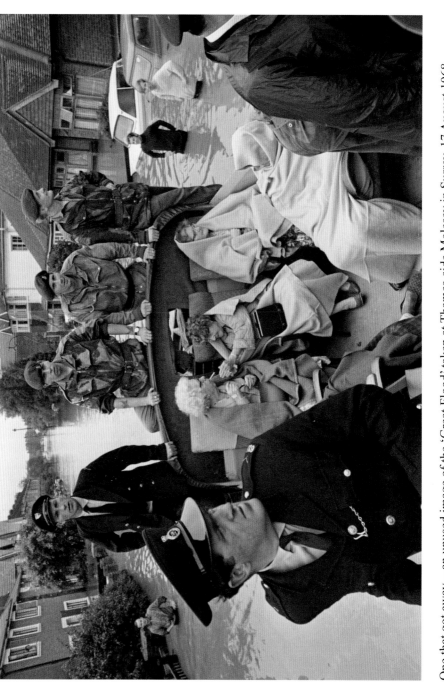

One that got away – an unused image of the 'Great Flood' taken at Thames-side Molesey in Surrey, 17 August 1968
(Credit: John Downing/Express/Getty Images)

Carol, a volunteer nurse with War on Want, attempts cholera vaccination during the Bangladesh Liberation War, June 1971

The cell at Kampala Central Police Station September 1972
(Credit: John Downing/Getty Images)

BABES IN HELL

WORLD EXCLUSIVE from inside Amin's terror jail

BY EXPRESS CAMERAMAN JOHN DOWNING

TWO little boys look through prison bars at a world gone mad.

Andrew Stanley is four, brother Robert two.

I took the picture in Kampala's Central Police Station at the height of the purge in Uganda.

The boys and their British parents, Mr. and Mrs. R. F. Stanley, were already there when I was held.

I thought of my own son at home.

But children are wonderfully tough and adaptable.

And boys will be boys. Amin or not. So Andrew and Robert were soon climbing the prison bars as if in a gym.

They have now been released, with other Britons.

My picture is a tribute to their courage.

Freed Expressman John Harrison's own story

Now I know what fear means

I CAME home to London yesterday from the terror and torture of Uganda's most notorious and sinister prison — Makindye.

I was kicked into this hellhole on the outskirts of Kampala on the orders of General Idi Amin Dada, the vicious dictator who calls himself president.

The dreaded Makindye is a military prison—a place where you learn the meaning of fear.

Welcome home! Sir Max Aitken with Expressmen John Downing (left) and John Harrison yesterday

THE CALL

THE ARMY

THE NOTE

so you'd like to convert a good income into solid capital?

London Life

MORE OF DOWNING'S ASTONISHING PICTURES: See Pages 4, 5, 6 and 7

GUN-LAW IN KAMPALA: Page 2

INTERNMENT TO END: Page 11

Missing wife: Army captain held: Page 11

LATEST

TV-Radio Programmes Page 17

BUS CRASH HORROR

PHONE STD CODE 01
353 8000
TELEX 21841

The end of the Balcombe Street siege, 12th December 1975. Four IRA members had taken a couple hostage in their own home

(Credit: John Downing/Getty Images)

An Afghan Mujahideen 'holy warrior', fighting against the invading
Soviet forces in 1983

I stepped out, thrust the camera forward at arm's length and released the shutter –
taking the exclusive image of the Thatchers leaving the Grand Hotel at 3.00 a.m.
after the IRA Brighton bomb attack, 12th October 1984

(Credit: John Downing/Getty Images)

The victim looked as though he'd fallen asleep next to his unfinished drink.
A Mafia assassination, Sicily 1988

A mother cradles her dying son, Chernobyl, 1990

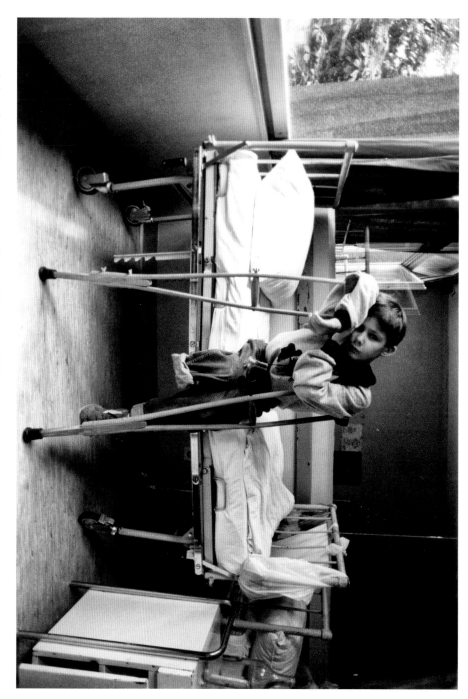

A young victim of a Serbian landmine, the Siege of Sarajevo, 1992

A mortuary in Bosnia, 1992

and dislodging the film from my fingers. I watched in open mouthed horror as it fell to the floor and the end of the canister fell off, exposing it to light. Letting out a cry, I swept it up and rammed it deep into my trouser pocket, doubling up like a man kicked in the groin to keep it hidden from the light. The darkroom staff were more than a little taken aback to see a sweating, swearing, bleeding, speeding, photographic Quasimodo bearing down on them, but once they'd grasped the seriousness of the situation they took hold of each arm and guided me into a single darkroom where I could quickly process my film. Fortunately very little light had penetrated it so – just as I'd hoped – we were the first to send half a dozen pictures and the story out of the country, much to the chagrin of the pack.

The rest of the day went smoothly, if you exclude the groom's car running over a photographer's foot and a French paparazzo making the intimate acquaintance of a policeman's nightstick. With our story in the bag, Liz and I opted to skip the monastery and go straight to the village for the final part of the party. We arrived just in time to witness the festive atmosphere as the villagers lining the road showering the newlyweds and their horse and dray with petals as they clip-clopped along the narrow lanes. It was certainly romantic and made for some lovely photographs – never published, sadly. By early evening, with everything done and dusted, it was time for a celebratory dinner. We joined with the other twenty or so foreign journalists in the bar, to hear one of the Scandinavians who knew Romania well announce that there was only one half-decent restaurant in Bucharest. Drinking up, we decamped there en masse to find it fully booked.

In a relaxed mood, we told the *maitre d*': 'No problem. We'll have a drink at the bar while we wait for a table.'

'Sorry sir, you can't wait. We don't have a bar.'

No bar? What sort of a restaurant was this? The manager was summoned and heavy negotiations were entered into that invoked the Kent/dollar formula until we had a successful conclusion. Escorted to the rear of the building, we grinned as the manager threw open a pair of double doors to reveal an elegantly panelled room with a large polished table, matching chairs and chandelier, all from a far grander era. Needless to say, we had a wonderful evening of good food, accompanied with much wine and laughter. Everyone was running on the twin octanes of high spirits and adrenalin springing from the knowledge of a job well done and a decent spread in our newspapers.

All that was left now was the Ceremony of the Blanks, a little journalistic foible which occurs with the paying of every bill. One person is deputised to hand over the money but as he or she does so they must stand close to the waiter and quietly ask, 'Can you give us some blank bills?' whilst noisily rustling banknotes. Don't get me wrong – the collecting of these blanks is purely borne out a desire to have yet another fond keepsake of a splendid venue and the good company enjoyed. The reason for them being blank is rather lost in the mists of time, but I believe it may stem from a journalist's need to always have a piece of paper to hand so that he can jot down notes.

That golden night in Bucharest the head waiter was summoned and the bill was duly paid. When the deputed journo whispered the magic mantra, he was met with a blank – not bill – but look. The Scandinavians, generous to a fault, started to scatter US dollars on the table like confetti, closely followed by the rest of us. This only had the effect of widening the waiter's eyes in still greater incomprehension. We were getting nowhere until one of the photographers took charge (you can always rely on a photographer to cut to the chase). Standing up, he collected all the money and proceeded to stuff it into our major-domo's jacket pocket whilst gently easing the book of bills from his hand.

Giving the hapless creature the indulgent smile we saved for people who were none too bright, we gently waved him away. He did as he was asked, shaking his head all the while. We could almost see him thinking: '*Why on earth would these people give me so much good black market money in return for worthless bits of paper?*' Stopping briefly at the door and with a little more enthusiasm, he turned and – holding his arm out at full stretch – offered us his cheap ball point pen, which we graciously declined. When we called in the next day for lunch he finally got the message. Our bill was presented on a silver platter and accompanied by not one but six books of bills. To his utter confusion, we also graciously declined. After all, what could we possibly do with so many?

Some years later – after the fall of Ceausescu – I returned to Bucharest, this time with Danny. We stayed in the same hotel that I'd shared with his wife (as I loved to point out), but not for such a happy reason. We were following up on a story that destitute homeless children were living in the city's sewers somewhere near the railway station. If true it was an extraordinary tale that would make extraordinary pictures so we were dispatched to check it out.

We arrived at the Intercontinental as dusk fell, dropped our bags, deposited all our valuables and most of our dollars in the hotel safe, and went straight out. We got lucky almost immediately for the first taxi driver we hailed not only spoke a little English but knew exactly where these kids hung out. 'This place dangerous,' he warned ominously, as he stopped to show us where. 'Gangs of children rob people here.' It seemed like the perfect place to start. We carried only a little local money in our pockets and had tucked more substantial amounts of dollars into our socks. I had also stripped my cameras down to the minimum – one body with a wide angle lens, flashgun, and a handful of films.

After some tense negotiations and the loss of a few more dollars, our driver reluctantly agreed to come with us and translate. Although it was dark, as we stepped onto the station forecourt we could immediately see a few kids flaked out on the pavement, sleeping off the effects of drink or drugs. We didn't have to worry about finding the rest of them for within minutes we were surrounded by a startling display of urchins of all ages, sexes and sizes, dressed in multiple layers of filthy, ragged clothing. The only thing they had in common was their matted hair and dirt-streaked skin. Danny questioned them through our interpreter and furiously scribbled down their answers. The novelty of two foreigners showing an interest in them not only seemed to fascinate them but I suspect it relieved the aching boredom of living on the streets or, to be more pedantic, beneath them.

For we quickly discovered that the story appeared to be true – they did live in the small underground tunnels that carried wide, sealed sewage pipes, and they were happy to show us in return for some food. This seemed perfectly reasonable so, having promised to feed them afterwards, we were directed away from the station. Danny and I felt like two latterday Pied Pipers of Hamelin as we walked along surrounded by kids pulling at sleeves, dragging at our jackets, pushing, shoving and shouting. It was a strange feeling to put your hand in your pocket to find another already there.

But first, they wanted to show off their skills. Our first stop was a tall street lamp with four large glass lanterns at the top, where the urchins slid aside a panel in the base to expose partially bare wires. To our utter horror, one of the little darlings grabbed these wires with his hands and touched them together. There was a bright blue flash and a sizzling sound as he was thrown backwards onto the ground. The lamps flickered off briefly before coming back on to light up the boy lying on his back, legs twitching, and his face locked in a grimace. For a moment, I went cold with fear as I stared down at him. Then, still frozen to the spot, I watched as his grimace turned into a grin, and then a broad laugh. The little monster and all his mates were laughing at his cruel party piece that had taken us in, hook, line and sinker.

Still a little shaken, we moved over to a round hole in the pavement about the size of a car wheel that disappeared into pitch darkness. A couple of the kids climbed in and signalled for us to follow them down a metal ladder. At this point our taxi driver-cum-interpreter who had been getting increasingly agitated, decided he had a pressing engagement elsewhere and – with a final warning not to go down into the hole – he fled. Danny and I exchanged worried glances and after a moment or two of assessing the danger, I shrugged and said, 'Well Danno, if I'm to get the pictures to go with your story then I'll have to go.'

Nodding loyally, he said, 'If you go, I go,' and with that I slung my camera around my neck and started down. As I descended cautiously, feeling with my foot for the next rusty rung, I was increasingly aware of the stale smell of bodies rising up to meet me on the warming air. After some fifteen feet or so the U-shaped rungs suddenly ran out, as did the wall, and my foot was flapping around in the void searching for something solid. Suddenly a hand grabbed my ankle and started pulling me downwards, a most unnerving feeling. This was rapidly followed by another hand and then another, all pulling – hard. I knew it was hopeless trying to fight these insistent troglodytes so I gave way and carried on lowering myself until – just as I was running out of hand holds – my foot finally touched bottom. Realising that the kids had been encouraging me onto the floor, I wiped the sweat from my face.

Peering right and left in the gloom, I could see that the tunnel veered off at right angles and was only about four feet high. Calling up to Danny, I said, 'I'm down. It's hot and smelly. Full of kids who grab at you but they're only trying to help. I think it's alright.' Ducking down to get out of his way, I crawled into the stiflingly claustrophobic darkness full of bodies I could hear and touch, but not see. As I rummaged around in my jacket for my small torch Danny joined me.

I will never forget what we saw down there that night – dozens of dirty, hungry children and a few adults living and sleeping alongside the broad terracotta pipes they clustered around for their warmth, especially in the winter when temperatures dropped to around -15. They were survivors, these sewer people. Danny called them the 'Lost Boys'. Roma mostly, they

were from an entire generation of a persecuted race that fled from Ceausescu's brutal orphanages once the Communist regime was overthrown in
1989. Beneath the streets they lived in an entirely different subterranean
world. The tunnels were stacked with garbage and rotting clothes that
served as dank bedding. There were toothless drug addicts sniffing glue
from bags and even men with dogs. Some of the shaven-headed teenagers
– many of them without shoes and covered in rat bites – had spent their
entire childhoods down there with only candles or pilfered electric light.
They had nowhere else to go. A frightening and dangerous place, it stank
and was full of disease. But it was home. In one dead end tunnel an old
cinema poster of a couple embracing adorned a wall, their only comfort.

Although the children we'd met at the station were friendly enough at
first, it was clear that they only survived by robbing and stealing. They told
us that the police who were afraid to follow them into their lair occasionally
lobbed tear gas grenades down the holes instead. Danny took copious notes
and I took many photographs but once we were trapped underground we
began to notice a constant jockeying for position amongst the older boys
as their demands for money grew. Nine-year-old Gabriel was one of the
most violent. Abandoned at the station by his father at the age of five, he
pulled a flick-knife and spat at us, his fingers constantly probing for money.
Sensing danger, Danny and I decided it would be prudent to leave. All the
way out we were badgered by Gabriel, who became increasingly aggressive
as we neared the entrance to the tunnels. Danny climbed out first but as I
started to leave, I felt my ankle being grabbed and looked down to see the
glint of a knife in the torchlight.

'Money!' Gabriel demanded and I resisted angrily at first. Someone else
grabbed my other ankle. 'Dollars! You have dollars!' he yelled and there
was something in his voice that gave me pause. I had children at home, I
thought. There were my parents to think of. It would be stupid to die down
here for the sake of a few dollars.

Slipping back down, as Danny called repeatedly to see if I was all right,
I reached into my sock and pulled out the one hundred dollars that was all
I had left. After a thorough search, Gabriel gave me a rare toothless grin
and finally allowed me to climb to the surface. I have never been more
happy to see Dan's smiling face.

SEVEN

I WAS JUST SITTING down to dinner at home one night in April 1982 when Tom Smith barged in. He was in an ebullient mood. 'You're washed up, Downing!' he cried. 'You can carry on covering skinheads kicking punks in Southend!' (referring to some of my recent photographs for which I won an award, I hasten to add). 'I've got the big one this time. The *Express* has the only newspaper photographer's pass to sail with the fleet to the Falklands – and they've given it to me!'

He was talking about the forthcoming battle for the Falkland Islands after the unexpected Argentinian invasion. The British government had given approval for twenty writers to join the fleet on its long voyage to the South Atlantic, but only two stills photographers – one newspaper, one agency. Many believed this was an attempt to control the photographic coverage in the press – especially anything that might be too graphic for the general public. Reporters' copy could easily be redacted but not pictures. Especially under war conditions, these would be almost impossible to censor and could ultimately prove far more damaging. The only two photo passes had been chosen by names drawn from a hat and the *Express* got lucky.

While Smiff continued teasing me about being usurped with the biting humour for which he was famous, a frisson of envy touched me as Britain going to war again was about the biggest story of our generation. My jealousy lasted all of a nanosecond before I flung an arm around his shoulder and, laughing with the pleasure one gets from seeing a friend on a high, guided him in the direction of a rather fine bottle of claret.

The truth was that few believed we would actually risk British lives over an uninhabited island called South Georgia that nobody had ever heard of, least of all for the trivial reason that a few scrap metal dealers had raised an Argentinian flag there. It was generally accepted that in the month it would take the fleet to get to the war zone, diplomacy would have played its part and all would end happily ever after. But then one shouldn't believe in fairytales, least of all when the fairy godmother at the time was Margaret Thatcher, known as the 'Iron Lady.'

Smiff was due to leave later that night so after loading him up with as much equipment as we thought useful, I wished him well and waved him off. Tales of his escapades in the Falklands thereafter are legion and always told in a self-deprecatory fashion. He boasted that whilst others on the ships were running around the deck keeping fit he was building the finest wine cellar in the fleet (purloined with a bribe from the officers' stores) and was devastated when he had to change ships mid-Atlantic, forcing him to leave most of it behind. His stories were his modest way of underplaying his extremely competent photographic and journalistic skills. Needless to say, and despite all the horseplay that masked the fact that his ship could be blown up at any minute, Tom's gritty photographs were as good as ever and some even iconic. They were used all around the world.

Not long after he had left on the flotilla and the country was gearing up for war, I had my own Falklands-related assignment that proved to be far less fruitful but was still quite the adventure. Desperate to cover as many angles as possible, someone on the desk told me, 'Get to the Falklands, Downing,' as if it were that simple. I'm sure they hadn't a clue how far away it was. After consulting those who knew more, I realised that as I couldn't get to the Falklands from Argentina for obvious reasons (being enemy territory), I'd have to fly to Santiago, the capital of Chile, and then try to get to the islands from the southernmost tip of Cape Horn. Once I landed I learned that there wasn't a direct connection between the two but there was an airstrip at Punta Arenas, the last point of civilisation before Antarctica. Along with a few other hopeful journalists and photographers we shared the costs and hired a small plane.

Punta Arenas is in the province of Magallanes and Antártica Chilena (part of Patagonia), but once we arrived we were stuck. The remote coastal town was a former penal colony that later enjoyed a gold rush and a sheep farming boom before becoming of national strategic importance to defend the Straits of Magellan. It was a strange place full of houses with corrugated tin roofs and it only had one hotel where my room was riddled with bed bugs (for which I was given free drinks by way of compensation). Once I'd stopped itching, I sat around with my fellow journos in the bar, trapped, bored to tears and hatching ever more crazy plans for reaching the Falklands.

When the ITN reporter Jon Snow arrived with his team I immediately teamed up with them, hoping for a better chance of getting somewhere hanging onto their coat tails. Jon was a lovely fella, and on my birthday (April 17) he and the crew took me to the town's Officer's Club for dinner. This was a rare treat for, although we'd been gorging on the abundant local king crab washed down with an excess of excellent Chilean wine, I was looking forward to something different. The local delicacy in the hotel and restaurants we frequented was a strange kind of barnacle called *picoroco*, which was served sitting upright on the plate and took all of my manpower to put in my mouth. Mercifully, there was no *picoroco* in sight at the Officer's Club and, better still, it had a grand piano so Jon – having discovered my love of music – played it for me.

Much of our time in Punta Arenas revolved around the hotel bar and was far from exciting however. That was until one night when a man sauntered in wearing a mac and a flat cap. He claimed to be in naval security and to start with I thought it might be a hoax but when he asked me where the reporters were, I directed him to Jon. Rather usefully, he gave Jon all kinds of useful tips including the fact that if the war started and the Royal Navy needed any assistance then they would come to Punta Arenas. He kindly arranged for us to get accredited by security at the docks in case that happened, and then to fly us to a meteorological research station in Antarctica, from which we hoped to hop a ride on a scientific boat or maybe even reach one of the lesser Falkland islands in a small plane. Our various desks back in London had arranged a makeshift landing strip with one of the sheep farmers there just in case.

No commercial flight had ever been to Antarctica, so we found a local pilot who serviced the small band of scientists stationed at Base San Martin on Barry Island. He flew us out with the warning that he carried just enough fuel to fly us there and only halfway back again two days later, so if we couldn't land there for him to refuel we'd be dead. We decided to take the chance. I had left the UK for Chile with a few warm clothes, as I knew it would be cold in the Falklands, but had nothing that would equip me for the ice cap where the average temperatures were -37 C, so I was glad we wouldn't be there too long.

Base Martin, as it was known, was the first ever human settlement south of the Antarctic Circle. The snow was too deep for planes to land for much of the year so its fourteen scientists were dropped there at the beginning of the season and picked up a year later. Even in the springtime huge bulldozers had to be operated continually by two men for twenty-four hours to sweep the small landing strip clear of snow before any aircraft could land. The base had housing for the packs of dogs they used to get about, as well as some warehouses, a radio mast and a power generator. The scientists were all closely cropped and we learned that they had a tradition of shaving their heads at the beginning of the year and allowing the hair to grow back over the next twelve months. They shared a cabin and an identical 'emergency house' in case the first one burnt down (as once happened). With long tables down the middle, these buildings looked exactly like the kinds of wooden huts that Ernest Shackleton and his men would have encountered circa 1915. It was like going back almost a century. Interestingly, their emergency cabin was only ever used for someone's birthday, so that those isolated souls felt as if they were going 'out' for a party. I loved the place; it was so photogenic and interesting that I couldn't stop taking photographs.

Our quest was to inch closer and closer to the Falklands and we hoped to connect with a scientific icebreaker named the *Magadan*, and either cadge a lift to the Falklands or at least speak to the crew to see if they could give us any information about ship or air movements. When that wasn't possible we heard that there was another small research station on an island called Signy in the South Orkneys with only two British scientists on it. Using the base radio, we tried to contact them to see if they had an airstrip on which we could land. I could see the snow falling heavily outside as Jon sat at the wireless in the radio room, headphones on, shouting 'Hello? Over.' into the darkness and getting nothing back for ages, until a voice finally echoed, 'Hello! Over.' in the most cultured BBC English I have ever heard. It was like something out of Pathé News.

Jon asked, 'Hello. Do you have a landing strip there? Over.'

'Oh, good God, no! Far too small. Over,' came the clipped reply.

'I understand there is a British scientific boat in the area? Over.'

There was the usual delay then, 'Can't say too much, old boy. Can't say too much. Over and out.'

Afraid of getting snowed in, we had to leave the next night without a story although Jon was at least able to file something from the base and I had stacks of (never used) shots. On the way home, the pilot told us, almost casually, 'If it's clear enough tonight I'll land in Tesco's.' We were confused. 'Tesco's car park,' he explained. 'It's closer to your hotel.' Sure enough, when we flew over the branch of the ubiquitous supermarket we realised it was close to our hotel but there was a single car parked in the middle and we had to go on to the airport after all.

Our single story from the entire six weeks I was in Punta Arenas was when a British Sea King helicopter from *HMS Invincible* was forced to land on the beach a few days later in a Force 10 gale with engine trouble. This was the first glimmer of a real news story that we'd had. We found out later that the craft was loaded with sophisticated radio equipment on a secret Argentinian monitoring mission and eight members of the SAS had slipped away into the hills the minute they landed, before making their way on foot to the British Embassy in Santiago. Piling into a mini-bus, we rushed down to the beach and took photos of the Chilean troops trying to cover up the wreckage. It made for a great story written back home by our defence correspondent Michael Evans under the banner headline Operation Eavesdrop, and it allowed me to return without shame. Oh, and yet another souvenir – a little flag from Base Martin signed by all the skinhead scientists we'd met.

My next trip in 1982 was much more entertaining and news of it came to me at the perfect moment. I was at another dreary party conference – this time in Blackpool in the most appalling weather. These events were almost as boring as election campaigns because they always followed much the same pattern, with speech after speech delivering the same boring message.

I arrived in the middle of the storm, ate something in the hotel and retired to bed at nine o'clock. The windows were rattling with the wind and the rain and I was throughly fed up. Just as I was about to nod off, there was a knock on the door. 'Mr Downing? Mr Downing?' a young man's voice called with increasing urgency. 'Your office is on the phone for you downstairs.'

Grumpily, I got up, got dressed and went down to the foyer. 'What is it?' I barked into the receiver.

The voice of the picture desk assistant at the other end of the line sounded contrite as he stammered, 'S-sorry to disturb you. I know you've only just arrived there, but…'

'Yes?'

'…but we'd like you to leave.'

My attitude softened immediately. 'Oh, okay….' Then, somewhat suspiciously, 'Why? Where do you want me to go?' (thinking it would probably be to somewhere even worse).

'Well,' said the voice, we'd like you to go on the Queen's Royal Tour of the South Pacific.'

I punched the air with my fist and cried, 'Yeess!' Within thirty-six hours I was drinking rum punch from a coconut shell on the beach. We then embarked on the tour starting in sunny Brisbane watching the Queen and Prince Philip close that year's Commonwealth Games before they boarded the Royal Yacht and we took to whatever transport we could find. That was the beginning of a journey that took us more than 18,000 miles in twenty-seven days in broiling heat and high humidity to some of the most remarkable places I have ever seen. But what a journey.

From Brisbane to Fiji via Papua New Guinea, the Solomon Islands, Nauru, Kiribati, Vanuatu, and Tuvalu (yes, really) and back to Fiji. The only down side was that the reporter accompanying me through malarial swamps, hepatitis lagoons, twenty-one gun salutes, exotic banquets and relentless ceremonial dancing was the constantly complaining columnist Jean Rook, but more about her later.

Trying to get a unique picture of a royal on an official tour is nigh on impossible, as each event is carefully stage managed with all the incumbent security, so I had to decide which of the pre-arranged photographic positions I wanted. At Funafuti, the capital of Tuvalu, the Queen was to be ferried to shore from the Royal Yacht in a ceremonial war canoe and then carried triumphantly with Prince Philip to the chieftain's hut. The gaily-clad islanders did this task with enormous pride and I got a nice head-on shot of her coming ashore.

Later on that warm South Pacific evening I joined Her Majesty's table, or to be more precise, Her Majesty's floor during a welcoming feast. She and the Prince sat on raised red velvet cushions and we guests sat in a circle on the ground as native girls in grass skirts delivered a huge coconut leaf piled high with crabmeat, fish, banana and rice. The dusky maiden assigned to sit in front of me fanned me to keep me cool (and to keep the flies off) in between feeding me small delicacies. After a while I found myself chewing on a black piece of flesh with the consistency of a Pirelli tyre. Come to think of it, the Pirelli would have been better. Curiosity got the better of me so I asked what I was eating. The reply was something no Westerner ever wants to hear – 'bat'. From then on I only ate bananas or anything recognisable and, looking around, I noticed that the Queen and most of my colleagues were doing much the same.

On Nauru – the world's smallest republic with the world's fattest inhabitants – the chieftain was a millionaire with a penchant for French wine. We soon learned that he had an excellent wine cellar and a sommelier named Christmas. There was so much wealth amongst the islanders that the chieftain's brother, a man called Newspaper, thought nothing of throwing a beach party for the visiting press where we sat around a camp fire drinking one of the finest vintage clarets I have ever tasted, cases of which were offered up like lemonade.

Then there was a tropical storm in Papua New Guinea, the likes of which I had never before seen. The ceremonial dancers, sporting exquisite feathers taken from the native birds of paradise, fled before their feathers were soaked through and everybody scattered apart from a loyal row of boy scouts who remained standing to attention in driving rain at an angle of 45°C as the Queen and Prince Phillip, who were undercover, watched them admiringly and we applauded their stoicism.

One of the high points of the trip for me was being invited onto the Royal Yacht *Britannia* for a reception and chatting to the Queen. I also enjoyed meeting a characterful one-legged parrot on the Solomon Islands presumably looking for his Long John Silver, but for Jean Rook the highlight of the whole trip was something that happened on our first day of the tour. During a Royal walkabout in Brisbane, we were following the Queen at a respectful distance and, to my amazement, a group of ex-pat Brits suddenly started waving madly. 'It's Jean Rook!' they cried, recognising the *Express* columnist. Jean's face lit up and she wandered over to her fans and did her best impersonation of a royal, shaking hands, posing for pictures and accepting bouquets they hadn't been able to give to the Queen. She never let anyone forget it.

'You're going to Afghanistan,' were the first words the picture editor said to me one October morning in 1983 as I arrived at work. 'And it's top secret.' There it was, that word again – secret – the one that I know knew really meant *dangerous*.

I was mighty relieved that my companion was to be the *Express*'s chief foreign correspondent Ross Benson, a man who looked more like Ian Fleming must have imagined James Bond to look than any actor who ever played him. With a mop of blond hair and piercing blue eyes, Ross was a picture of sartorial excellence wherever he went – even when facing the possibility of death. He was far more at home in the watering holes of London nightclubs like Annabel's or Tramp than on the road but he was nevertheless a first class journalist who relished the life of a roving foreign correspondent, because – as he frequently admitted – he was the eternal

Peter Pan who never wanted to grow up.

Surprisingly self-effacing for someone who lived in Belgravia and went to school with Prince Charles, he dined out on the tales of the lengths he went to in order to maintain his immaculate looks, even in the back of beyond. Never a mirror was passed without him stopping for an inspection and I can confirm that the man whose locks were bouffanted daily with cream cake precision (and who I'd just been on assignment with following Terry Waite in West Beirut) packed a hairdryer wherever he went. I do, however, think the story Bob Geldof tells of Ross standing in front of the propellers of an Ethiopian relief plane to dry his locks may be a tad far-fetched.

Impeccably turned out in his Savile Row suits, silk ties, Gucci loafers and Turnbull & Asser shirts (personalised, naturally), Ross carried himself with an air of self-assurance. I was his antithesis, dressed in the photographer's uniform of leather bomber jacket, chinos, casual shirt, and thin leather tie that went out of style years before I adopted it as a fashion statement. I still occasionally wear them today in the hope that they might become chic again. Since boyhood my hair has been a talking point and was, in the words of one past girlfriend, like an 'unmade bed'. This unruly mess tops a face once described as 'having more lines on it than Charing Cross Station'. Personally, I'm more drawn to Ross's quip: 'Face of a truck driver, soul of a poet.'

Briefed by the foreign desk before we made preparations to leave, Ross and I were told that they'd made contact with Afghan Mujahideen 'holy warriors' fighting against the invading forces in the complicated Soviet-Afghan War. These insurgents had agreed to lead us into Afghanistan from neighbouring Pakistan, making us the first British journalists to live and travel with the 'Muj' inside that war-torn country. To set the plan in motion, we had to use the same trick we'd deployed to get into South Sudan – send our business cards to a contact in Pakistan who would then find us at our hotel in Peshawar, a town in the North West Frontier province close to the border. He'd return it with the cross in the top corner, signifying that it was safe to talk openly. If the cross wasn't there, we had to pretend we were tourists as there was a risk our 'contact' could be a member of the secret police.

Two weeks later we flew out to Peshawar, booked into the hotel and waited. Unusually, we didn't have to wait long this time. Within twenty-four hours, we were informed that two men were downstairs and wanted to see us. They informed that we'd be starting our journey at the North West Frontier and from there to Kabul, photographing the Russian military presence – a first glimpse of Soviet activity inside Afghanistan. The direct route over the Khyber Pass was impossible as it was held by enemy forces. Instead we'd have to circle around, crossing mountain ranges and travelling via the Paktia province, passing Miran, Ghazni and Jaghtu in the Wardak region and even then getting across the border would be far from easy.

The next day we were taken to a local market and kitted out in authentic Afghan outfits, including turban-like scarves that could be unwrapped to cover our faces. We were told to buy a knife, sleeping bags, and *patus* – traditional shawls like blankets worn over the shoulder that have multiple uses. 'Under no circumstances are you to take photographs of any women on your journey!' I was warned most firmly. Once we'd bought our supplies we were blindfolded and driven to another part of the city where we were ushered into a small, nondescript dwelling. Here we had our photos taken in our Afghan garb, given local names and issued with fake identity cards. We were then dropped off at our hotel and told to wait.

Two days later one of our contacts returned and, telling us to pack only what we could carry on our backs and meet him at midnight in an area of the town far from the hotel. After he had left we filled our rucksacks and left for the rendezvous where a wreck of a car was waiting. Driven to a secret location on the outskirts of the city we had our first face-to-face with some of the freedom fighters with whom we'd be living (and hopefully not dying) for the next six weeks.

These ten Mujahideen were all from the same tribe in the Wardak province. War veterans in their thirties, they were heavily armed and extremely fit. They were such tough people but wonderfully photogenic, with eyes that spoke of centuries of bitter conflict. Communication was a major problem as neither of us spoke their language (a Pashto/Persian dialect) so we learned early on that *tic* meant OK so after that everything boiled down to *tic* or non-*tic*. A few of them had a smattering of English and one offered to act as our translator. Then there was Ahmed, the son of the local warlord. At just twenty years old and slightly overweight, this moon-faced boy was the leader of our group and, worryingly, it was his first excursion into a conflict zone. In spite of his obvious inexperience (or perhaps because of it) he was extremely arrogant and full of his own self-importance. The far more experienced Muj warriors resented his boastfulness.

We sat together on the floor drinking tea and after an hour or so we slept a little in preparation for our dawn departure. At first light we travelled in two battered cars to an area near the border where we met another twenty veterans, all armed with Kalashnikov machine guns. After we'd been introduced, an old ambulance arrived and we were told to strip and put on women's burkhas to cover us up from head to toe. Feeling a bit like Tony Curtis and Jack Lemmon in *Some Like It Hot*, we did as were told and settled into the back of the vehicle with six men for the drive to the border. As we both had blue eyes, a dead giveaway in Afghanistan, we were ordered to adopt the traditional female pose in Afghanistan and not look up under any circumstances.

As soon as we approached the border the vehicle was stopped and searched, as we'd been warned to expect. The atmosphere that was already extremely tense almost reached breaking point when the guards started shouting that they wanted us 'women' to get out. We thought the game was up. The men argued furiously, accusing the guards of being disrespectful and warning them that they shouldn't even be looking at us. After an agonising stand-off, a bribe was paid and we were finally waved through.

Once inside Afghanistan, we travelled to the small town of Darra Adam Khel a place with streets of dust, houses of mud, and wooden shacks and walkways that gave it a Wild West feel. The difference here was that at every stall and store men and boys were making and selling the kinds of weapons the Muj needed to purchase for our excursion. The noise was incredible because guns were being fired all around us with every seller operating a policy of 'try before you buy'. One of the stallholders was happy to display his anti-aircraft gun in the street, creating the first photos of my assignment.

The traders boasted that they could copy any gun brought to them and the one weapon the Muj were desperate for were surface-to-air missiles, preferably US-manufactured SAM's. These would have been particularly effective against airborne attacks from the Mil Mi-24 or Hind assault helicopters that were proving to be a deadly foe. With their armoured fuselage, ballistic-resistant glass and titanium rotor blades plus speeds of up to 360kms per hour they were practically impossible to shoot down with conventional weapons. The guerrillas called them *Shaitan-Arba* or Satan's Chariot, and I was soon to find out why.

As I wandered around town, marvelling at the sheer quantities of murderous weaponry on display I suddenly noticed something I recognised.

A few years earlier I'd been sent to photograph Simon Wiesenthal, the Holocaust survivor and Nazi hunter. Whilst sitting in his office, he handed me a fountain pen that wasn't what it seemed. Like something out of a Bond movie it was a small and discreet weapon that fired a single bullet but could still – the Afghan stallholder assured me –'kill a man at six feet.' I couldn't resist. After a couple of practice shots into a bullet-pocked tree trunk at the back of his stall, I bought the weapon for $5 along with three bullets for a dollar each. My first Afghan souvenir.

Our rugged companions were meanwhile busy buying something far more heavy duty. After a shopping spree lasting several hours, they carried their terrifying new arsenal to our ambulance and, after clambering in awkwardly to find a place to sit with our hazardous and deeply incriminating cargo, we moved on.

The next day and night would be tough as we'd have to cross the Plain of Zurmat, a desert wasteland that would take some twelve hours to traverse. We carried little water and although we'd travel mostly at night, we'd also have to walk part of the route in the daytime because our scout Amir needed to spot key landmarks to ensure that we didn't get lost in the barren wilderness. Aside from dehydration, our biggest danger was that the Russians – who had a heavy tank presence on the plain – might spot us. If that happened, there would be no escape.

Within hours of setting off a small convoy of enemy tanks appeared on the horizon heading straight for us. We were quickly told to drop to the ground and cover ourselves with our earth-coloured *patus* as the convoy sped past without giving us a second glance. As the hours passed and the heat intensified, both Ross and I became increasingly sick with heat exhaustion until he finally collapsed and Amir and I had to help him the last few miles. When we finally arrived at a small village on the other side of the Plain, we could rest and recover.

Every day in Afghanistan was more physically punishing than the last. The landscape was so rocky and uneven that it made the walking extremely hard. We had to negotiate mountain passes as high as 12,000 feet that were mainly shingle with little or no vegetation. There was hardly any wildlife. We used donkeys to carry the heavier supplies including my camera case, but on my person I carried a Nikon, some film, and a lens at all times as well as a Polaroid for instant shots to hand out to the locals in return for their permission to capture their images. I almost had a disaster in the early days when one of the donkeys carrying much of my kit lost his footing and crashed to the ground, crushing the delicate tools of my trade but I managed to cobble together what was left.

Most mornings we were up at 3am to walk nine hours until noon when we'd stop and rest for a few hours as the heat rose to an unbearable 100-plus degrees. Our only respite came five times a day when the men, devout Muslims, stopped to pray and drink tea. Once we made camp, we'd sleep. When it was time to eat, a piece of ragged grey linen about seven feet by three feet was unfurled on the floor around which we all sat, barefoot and cross-legged. One of the warriors would bring a bowl and a jug of water, similar to those long-necked brass coffee pots with a swan-neck spout so beloved of Moroccan tourists. Ours were made of recycled gunmetal or gaudy plastic. Water was a precious commodity but, with deep religious significance, the precursor to every meal was to wash one's hands and feet, which we did – rubbing them vigorously as a trickle of water ran over them. It just about took off the day's dust but never the adhesive mud from a hard day's march.

Once we'd finished washing, large flat rounds of a naan type bread, the size of small dustbin lids, would be lobbed down the twelve-foot 'table-cloth' by the filthiest old man I'd seen since the invention of the dirty raincoat. His two young sons who helped him were just as dirty. I asked our translator why they were so grubby. His indignant reply foxed me – 'Because he is the cook!' The bin lid of bread was accompanied by an even larger bowl of rice with a handful of raisins or a piece of lamb mixed in, all covered in a congealing skin of lukewarm sheep fat. The men thrust their dirt-ingrained hands into the communal bowl to scoop up a handful, squeezed it into their palms to firm it up before projecting it into their mouths with their thumbs as though tossing a coin. This might have been acceptable had it not been for the Mujahideens' love of nasal excavations, which rather took the edge off the meal for me.

Naively, I managed to upset the social and religious etiquette on my very first day. Being left-handed, I automatically reached towards the bowl of rice, causing an audible intake of breath from all those seated around me. I was immediately reprimanded and told that in Muslim countries food is only eaten with the right hand as the left is used for more prosaic duties (there's no toilet paper in the wilds of Afghanistan). Duly chastised, and trying to recall if the nose picking was only ever left-handed, I never made that mistake again.

The food was almost always the same and there wasn't much of it so we were constantly hungry. During that trip, I lost 28lbs in weight. The only variation to our diet came when we called on a local warlord who might prepare us a feast. This was always a real treat as we were then able to sample the local yoghurt and enjoy fresh fruit such as plums, apples and grapes. After any feast we'd go to 'bed', digging a shallow trench to lie in overnight as the earth was warmer than the cool night air. Then at 3am we'd set off again.

Walking up to twelve hours a day, we'd devotedly follow Amir the scout who sported a pair of cut-down Wellington boots. He was about my age but looked much older because of his leathery skin and full beard. Despite being forty, he was extremely fit and an expert at finding the hidden tracks and paths that crossed the mountains. His agility, knowledge of the flora and fauna, and his excellent sense of direction saved our lives and earned him the respect of the entire group. One day he stopped and signalled for me to come and look at a bush further along the path. He crushed the seeds of the bush and gave them to me to smell. The overpowering scent was of aniseed, which transported me straight back to Morgan's, the corner shop in Llanelli, and the little black seed that lay in wait in the centre of my favourite aniseed balls. Ever hopeful, I took a handful of Amir's seeds, crushed them up as best I could and trickled them into the bottle of pure alcohol I had in my first aid kit, hoping that I might be able to create something vaguely resembling Pernod.

Later that same day we came across an exhausted four-man team from the Médecins Sans Frontières charity on their way out of Afghanistan after a three-month tour of duty. This is an excellent organisation that specialises in ferrying doctors and medical aid into war zones. They joined us for what was laughingly called dinner. As I took some pictures we chatted in the gentle light of an oil lamp and they spoke longingly of their return to civilisation – Paris, good food, street cafés, post-prandial Pernods.

Pernod! An idea leapt into my mind. I'd seen that they had an unopened half bottle of Johnny Walker Black Label whisky, which they'd kept for their last night in Afghanistan. Offering them my homemade 'Pernod,' I asked if they wanted to trade. The doctors sniffed my concoction suspiciously but the memory was too much for them. They insisted we swap; a deal I was only too pleased to oblige. That night – and every night until it ran out, Ross and I had a little tipple, toasting the French whilst wondering what they made of my artisan hooch.

The next night we arrived in a small town in pitch blackness. Fumbling our way down narrow alleys we could hear villagers passing close by as they scurried away. Most were scared to be associated with the Mujahideen, chiefly because if the Russians found out that they were giving refuge to insurgents they risked being imprisoned and tortured. Arriving at a small door we were ushered into a dark corridor with dim candlelight shining from a distant room. Men and women brushed past us but we couldn't see them, we could only feel the touch of their robes. The women started giggling nervously at the sight of us and were immediately ushered out as we were led on to the candlelit room to meet the village elders. Welcoming us, they invited us to sit and drink tea with them before allowing us to bed down for the night.

The following day, our plans to move on were thwarted when we learned that there were Russian patrols nearby. Ross and I went up onto the flat roof to see if we could spot anything, but in the myriad of roofs of differing levels in that souk of a town, there was no sign of them. While we lay there waiting, we got so hot that we stripped off our shirts without thinking. Hearing female laughter, we looked across the sea of rooftops to see a group of young girls watching us and giggling. They were pointing at us and waving so we waved back. We then watched in horror as the girls' father appeared and started beating them angrily with a stick.

When they heard what had happened, the Muj warned us that we must never strip off in public again as we could be severely punished for such a crime. We also had to say sorry to the father of the girls, which rather stuck in our throats after what we'd witnessed.

Once the Russian patrols had left the area we travelled on towards the fortified city of Ghazni on Highway 1, the main route from Kabul to the south. An ancient city with a rich history, it was recognisable by its landmark citadel. Knowing this was a place that had witnessed the death of many British soldiers in the days of Empire and the history of the North-west Frontier, we had no intention of adding our names to the death toll.

Worryingly, when we arrived at night we found a fierce battle raging. Tracers lit up the night sky as the Russians, based in the castle at the top of the hill, fired shells and rockets down into the poorly defended town. A chatter of machine guns echoed back from somewhere in the darkness. Ahmed, our young leader, insisted that we continue into the town, as it was the only place to stay. Under effective fire, we ran ducking and diving down narrow, unmade alleyways as overhead the air was cut and sliced with the whizz and fizz of death. We finally tumbled in through an ancient door into the courtyard of a 'safe house' without incurring any injuries. The night had been our friend. Panting to catch his breath, Ross ran his hands through his dishevelled hair and told me, 'You know, on the whole, I'd rather be at Annabel's.'

When my heart had stopped hammering in my chest (and against the express wishes of our leader), I crept up a rickety ladder and shot a long exposure picture of the tracers raining down from the sinister looking castle. Many innocent people were killed and injured in the town during that relentless attack and I knew it was my duty to at least record their suffering.

The next morning we moved out early and walked all day. By nightfall we reached a zone that was heavily manned by the Russians and fortified with six small fortress-like structures half a mile apart, each with its own watchtower. If anything suspicious was spotted, the nearest watchtower set off a flare to warn the others. This flare became a marker for the gun crews who would home in and shoot.

The area in front of each watchtower comprised flat scrubland. Alarmingly, Ahmed announced that we had to cross it at night to reach the mountain pass as it was too dangerous to attempt during the day. At midnight we gathered on the outskirts of the village with about thirty of the Muj and, after some tea and a discussion of the dangers, we set off into the moonless, silent night. Several foot-slogging hours later we were called into a huddle for a final whispered warning that we were about to break through the line of Russian forts that were a few hundred yards apart, and that complete silence was paramount. To add to the excitement the area was mined.

In what was an intense hour, we set off again one behind the other with Ross and I roughly in the middle. Following Amir through the minefield, hoping not to be blown up or spotted, we climbed over a small wall and crawled along its lea before reaching a scrappy hedge of stunted trees and thorny bushes that provided the only cover between two of the strongholds. The tension was palpable. There was a water-filled ditch either side of the hedge, forcing each of us to cling onto any prickly handhold as we made our way along. Wading through the water wasn't an option as we were told there could be trip wires.

We were going well but halfway along I suddenly lost my footing in the darkness, plunging both legs into the muddy water and letting out a whispered oath. My compatriots turned to me as one and, like a punctured tyre, let out a mighty, 'Ssshhh!' Within five seconds all hell broke loose. The sky lit up with red and green flares and a couple of mortars dispatched their lethal shrapnel. Ross noted later that when the first mortar exploded I didn't even flinch and I pointed out that if you heard the bang it was probably too late to be ducking. By one of those quirks that night can play on the senses, it must have seemed to the Russians that the noise I'd made had come from a different direction because the mortars exploded at some distance from us, but it was still some time before we dared move on. Crouching, we didn't move a muscle in the hope that they'd think an animal was to blame. After a few minutes the firing stopped but it was still some time before we dared move on to safety.

The next day we met up with another group of warriors returning from Kabul. They told us that there had been heavy fighting further up the next mountain pass and warned us that Russian attack helicopters were in operation. The Soviet Spetsnaz Special Forces had inflicted heavy casualties on the fighters and were the only group that they genuinely feared. An elite SAS-style brigade, they would be dropped behind enemy lines to attack unsuspecting enemies.

As we were talking, two young boys rode up on a bicycle out of nowhere so I grabbed my camera to take a picture of what seemed an incongruously innocent scene. When I did, the boys abandoned their bikes and started running. The next thing I knew, sub-machine gunfire was spraying all around us, missing us by inches. A Russian patrol further down the mountain had spotted the sudden movement. We all dived for cover but it was impossible to see where the shots were coming from. In the commotion the other group of fighters suffered some casualties but we managed to crawl away unscathed.

Further along the mountain paths we came across one of the *caravanserais* that provided refreshments for a few Afghani. These *serais* provided two types of sugar-laden tea – *tor chai* (black tea) and *chin chai* (Chinese tea) and were the only places in the mountains where travellers could revive themselves. Sipping at my drink, I spotted a rugged-faced man with a beautiful hawk on his shoulder, and learned that he had trained the bird to hunt for small animals that the two of them then shared. He agreed that I could take his picture and, as a reward, I gave him an instant Polaroid of himself. The falconer was so delighted that he shared his only apple with me, a rare gift.

During that trip I took so many Polaroids for the locals that I eventually ran out. The Afghans were amazed and had never seen anything like these instant pictures. I'd given our guards prints of themselves from the beginning and immediately had them watching my back. Many locals would plead with me to take a *puri* or picture of them. Word spread so quickly that when we arrived at some villages crowds of over-enthusiastic people would run up to me shouting, '*Puri! Puri!*' When I ran out of film I offered them sweets and cigarettes but they still wanted Polaroids and I ended up needing minders to fend them off.

One afternoon, as we were travelling across another rocky region, Ahmed the leader suddenly spotted a large white bird similar to a crane resting on a stone, which surprised and delighted me as we'd seen so little wildlife. Before I could stop him, he lifted his rifle and shot it. I was sad about that, 'Are you going to eat it?' I asked, but he just laughed. He had shot it purely for sport. I was tired and hungry and his arrogance rattled me unduly. We were all famished and if he wasn't hunting to feed the group then it seemed a waste of a life in a place where the fragility of life seemed that much more precious. Before I knew it, I was arguing with him, which he clearly didn't like. It was an uncharacteristic display of anger on my part, sparked in part by my frustration at the endless dust, legions of flies and blistering heat. Plus I had a desperate urge that day to be back home with my family – anywhere but there.

Our dispute festered into the next few days of endless walking and when we stopped to rest Ahmed started playing a game by pointing his gun at me as if to shoot me but then firing at a rock or into the air. Riled, I lectured him on the dangers of playing with guns and rather haughtily concluded, 'Any fool can shoot rocks on a mountain'. Feeling threatened, he immediately challenged me to a shooting match, insisting he was a great shot, whereas he quite rightly suspected that I had only limited experience with a gun. Even so, a principle was at stake so I took up the challenge.

It was only as Ahmed picked out a rock further down the mountain that he added, almost casually, 'You win – you shoot me. I win – I shoot you.'

'Wait. What?' Everyone was watching so, with the pride of Fleet Street on my shoulders, I accepted with all the panache I could muster. Borrowing the nearest gun I dug deep into the memories of my teenage shooting lessons when I had briefly joined the Territorial Army in south London.

The men all watched and silence fell as Ahmed announced that he'd go first. He picked up a Kalashnikov and fired, missing the rock. I was mighty relieved. Then it was my turn. Trying not to think of the consequences, I tightened my grip, took aim and squeezed the trigger. On opening my eyes, I found to my unutterable joy that I had hit my target dead centre. The whole group gave out a cheer, clearly backing me over Ahmed, who they only put up with because he was the son of their chief. Furious, Ahmed declared that he'd used the wrong gun, so he grabbed another and tried again. Mistake. Even from the basics I'd been taught in the TA, I knew he should have used the same gun and adjusted it. He missed.

Quietly confident, I took one last shot and hit the rock for a second time. There was an uneasy silence and I wondered if Ahmed might shoot me anyway just to impress his men. Leaning towards him, I said quietly, 'Where would you like to die?' He pretended not to understand at first and asked someone to translate. When they did there was a huge laugh from the group and Ahmed blanched, uncertain if I was serious. Smiling, I returned the gun and walked away but Ahmed had lost face in front of his men and I had myself made an enemy. We had several disagreements after this and on many occasions he would ride the supply donkey up the mountain just so that I'd have to carry my camera case. And all for a stupid bird.

Keeping a low profile as we moved on, we tried to stay in villages and towns for just one night at a time, for fear of being turned over to the Russians by local informers. But because of nearby patrols we sometimes had to stay longer. In one town where this happened, we were woken at first light by the sound of panic in the village. Russian HIND attack helicopters were approaching. We guessed somebody had tipped them off about our presence because capturing two Western journalists would have been a prize.

As we fled through the narrow streets two helicopters strafed the town and fired their rockets, injuring many. Stopping just for a moment as they flew overhead I managed to take a few shots of the intimidating new craft. Although we escaped unharmed that morning, the Russians now knew we were in the area and over the next couple of days we had to hide repeatedly from a number of air patrols searching for us. The *patu* we carried over our shoulders proved a vital tool against detection. On many occasions as soon as we heard a helicopter approaching, we'd spread out and hunch down on the ground, pulling our blankets over us. These acted as the perfect camouflage and must have made us appear from the air like another cluster of boulders.

Later that day, we stopped in a small fort to rest while the men drank tea and played chess. That was the day I have already described when the warriors suddenly jumped up and ran from the building as Ross and I looked on, confused. When the HINDs closed in on us, the fear that flooded every blood vessel in my body and drove me down that stepped valley to safety will always be embedded in my memory banks. Cowering as those screaming metal monsters rattled a stream of bullets at me from immediately overhead, I was convinced I was going to die. Even now, it still amazes me that I had the energy to shoot off a couple of frames and capture the infamous machines.

As if that wasn't bad enough, the next few days of walking were probably the most brutal and at the age of forty-three I was the old man so I found it staggeringly tough. One day we walked for sixteen hours, waded a river, stopped at about 9pm for a cup of tea (there was always tea), then marched again from midnight to 6am before another tea break and then walked until noon. We were finally taken to the top of the mountain from where we could look down on to an isolated Russian military base that had around a hundred soldiers and many armoured vehicles. Ahmed announced that his men would attack the base the next day, but first they'd warn the Russians that they were all going to die unless they moved out. I was so surprised and queried that decision but was told that it was the right thing to do. The Muj were honourable like that, perhaps because of their religious fanaticism.

Amir the scout was sent to deliver the message, and to our astonishment, it worked and the Russians abandoned their post the next day, so fearful were they of an attack. The Muj had quite a reputation as fierce fighters and those young Russian soldiers were eager to escape. I was desperate to go in and photograph the place afterwards but was told that they would have laid booby-traps all around and it would be too dangerous.

I don't know how many days later it was that we arrived on the outskirts of Kabul. As we approached, we came across yet another group of exhausted fighters who'd suffered heavy losses in a gun battle with an armoured patrol. One of the men was carrying a sack containing his brother's head, which he was taking back to his family. He refused to take it out of the sack and show us but allowed poor Ross to confirm its grisly existence.

Finally we reached Kabul, from which all foreign media were banned, still hopeful of capturing exclusive images of Russian troop movements, armoured convoys, and supply trains as they travelled out of the city. To get the best shots I'd need to get as close to the road as possible. The problem was that there was very little cover, so I hollowed out a space in a stone wall in which I could hide. Lying there alone, I was able to get some unique pictures over the next few days. It was risky, as I would have been blasted from my hidey-hole in an instant if anyone spotted me. There was just one close call as I was taking a picture of an armoured convoy. The officer in the leading tank was framed perfectly in my lens when he suddenly turned towards me and my heart leapt into my mouth. Unnervingly, he appeared to be looking directly at me. Had the sun reflected off my camera? I desperately wanted to lower it in case it was mistaken for a gun but I knew that I couldn't move an inch. Fortunately, the convoy rolled on and I managed to get the first ever photographs of a Russian convoy in Afghanistan, thereby fulfilling my brief.

Our work finally done, Ross and I began our long journey back to Pakistan with our armed companions. We took a different route, which was slightly faster but still arduous and seemed to take forever. It was with great relief that we finally crossed the border and bid farewell to the fighters we had travelled with. Just as we were leaving, Ahmed – my old adversary – took me to one side and shook my hand. Smiling, he told me, 'John, you will never grow old.'

Emaciated and exhausted, Ross and I returned to England with our world exclusive story and pictures. To its credit, the *Express* ran a full week of coverage and my pictures won a number of awards. The photo that I'd managed to take of the HIND helicopter during that deadly attack was of special interest to some. The day after it ran, someone from MI6 rang the Editor and asked for a copy. It was the first close-up of a HIND that they had ever seen and they were eager to study it.

James Bond, eat your heart out.

EIGHT

WITH WORK LIKE THIS, I was enormously proud of our profession and, of course, I always took my photography extremely seriously. Far too seriously, some might say. I never used studios, for example, and I tried never to use flash, as the medium we work in is natural light. If you study the lighting of early photographs and old black and white films like *The Third Man*, especially as I did, you can learn a lot.

I'm especially proud of some of my portraits that were shot on scene using only available lighting or where I had to be especially inventive. Photocalls in hotel rooms where the worst, but I'd change the lamps around, move mirrors and use the natural light from the windows to try and get the best effect. On one photocall with Jack Lemmon in his hotel suite, everyone was given no more than thirty minutes for words and pictures and most photographed him as he sat on the sofa. When it came to my turn I took him into the bedroom where I sat him in front of an old-fashioned dressing table with three mirrors. When I explained to him what I wanted to do he laughed and said, 'Gee, John, you must be one those special photographers!' Propped in place with a box of paper hankies I positioned each of the mirrors in such a way that I could see his face three times, then I sat on a stool behind him with a blanket thrown over me so I wouldn't be seen, and shot the picture over his head giving three different portraits. I thought it worked well but it didn't make a paper. That didn't matter, though, for they were the kinds of photos I shot for myself more than anyone. If they made it to publication then that was a bonus.

Another picture I'm proud of was of a trade union leader called Joe Gormley who had a wonderful way with the press. He was a nice, ordinary guy but when he was up on the stage at a trade union conference he reminded me of a headmaster, especially as I'd noticed that he peered over the top of his glasses at people. That is what I wanted to capture so I took a gamble. I waited all the way through the conference, right to the end, with the risk of getting nothing at all and then it happened. Just once. Bang.

I knew then that I had a better picture than anyone else there.

My pedantic ways didn't always make me popular with my peers, however. On one Royal Tour of Kenya by the Queen in 1983, she returned to Treetops – the luxury hotel she'd been staying at in 1952 when she discovered that her father had died and she'd succeeded to the throne. I was sent there on a rota with the *Sun*'s legendary royal photographer Arthur Edwards. That afternoon, he had taken all the photos he wanted but I was holding him up as I waited for the right light and the perfect moment when a water buffalo slowly sauntered into frame. Exasperated, Arthur uttered the immortal lines, 'For fuck's sake, John. Get a move on! Better a smudge today than a Botticelli tomorrow!' That made everyone laugh, including me and he was right, of course, but I still waited until I had the perfect shot.

With passion like that, I wasn't the only one who was deeply concerned how the increasing numbers of paparazzi were denigrating our profession. A lot of the new bloods were cutthroat, intrusive and disrespectful but their pushy methods were sometimes getting the kinds of shots that many of the tabloids increasingly demanded. This put even more pressure on us and meant that a lot of our quality pictures were either not being used at all or not well enough. To add insult to injury, the public started to call us paparazzi or 'snappers' and that used to drive me mad because we weren't. The paps would snap anything any old way whereas we would aim to make a photograph of it. At the Aberfan disaster, where an entire town and school was smothered by coal waste killing 144 people, there were shameful stories of photographers planting dolls and other toys in the mud, when the story was already so grim. It was always down to the photographer's own moral compass. I tried to be as honest as I could towards a job and I knew that the more honest we were the more we would raise the standards not only of photographers but of photography itself.

Not long after I returned from Afghanistan, I decided to set up the Press Photographers' Association to set a gold standard and show the public that the majority of news photographers were highly professional. I hadn't a clue how the organisation might work at first. I just wanted to see if there was any interest. To begin with I chose a photographer from each newspaper who I knew personally, and suggested the eight of us meet down at the City Golf Club to see if such an organisation was viable. I didn't want to exclude anyone so I also asked the PA/Reuters photographer, but I put a few noses out of joint because I probably should have invited more people.

Having got together, we decided to proceed so we published a leaflet asking any photographer who agreed with us if they'd care to join. We wanted to filter out those who were more in the 'flash, bang, wallop' mould and not as interested in the art of photography as we were. I was interviewed in the *UK Press Gazette* about our goals and there was a mixed reaction at first; some people wanted to join straight away and others were reluctant, seeing it as too exclusive.

There was the usual jealousy and rivalry, of course, and someone stuck a sarcastic note on my locker that read, 'We can't wait for the arrival of the great PPA!' And when I went to a job at Gatwick airport soon afterwards the other photographers, already banked up, started shouting out quotes from my article: 'Oooh, here he is – the founder of the PPA. We hear you're going to create 'a cocktail of talent,' Downing?!' I took a lot of flack like that at first but I stuck it out.

I was elected the PPA's first chairman and Eamonn McCabe, a brilliant sports photographer for the *Observer* and *Guardian*, was voted in as deputy. Once we had enough members our goal was to set up an annual exhibition to show the quality of the work and the kinds of pictures that the papers weren't using. Our peers would choose the photographs and the reward would be to have them exhibited and printed up in a yearbook called *Assignments*. We decided against an annual award as the Press Photographer of the Year was already in place and had been going for some time, sponsored by different companies over the years. When I first started out, by the way, Encyclopaedia Britannica sponsored it on the proviso that they could use the winning photos in their books. By the time I was established in Fleet Street, the film manufacturers Ilford had taken on the mantle, and recently the online agency Shutterstock was the sponsor.

I wanted the first PPA exhibition at the National Theatre in April 1985 to be special so I suggested that we try to find a Royal to open it. We were lucky enough Princess Michael of Kent accepted our invitation, who was always a good *craic*. When I invited her to peep under the curtain at the back of on an old-fashioned wooden camera, she quipped, 'If you knew how much my hair-do cost, you wouldn't ask me that!' A photo of the two of us made the *Express*. The show featured more than three hundred images and was one of the most successful photographic displays in London that year and the theatre's most successful exhibition ever. When it was over, I dug out the sarcastic note that had been stuck on my locker and put it back up for everyone to see.

Two years after the exhibition, Phaidon Press published *Assignments*

1, our first book, featuring one of my Afghanistan portraits on the cover. Harold Evans, former editor of the *Times* and *Sunday Times* and a newspaper legend, wrote the Foreword:

> There are 146 photographs in this book and three good reasons to celebrate every one of them. Firstly the photographers who have given their work have done so co-operatively in the new Press Photographers' Association; secondly, the images they have provided are independently provocative and collectively compelling; thirdly they are herewith preserved.
>
> The cheering thing about the PPA is the people in it. They are working photographers who are proud of their craft but acutely conscious of their part in the profession of journalism. They want to raise questions about standards and conduct and ethics and they are right to do so. There has been gross intrusion and sometimes deception – but there have been more instances of bravery and grace. It is time that public recognition caught up with the reality of the contribution the press photographer can make not simply to our entertainment, welcome though that is, but to our knowledge of ourselves and our time.'

I remained chairman of the PPA for the first three years and then I stepped down but was invited back to be one of the judges. The organisation later morphed into the British PPA and is still going strong with almost four hundred members and ongoing campaigns for press freedom. The present committee chaired by Lindsey Parnaby has been extremely supportive. They recently held a retrospective of my work and are creating a trophy in my name to be given to the promising young photographers of the future. At their meeting to decide what it should be someone suggested a permanent scaffolding tower opposite 10 Downing Street and there were plenty of other jokey suggestions. The main thing is that the winner and two highly commended runners up will be chosen by their peers and all the entries will be displayed together on a giant contact sheet at the awards ceremony. I had no idea what the award would look like but I wanted it to be tasteful and was hopeful when one of the committee told me, 'I wouldn't want to drop it on my toe!'

Touchingly, I learned recently the John Downing Award will be made of Welsh slate. I couldn't be more delighted.

The same year the PPA was founded I was sent to Nicaragua, Honduras and El Salvador, once again in the company of Ross Benson. Although he and I were complete opposites we got on like a house on fire, travelling the world together with never an angry word between us. One thing we never did, though, was socialise together out of work hours. I always thought of us like those two soldiers who rowed the Atlantic, one of whom was an officer and the other a squaddie. The pair worked brilliantly together but were in a different class, so when it was over, they never met. In our relationship, I was most definitely the squaddie.

Being in Central America was just another adventure with Ross and I was delighted to be with someone who was both extremely good at his job and also endlessly entertaining. Which was just as well because our brief this time was to take an eight-hundred mile 'Trail of Terror' through war-ravaged Central America, thumbing rides with the drivers of the lorries that ran the gauntlet of *Camino de la Muerte* or 'Road of Death', better known as the Pan-American Highway.

The first truck was arranged in advance for us and then we'd be on our own. Our driver was a foolhardy Costa Rican named Hugo, who'd earn the equivalent of £14 a day for braving the treacherous five-day trek in his 32-ton, 18-wheel juggernaut. Our journey would take us from the relative safety of Costa Rica north to Nicaragua and Honduras, up through El Salvador and into Guatemala. The downside was that there was either a guerrilla war or a civil war raging all the way along the route. 'It is the most dangerous highway in the world,' the owner of the haulage firm confidently assured us, explaining why he needed men like Hugo to deliver food, electrical goods and vital supplies along this shot-up lifeline. Shaking his head, he added, 'Not every driver lives to collect his wages.'

Ross discovered that forty trucks had been ambushed or destroyed in the previous few months. He wrote later, '*One truck in five which tries to run the guerrilla gauntlet of Eastern Salvador never makes it to its destination.... In Guatemala the death squads are back in nightly action and the toll in that country's chronic civil war now stands at over 30,000.*' Even the children seemed immune to the lethal way of life. Gathering around us in a cemetery in San Salvador where three mutilated corpses had recently been dumped, they came to stare not at the bodies but at us, the 'gringos'. Corpses were commonplace.

The lawless road on which we travelled was pocked and peppered with debris and death. A £5 million suspension bridge had been blown to pieces and we had to cross a makeshift 'Bailey' bridge instead. In places the tarmacadam ran out so we crawled painfully slowly along bumpy dirt tracks, a sitting duck in a shooting gallery. Two days after we passed through, twenty-nine young soldiers were killed on that same spot. Finally arriving at our destination, we celebrated with a meal of refried beans and eggs as our driver – who had more than earned his wages of fear – contemplated his next trip.

As if we hadn't had enough of Central America, Ross and I returned to Nicaragua a year later to take a foray into the jungle with the US-backed Contra rebels in order to witness their guerrilla war against the revolutionary socialist Sandinista government. We arrived and checked into the Hotel Torremolinos on the outskirts of Costa Rica's capital city San Juan where we waited for a contact arranged in London to let us know where we had to be and when. We had no idea what to expect.

A few days later, as he lay beside me, Ross murmured: 'War's hell, isn't it?'

I was too tired to respond, as a trickle of sweat ran down my chest.

Stirring himself, Ross gently eased himself onto one hip and squinted into the noonday sun. Everything was uncannily silent.

'Hey, look at that!' he said suddenly.

On reflex, I grabbed my camera and rolled onto my stomach, blinking into the heat haze.

'It's a woman,' he added.

Sure enough, walking towards us was a bikini-clad beauty, iced drink in hand. As we watched transfixed, this vision of loveliness put down her tumbler and plunged into the swimming pool next to us.

Collapsing back onto my sunbed, I laughed. 'You're incorrigible, Benson.'

We had learned from previous covert meetings with guerrillas that, whilst insisting on *our* punctuality, they are often far from punctual and keep us hanging around for days. This meeting was no exception, which is how we found ourselves sunbathing during the day and killing time consuming pizza and beer at night whilst watching endless re-runs of Julie Andrews in *Victor/Victoria*, the only film on the in-house television. Ross had experienced the mindlessness of a continuous film loop once before whilst stuck in some hellhole, watching Bugs Bunny cartoons back to back. He blamed this indoctrination on one of his catchphrases, which (regardless of his inability to speak a foreign language) he pronounced in perfect Spanish – '*Que passa, Doc?*'

Eventually, and when we'd almost given up and were worrying how to justify the not inconsiderable expense of our trip, two swarthy men made themselves known to us. After a couple of beers we were whisked off, not as we expected to a secret meeting place but to the local market, where we were instructed to purchase what they assured us was indispensable equipment – a hammock and a machete. Only then were we escorted to our first meeting in an airless little office in the back streets of the city where, over cups of heart-pumping coffee served by an attractive, dark-eyed woman the arrangements were outlined to us.

That night at dusk we would be flown from a secret airfield over the border in a small single-engine plane, hugging the treetops to avoid radar. Then, at last light we would drop into a field, identifiable by a small fire lit by a sympathetic farmer. From there we'd cut our way through the jungle to the frontline, just over a day's hard march to join guerillas loyal to a leader known locally as 'Commander Zero.' That was the plan. Of course it never worked out anything like that – plans rarely do. The Contras had been losing ground over the past few weeks and our proposed landing site was on territory recently reclaimed by the Sandinistas, so after three false starts it was agreed to make the journey by foot. Not being especially fit, Ross and I were less than happy with the new arrangement but the only alternative was to run home to the *Express* empty handed and we preferred our chances in the jungle.

In the early hours of a chilly Costa Rican morning we slipped out of the hotel and jumped into one of the two beat-up 4x4's that would take us to the border. It sheeted down with rain the whole day turning our route into glutinous potholes that made the journey even more perilous. Having had our insides thoroughly shaken and stirred, we finally arrived at the broad San Juan River that marked the border. Sheltering under some dripping trees we came across some heavily armed, sullen-looking guerrillas. It was immediately clear that, though undoubtedly fearless, they were very poorly equipped and had little ammunition. Some of them were without boots. They were lethargically guarding two dug-out canoes crudely hewn from trees and powered, incongruously, by modern outboard motors.

Sceptically, we climbed into our Fred Flintstone craft, sitting one behind the other like children playing trains. As well as the six precariously balanced men that climbed in after us, our cargo comprised tinned Canadian herring and rubber boots. The boats took off at a good lick, hugging the overhanging trees on the Costa Rican side of the border until nearly an hour later when we suddenly swept across to what I thought was the far embankment, but turned out to be a large mosquito-ridden island sitting midstream. The rain came down unremittingly as we scrambled up the slippery undergrowth onto a well-used path through the rainforest. It was the width of two men but ten inches deep in thick, cloying mud. In a few places logs had been laid in an attempt to make the passage safer but this had the opposite effect for those of us wearing boots, as it just made everything more slippery. Nothing, it seemed, defeated this mud and we suddenly understood why some of the men had chosen to go barefoot. Eventually, the path led us through some tall bushes and trees until it opened up into a small clearing where a few simple shelters were randomly dotted about, most without walls. The camp was surrounded on three sides with zigzag trenches that were knee-deep in muddy water and redolent of the First World War, some of them protected by artillery.

In one of the shelters, a cheery 'Mama' was cooking over a smoky open fire under a large tarpaulin about eight feet square and tied at the corners to trees. We ate her unidentified stew (only to discover later that it was monkey) and watched as the guerillas were reunited with their women and children who appeared to be willing camp followers, despite the conditions and the constant sound of gunfire. As the light faded, we were shown how to sling our hammocks criss-crossing in rising tiers amongst eight others, all swinging perilously above the open fire. Those with the least bedding took the lower positions nearest the smouldering flames while Ross and I were placed inches from the sagging wet canvas roof.

Once embedded, we formed a pile of humans that brought flashbacks of the mass grave I'd seen in East Pakistan, bodies piled irreverently atop one another, their limbs at crazy angles. In our case it was wreaths of smoke that separated us instead of shrouds of earth and our choking fumigation helped keep wild animals, snakes and the endless mosquitos at bay. Cocooned inside my warm, dry sleeping bag I was surprisingly comfortable and fell quickly into a deep sleep to the constant drumming of heavy rain inches from my face.

Early the next morning, just as we were finishing our hair-curlingly strong coffee and chapati-like bread, two Scandinavian journalists appeared. After exchanging pleasantries we discovered, to our annoyance, that they were to join us on our march. Goodbye exclusive. On the up side, though, they came laden with tinned food including sardines, corned beef and spam fritters, which softened the blow. Together, our little troupe marched off to the river where, hidden amongst the reeds, we found two more dugouts sitting dangerously low in the water and full of armed fighters. Ross and I boarded the first, the Scandinavians the second. Pushing off, we hugged the embankment shrubbery once more, the men paddling silently. It was only then that I noticed my feet were getting wet and spotted a six-inch split in our vessel's bow. One of the men was baling us out with an old tin can at the back but he wasn't fast enough and the river was winning.

As we reached the far end of the island, the Scandinavians insisted on being put ashore, 'before we all drown!'. They were duly landed and, to their credit, tried to persuade us not to go on. When we insisted, they told us, 'But you will die!'

Ross, never one to miss a trick, said cheerily, 'Don't worry chaps, we'll be all right. I don't suppose you could spare us some of your food?'

We struck off again, heavier by two tins of sardines, and this time across the main stream towards the Nicaraguan bank. We'd only just passed the halfway point when, roaring low from above the trees and smashing the silence with an explosion of noise, a government M18 helicopter gunship flashed above our heads, scattering birds and shredding nerves. Our boys made a desperate attempt to reach the far bank, striking still harder into the water with their paddles as we urged them forwards. But it was too late – we'd been spotted. Having overshot us, the helicopter arced sideways in an attempt to bring its guns to bear. We'd almost reached the protection of the bank when a second chopper tore out from behind the screen of trees, its guns chattering. Our men bent forward and thrashed even harder at the water, sweating profusely with open terror in their eyes. Expecting to die at any second, I suddenly saw where possible salvation lay. Directly ahead of us was the entrance to a small tributary almost completely hidden by a flimsy counterpane of thick bushes, vines and overhanging foliage. The first gunship completed its curve, lined us up and, just as our little convoy slipped into the gloom of the leafy corridor, it opened fire.

The undergrowth around us zipped and whizzed as bullets ripped through the vegetation. Frantically, we decamped, scattering in all directions. Foolishly, some of the fighters returned 30mm and small arms fire through the canopy, the daft buggers. This had no effect other than to pinpoint our position to the pilots. Ross and I took one look at each other and dived into the exposed hollow of an enormous tree, but not before I shot a frame of him cowering there. The battle raged on for probably only a few minutes but it felt much longer, as we came under increasing fire. Finally, when the predatory Cuban pilots were unable to locate us precisely enough to kill us, they moved on, hunting their next prey. That was probably my closest brush with death. If the helicopter had appeared thirty seconds earlier it would have been goodbye.

Ross and I spent an interminable three weeks in that sweaty jungle, creeping further and further in on our trail for government troops. Sometimes we were lying flat as we paddled under low trees; other times we were soaked to the skin in clay-stained water dragging our craft over rocks and logs. As we went deeper the rivers became too small to paddle in so we were reduced to using our machetes to cut a route through the thick undergrowth. A favourite photograph of me 'at work' was taken in that jungle. My trousers were soaked through up to his knee and my top was soaked through from head to waist from the rain. Only my midriff was dry, which is where I tried to keep my cameras, but one got so wet that it packed up altogether.

Each time we approached the frontline it moved further ahead of us and there was always the threat of the gunships that came back with frightening frequency, breaking the silence and reminding us of our vulnerability as we hid in tree roots or dived into water-filled gullies. Every time they came, Ross and I would hide but the foolhardy rag-tag rebels always raised their weapons, wasted their precious ammunition and then slapped each other on the back, laughing and cheering as the machines of death twisted away. 'You see, you see!' they cried. 'The helicopters are no problem. No problem.' Having staggered around in the rainforest for weeks we finally accepted that there was nothing for it but to return home. Pushing our way back out on our last night, we found ourselves accompanied for a good part of the way by thousands of fireflies. It was a magical spectacle that cheered us up and slightly eased the pain of our failed assignment.

Coming home after that job, I thought I'd adjusted well to normality until jogging one day in the leafy suburb of Weybridge, naively hoping to maintain my jungle weight loss, when a chopper suddenly flew overhead. Involuntarily, I threw myself to the ground and covered my head. It was a reflex reaction and, apart from a few old nightmares, my first real taste of PTSD. Looking around me at the startled expressions of those I was with, I felt a complete fool.

Once again, being back home brought its usual strange mix of relief and regret. I was glad to be safely home in the bosom of my family and wracked with guilt over what I'd missed. There was a penalty to be paid for doing what I loved doing and it was my home life that always suffered. I knew I hadn't been much of a father when I was away all the time and that weighed heavily on me. It still does.

Mind you, Bryn always tried to put my mind at ease by assuring me that although I wasn't always around I made what he calls a 'massive effort' when I was, attending his school performance as Huckleberry Finn in *The Adventures of Tom Sawyer* as well as many other events. I even insisted on photographing him secretly through the bushes at sports day once when his school decided to ban parents from attending. This backfired slightly, as – knowing I was there with my camera – he tried too hard at the high jump, breaking his arm. I was also on the sidelines at many of his rugby matches with the local team, the University Vandals, secretly hoping he might get picked to play for Wales one day – if only to appease my uncles.

Gareth had gone to state schools when he was Bryn's age as I couldn't afford anything better back then but, once I could, I wanted Bryn to have the education I never did. He went to Danesfield School in Walton and later to Claremont in Esher, travelling by bus to a child-minder or my parents' house after school and for the holidays until one of us got home from work. My parents were great with him, and with my nephew Paul, who was a year younger. They fed their beloved grandsons on homemade cakes and other delights, allowed them to play with my old tin soldiers, making papier-mâché puppets and teaching them card games fought over for a penny. Bryn called my Dad by the affectionate name of *Dadcu*, Welsh for grandfather, something his two girls now call me.

Mum had kept all our childhood toys so Bryn had his pick of books and games. I also encouraged him to learn a language, read music, and take up an instrument. When he picked the recorder, I bought one for myself to practise with him but the cacophony was too much for him and for Jeanette so that was quickly abandoned. Bryn switched to guitar, which served him well later when he joined a successful pop group called Optimystic that did pretty well (Mum could never remember their name and kept calling them Obstinate). They were offered a contract by Warner Brothers, did some TV and Radio One Roadshow appearances and even went on tour with Take That.

I was nevertheless keen to introduce my boy to Wagner and Beethoven, particularly by the Berlin Philharmonic and conducted by Herbert von

Karajan and played at full volume on the £1,500 stereo system I treated myself to with the money from one of my awards. I had always enjoyed concerts at the Royal Albert and Festival Halls so I took Bryn along to a few but he wasn't so keen. Hoping to fire up his interest, I picked a few current pop songs that were based on the classics and then played him both so he could see where the original inspiration came from. I also used to play him 'In The Hall of The Mountain King' by Grieg. Spinning him a story about monsters who couldn't stop dancing and went faster and faster until the castle came crashing down around them, I'd chase them madly round the room as the music got faster and faster, leaping over furniture to grab at them with a roar. Bryn loved it and when it was all over, we'd roll together on the floor laughing. This is a game I have played since with every child who has ever come to my house. The quid pro quo of this with Bryn was that I had to learn about people called Adam and the Ants and The Police to keep up with a boy who – given half a chance – would have their discs spinning on my prized record player instead.

Saturdays at home were always fun, and usually involved us all going to The Swan pub in Walton-on-Thames to meet up with Tom Smith and any of our other mates with children. Gareth would join us on the weekends that he was allowed. The kids would have the run of the pub garden while we slaked our thirsts. One Saturday night at a riverside pub we also frequented in Shepperton it was so warm that Tom challenged me to race him across the Thames. Well, drink had been taken. It wasn't such a great idea once we were in, though, and by the time I made it to the other side – where Jeanette was waiting with the white Afghan coat I loved to wear back then – I was covered in wet mud that completely ruined it.

On Sunday mornings, we'd usually be back in the pub before heading home for a traditional roast followed by a game of snooker – played on a specially adapted dining table that flipped over once the plates were cleared away. Christmases were always epic there too, with champagne served for much of the day and all our friends and neighbours chipping in. One year, Dr Stedman who lived two doors away was having so much fun at ours that he didn't want to go home so he went and fetched his cooked turkey in a wheelbarrow to add to ours.

In the summer we'd head to a villa in Javier, Spain with friends and Bryn would come too, always with a mate so he had some company. Gareth, sadly, wasn't allowed. What I could do with him back home, though, was get him and Bryn a ringside seat on the sidelines at Twickenham for the rugby, taking a few shots and they pretended to be my assistants. And Bryn still talks about one of the most memorable trips of his life – a visit to India when I flew him and Jeanette out for a week after another Jean Rook job.

Rook was a piece of work. She was famous for being the 'First Lady of Fleet Street...Britain's bitchiest, best known, loved and loathed woman journalist', and the original model for *Private Eye*'s character Glenda Slagg. To those who worked with her she was one of the most ungracious, vulgar, money-grabbing people I have ever met, and yet she was considered a superstar and allowed to get away with murder. She dressed like a brassy East End barmaid, resplendent in chunky gold jewellery that clanked with every movement as she expressed her loud and usually poisonous opinions of everyone. She worked the system to her advantage as much as she could, even to the point that when we went to interview a headmistress of a girls' school – a story I couldn't fathom her being remotely interested in – I found out that the woman was married to a master at Eton, which Jean was hoping her son would attend.

We went on numerous jobs together, and she liked my photography but didn't like the way I dressed. On one trip to South Africa in 1979 we arrived at our five-star hotel, the Mount Nelson, where she went into her usual routine, asking to see my room as well as hers to make sure she had the best. Mine was better because it had two windows not one, so she returned to hers and I to mine, where I didn't bother to unpack and waited for the inevitable phone call. It came a few minutes later: 'Would you mind terribly switching rooms, John? Mine overlooks the swimming pool and people are making so much noise it will put me off my writing.' I did as asked only to find that there wasn't a soul by the pool and it was quieter than mine. Best of all, the hotel later lost her laundry, never to be found, so there is a God.

She also arranged for us to visit a diamond mine where she was so desperate to get a free sample that she agreed to go down into the mine where they had just blown the rock with dynamite. It was a horrible, hot, dangerous place and not her thing at all. To have her photograph taken down there, she decided to take off all her rings and handed them to me for safekeeping. I put them in my top pocket but then completely forgot about them. When I bent down to pick up my camera bag they fell out into the dirt in the dark. Panicking, as I knew that if I lost one she would make sure that I was sacked, I had her turn away from me for a pose as I scrabbled around in the earth picking up all that I could find. To this day I don't know if I got them all but she had so many I don't think she would have noticed until later. Having done what she considered to be her duty, she fished for a free diamond from the mine owners but none were forthcoming so she left in a fit of pique.

She pulled a similar trick in China at a place called the Palace of the Seven Wonders. We were led from room to room filled with treasures and shown some tiny stone carvings and then some origami. Jean was only interested in the final room – the gold room. Her eyes glinting as we entered, she was asked if she might like a memento of her trip. 'Oh, I would!' she cried delightedly. Her face fell when the tour guide pointed to another door and said, 'The gift shop is this way.'

We hired a luxury BMW and I drove Jean over the veldt to the battle-field of Rorke's Drift from the Anglo-Zulu War but found virtually nothing there apart from whitewashed headstones and a small church. I got out and took some pictures as Jean sat in the car writing her notes and then we headed back. It was almost dusk when we spotted a tiny dot in the distance and, as we drew closer, came upon a little boy in the middle of nowhere, carrying a tin pail of water. Jean barely looked up but I stopped the car at a distance wanting a photo of him in the middle of nowhere with nothing in sight. The boy turned, took one look at my long lens, and almost abandoned his hard-won water. He was terrified and I realised that he thought I was pointing a gun at him. Getting back in the car I drove after him and pulled over.

'What are you doing?' Jean asked.

'We need to find out where this boy belongs,' I said, leaping from the car.

'It's all right,' I told him, approaching with a smile. 'Nobody's going to hurt you.' Once he had calmed down he let me take a few shots and then I held out my hand. 'Come on,' I said, 'We'll give you a ride to wherever you're going.' The idea of getting into his first ever car was even more frightening than my camera I think but I coaxed him in gently, despite Jean's protests. The last thing she wanted was a dirty, smelly little African boy in her fancy BMW but I ignored her and sat him on the back seat with his can of water.

Every dusty crossroad we approached I'd point and ask him, 'Here?' but the boy kept shaking his head. And so it went on for what seemed like miles until eventually he pointed and I swung our car left and up a track to a lone straw hut. Hearing us approach, curious, fearful people spilled out of the hut and stood eyeing us suspiciously. Opening the door and stepping out with a wave, I turned back, offered the boy my hand and helped him out as I saluted him.

The look on his face was priceless and the expressions on those of his family were even more special. Laughing, he skipped up the hill to his mother, eager to tell the story of how a white man came to chauffeur him home.

NINE

I RATHER LIKE Brighton despite the fact I nearly died there. The place has a certain air about it, not just super-oxygenated, but sensory. I suppose it's due in part to its glorious pleasure dome, the Royal Pavilion, and the district of narrow streets known as 'The Lanes' with their discreet antique emporiums and seductive jewellery shops.

It certainly has its share of chip shops and burger bars but they seem not to dominate the area in the way they do in other seaside towns. The eateries are more brasserie than brassy, and this might be related to the fact that every year one or other of the major political parties or the TUC held their conference there. Generally I try to avoid these events, which are a hard slog: boring, self-congratulatory, and almost impossible to get an unusual picture out of, but I'm happy to compromise when it comes to Brighton.

Two conferences there especially stick in my mind. The first was back in the autumn of 1977. It had been a mind-numbingly boring week, and on the Friday afternoon I had to take a break from the tedium and get some sea air into my lungs. I was also looking forward to a musical concert I'd booked tickets for that weekend at the Albert Hall. Asking a fellow photographer and friend Barry Gomer to cover for me in case anything happened I took myself off for a short amble around The Lanes. Window-shopping, my eyes fell upon a bronze Art Deco eagle mounted on a black marble plinth. It was love at first sight. Knowing only too well that I wouldn't be able to afford it, I nevertheless entered the shop to enquire about the price. It was a whopping £300 and even when I mentally juggled the numbers in my bank account, totting up my overdraft and debts, it all came crashing down in the red so I took one last look at my bird of paradise, shook my head and made for the door.

'Okay, £250 then.' The shop owner's voice stopped me in my tracks. He had either taken pity on me or was desperate for a sale, but it had the desired effect – my mental calculator went into overdrive. Still, I reluctantly concluded, it was futile. I simply couldn't afford it. Sadly, I wound my way back to the conference.

Finishing the afternoon off, I made a last visit to the railway station to dispatch all our films to London then drove home, my heart as heavy as the traffic. I had hardly taken a step inside the front door when the phone rang and Jeannette called out, 'It's the office for you.'

Now what? I thought as I wearily picked up the extension. I was relieved to hear the voice of my picture editor, Ron Morgans (later picture editor of *Today* and the *Mirror*). Ron was a laid back, easygoing boss who'd encouraged me to develop a photographic style of my own and given me the freedom to pursue it. There was little I wouldn't do for him.

'Are you sitting down?' he asked.

'Yes,' I lied, wanting him to get to the point.

'Congratulations. You've just won British Press Photographer of the Year.'

This was my first ever win and, almost involuntarily, I did sit down. It took a moment to pull my thoughts together. I knew that Ron had entered a set of ten of my photographs from the previous year, including one of a National Front march in Birmingham that turned violent (taken as I dodged bottles and bricks) and a funny shot of Morecambe and Wise with Penelope Keith in a *Cyrano de Bergerac* sketch. I wondered which had specifically attracted the attention of the judges.

'Which section have I won?' I asked.

'Not section!' Ron replied. 'You've won the overall prize, you idiot. Photographer of the Year! They said you showed 'skill and individuality.' Prince Charles is presenting the awards at the Savoy Hotel.'

To add the cherry on the cake, he told me that I had also come third in the World Press Awards for a set of photographs I took at a memorial for Elvis Presley in North London including a young 'Teddy Boy' rock and roller, sporting an Elvis quiff and blue suede shoes, weeping openly.

'There's prize money for the first one,' Ron added.

'Really? How much?'

'£250.'

I had to laugh. And that's how I came to be driving back from Brighton the next day with a two-foot high bronze eagle strapped in the passenger seat. It is still one of my most treasured possessions and has lasted pretty well apart from a couple of chips to its plinth after an unhappy ex-girlfriend threw it at me one night some years later. It has been referred to ever after by my friends as, 'The eagle has landed.'

After another of our many arguments one night, that same woman hurled a full cut glass decanter at the back of my head, knocking me down. As I lay there dazed, I remember looking at the carpet and thinking 'I hope this red stuff is blood', because the decanter had contained a particularly expensive port.

My second vivid and rather more dramatic Brighton memory took place seven years later and happened at the Grand Hotel at precisely 02:54am on Friday October 12, 1984. I was back in the town for the Conservative Party Conference, which proved to be as boring as the rest, sitting around listening to people babbling on and only able to take pictures of talking heads.

The week was drawing to a close and the only speech remaining was the much-awaited delivery from the Prime Minister, traditionally the last of the conference. As always with Margaret Thatcher it had been a hectic week, not just at the convention but also at the lunchtime meetings, visits to local events, and the endless round of nighttime parties, get-togethers and dances. With boundless energy, 'Mother' as she was affectionately known at Tory HQ (but never to her face) strode through it all without flinching, while her staff slowly wilted beside her. They weren't the only ones. We photographers were feeling the strain too.

A photographer's hotel room was a sight to behold in those days, resembling nothing less than a mad scientist's laboratory. The bathroom would be converted into the darkroom with bottles of highly toxic, noxious chemicals and other developing paraphernalia, including tanks, a squeegee, a thermometer, heating elements, a hairdryer, disused cassettes, films washing in the sink and yet others hanging from the ceiling like panchromatic streamers. Having a pee was a major operation involving a high degree of balance and accuracy. The bed was completely buried beneath a welter of cables, wires, extensions, tools, cameras, light box, negative files and an extension telephone. The bedside tables supported the scanner, modem and computer with its umbilical cord attached to the phone socket, which disappeared out of sight behind the headboard, which had usually become mysteriously detached from the wall.

Most newspapers accredited two photographers for the week, easing the pressure at night by allowing us to alternate the late watch, the off-duty man making the 'early bird' cover in the morning. On Thursday night, I joined *Express* man Terry Disney and a group of other photographers for our first real meal of the day. It was something of a mixed evening with those who were finished in high spirits (not to mention wine), while the rest of us were showing admirable restraint due to a pending 10.15pm job in the ballroom, where the Prime Minister was to make an appearance at the Conservative Agents' Ball.

Shortly before ten o'clock those photographers on duty – myself included – started straightening ties, slicking down hair, and generally loading up with photographic impedimenta. We left the others and walked the short distance to the ballroom's back door, where we were checked by security. The PM dutifully arrived to rapturous applause and was in radiant mood with her husband Denis at her side. They went through all the formalities good humouredly, which included a short speech smothered in thank yous and a quick spin around the dance floor for our benefit. My last picture of the night was the two of them holding a very large teddy bear, the reason for which is now lost in the mists of time. Then they left as the clock struck eleven o'clock.

We repaired to the bar for a 'swifty' before drifting off in twos and threes for our last duty of the night, a quick trawl through a few of the hotels in the hope of picking up a scoop. This invariably found us in the early hours of the morning at the watering hole of the party HQ, the elite Grand Hotel block-booked by the Tory Party, and the beehive of activity where the worker drones kept close to their Queen, Margaret.

At 02:49, the bar was still very busy. My last two photographic companions, Mike Moore of the *Mirror* and the Irishman John Minihan of the *Evening Standard* wished me goodnight and left.

02:50: A minute more slipped by and I fell into easy conversation with a young married couple. He was in his dinner jacket and she was dressed in a dark party dress, sitting prettily on a cane-backed chair.

02:51: The large hand on the clock in the corner stuttered forward.

02.53: My exhaustion was starting to get the better of me and my legs aching so pretending that the crowded bar was too noisy I crouched down on my haunches alongside the young lady's chair. Something amusing was said and we three burst into laughter. It was the last of the night.

02:54: An almighty bang assaulted my senses and threw me to the floor. I knew immediately that it was a bomb.

For one brief second there was a hollow-echoing silence, then I heard myself shouting, 'Get down everybody! Get down!' To my amazement, everyone reacted immediately, hitting the deck without a further word. Well, not quite everyone. As the lights flickered out and what seemed like every burglar and car alarm in Brighton started going off, I saw through the dusty half-light that the young woman I'd been chatting to was still sitting frozen in her seat, her head and shoulders covered in what looked like snow after the ceiling plaster collapsed and coated us all in white shrouds.

Strangely, in a dreamlike state akin to slow motion, I recalled a film I'd been shown in a London police station demonstrating the effects of a car bomb blast on a building. The window glass splintered into hundreds of tiny triangular arrowheads, before being forced inwards with lethal speed, twisting and ricocheting as it searched out flesh. Realising that the pretty young woman was about to lose her looks, I grabbed the back of her dress and, almost without thinking, pulled her backwards over her chair and onto the floor. As the sound of crashing masonry and breaking glass filled the room I threw my body over her head and, covering mine with my hands, waited for an impact.

When I accepted that we both seemed to have survived the experience, I became aware of people stirring around me. Many of them were moaning in pain. 'Keep down!' I shouted again. 'There might be another one!' My order was obeyed. A short time passed before a voice of authority yelled from the darkened back door, 'Security. Ladies and gentleman please stay calm, follow me, and I'll lead you to safety.'

This was my moment. I leapt to my feet, grabbed my faithful Nikon, and blitzed off six frames into the darkness, not having a clue if any of them would come out. Minute by minute, the air in the bar was filling with the swirling dust of broken plaster and exploded concrete. The effect on my flashgun was that of headlights in the fog, the light bouncing back as an impenetrable wall of white. Limping, coughing and gasping for breath, everyone started vacating the room, leaving me behind.

After making a quick sweep of the room, I called into the darkness, 'Is anyone here? Anyone hurt?' Silence. Time to go to work.

My initial plan was to get out through the front door of the hotel and photograph what remained of what I wrongly assumed to be a car bomb. Pushing my way through the gloom and picking carefully over upturned tables and chairs, glasses, handbags and coats I found my route through the front of the hotel completely barred by vast chunks of fallen masonry so I retraced my steps to the bar and climbed out of the glassless window.

The first thing I saw was an injured policeman laid out on the pavement being attended by two of his colleagues. I took a couple of shots that brought the wrath of the coppers down upon me, although I don't believe it made a blind bit of difference to the poor bobby on the ground. (This often happens when people are frightened or feel inadequate. They need to do *something*, even if it's only to shout at someone – in this case, me).

I moved away and as I did so, Mike Moore, one of the *Mirror*'s top photographers, came running up, looking badly shaken and with some justification, as this was the third IRA bomb he had witnessed. Grabbing my upper arm, he asked me breathlessly, 'Are you all right, John? Are you all right?'

'Yes, yes, I'm OK,' I assured him, completely unaware of how ghostly I must have looked, covered in plaster. In hyper mode, Mike started babbling: 'I heard the bang and as I looked back the whole front of the hotel disappeared in a wall of dust and I thought it had completely collapsed. I was sure you were a goner!' In fact, he thought everyone inside was killed. When they heard the bomb go off he and John Minihan immediately jumped to action. Mike came straight to the hotel as he had his cameras on him and John ran to his car to fetch his. It was the source of much amusement in Fleet Street later when a report stated that 'an Irishman' had been seen running from the building.

Incredibly, despite the ringing in my ears, my mind still seemed remarkably clear. I knew exactly what I needed to do – take pictures. I grabbed Mike by the lapels of his jacket, gave him a quick shake and said, 'Come on. We've got work to do.' My words must have touched something deep inside him for he changed immediately, dropping his panicky demeanour and regaining the poise of the true professional that he was. 'Right,' was all he said, and as we went our different ways to photograph everything, I knew he would be all right.

A few yards away from me a young couple loomed into view, assisted by a policeman. The man in a dinner jacket was covered in the ubiquitous film of dust and she, in an elegant party dress and fur jacket, was barefoot and carrying a pair of silver heels that would likely never trip across a dance floor again. Her stockings were in shreds and slashes of blood zigzagged tellingly across her face where glass had embedded.

As more and more stunned and uncomprehending guests emerged into the street in various states of injury, I worked my camera. This was a monumental event and I knew deep inside it was not only my job to record it, but also my duty. The first of the fire engines roared up and screeched to a halt and, as they did so, my eye caught a hurrying figure running along the pavement. It was the very man I wanted to see, the Prime Minister's personal detective. The PM would not be far away. I ran up to him as fast as my straitened lungs would allow and gasped, 'Is she alright?'

'Yes.' Then, a brief hesitation. 'I think so.'

I instantly realised that this meant, 'I don't *know* so.' Together, we ran round to the rear of the hotel and as I followed him into the small car park his professionalism kicked in. Stopping me, he said, 'You can stay here but keep out of the way.' I thanked him, but just as he was leaving two very agitated uniformed policemen arrived and started manhandling me, shouting, 'Clear off!'

Maggie's detective noticed the trouble I was having and called back to the two Bobbies, 'It's all right. He's OK.' It was an extraordinary moment of kindness, particularly at such a traumatic time for him.

A minute or so later, and as cool as a cucumber, I watched the Prime Minister march down the fire escape accompanied by a phalanx of police and officials. Her husband Denis and personal secretary Cynthia Crawford were both with her, wearing their nightclothes. Mrs Thatcher was still wearing the evening gown she'd had on at the party. As everyone fussed around her in a collective state of shock, she completely ignored all the security urging her to get out of the hotel and away from the area as quickly as possible (I, too, was willing her to hurry for I didn't want some other photographer to happen upon my exclusive). Oblivious to us all and unbelievably calmly, instead she walked to the back of the waiting Jaguar and placed her briefcase in the boot. Seemingly unfazed, she took care with her dress as she slid into the back seat flanked on either side by her companions.

Finally, the armoured Jag cleared its exhaust with a deep-throated roar, its headlights flicked on full beam, and it began to power out of the car park straight into my path. This was it – my big chance. Just one shot. In that 250th of a second that the shutter blinks its eye I would be a hero or a failure.

All those years of experience, knowledge and commitment were rushing towards me like that dark limousine. My reputation was riding on the frail back of Lady Luck. Should the PM be looking the other way, my flash fail, or there be a reflection on the window – things over which I had no control – all would be lost. Placing myself at the corner where the car would have to slow I quickly glanced at the little red neon on my flash, winking: 'Ready.'

As the car roared up alongside me, barely slowing at all in preparation for its hard right turn, I stepped out, thrust the camera forward at arm's length and released the shutter. The dark interior of the car mercifully bleached out in response to the flash, momentarily blinding me but freezing three ashen faces for all time. As the car sped past, I heard a sharp metallic crack as my lens hit the bulletproof glass. And then she was gone.

There was no time to worry if my camera was broken. I looked at my watch and saw that it was almost 03:15. I had one more important job to do. I cut down to the seafront and ran hell for leather to the nearest hotel. Charging into the foyer of The Old Ship I ran up to the reception and blurted: 'A bomb has gone off at the Grand! Can I use your phone?' The dazed receptionist nodded and directed me to an old-fashioned wooden phone booth that I squeezed into.

Shoving as many coins as I could into the slot beneath the phone, I dialled the number of the *Express* I knew so well and gasped, 'News Desk! And please hurry.'

'Just one moment, please,' replied a lethargic telephone operator with a well-practised air. As I waited my mind ran riot. The newspaper was about to shut down. It was too late for pictures that night, but we could run them the following day. If I could just catch the news desk I might make the last edition with that coveted headline: 'EXPRESS EXCLUSIVE!'

'Hello, news desk – this is John Downing – a bomb has gone off in The Grand Hotel in Brighton – Maggie is okay – can we make the last edition?'

There was a sudden commotion down the line, with lots of shouting in the background as the desk reacted instantly to the news. Then, joy upon joy, I heard those immortal words: 'Stop the press!' Then: 'Okay, we can hold the front page. Shoot!'

My mind working overtime, I ad-libbed an instant newsflash on what I had just witnessed: '*In the early hours of this morning a bomb exploded* ...' The next call I made was to wake my then picture editor John Mead, known as 'Gentleman John' and quite the nicest boss anyone could wish for. As if to prove the point, he was the only one to enquire after my health. It was only then that I realised that beneath my thick plaster coating I was completely unscathed.

Once I'd done what I needed to do, I called Jeanette and Bryn, who were fast asleep at home in London. 'There's been a bomb at my hotel,' I told her when she answered groggily. 'But I'm okay. I just wanted to let you know I was safe.' I put the phone down, little appreciating that she and Bryn would lie awake for the rest of that night waiting for me to come home so they could reassure themselves that I was really okay.

Exhausted, I tumbled out of the phone box around 4am feeling absolutely shattered as the adrenalin that had kept me going started to ebb away. One of the hotel receptionists kindly made me a strong black coffee, which I accepted gratefully and drained in one. I knew that I had to keep going and get back to the scene. By the time I did the police were far more organised and had sealed off the area, so I was forced down onto the beach where I spent the remainder of the night.

The IRA assassination attempt at the Grand Hotel that night killed five people, including the MP and Deputy Chief Whip Anthony Berry. Another thirty-four were injured, including Lord Tebbit and his wife Margaret, who remained in a wheelchair for the rest of her life. The bomb was set up a month earlier on a long-delay timer by terrorist Patrick Magee, who was later caught and sentenced to eight life sentences although he only served fourteen years.

Denis Thatcher was asleep in bed at the time of the explosion but his wife had been sitting up, polishing her closing speech – something she delivered an adapted version of to a standing ovation that morning at 9:30 prompt. In a rallying cry to the faithful, she said, 'The fact that we are gathered here now – shocked, but composed and determined –is a sign that not only has this attack failed, but that all attempts to destroy democracy by terrorism will fail.'

My photograph of the Prime Minister leaving the devastated scene that night in her ball gown, twin set of pearls, and diamond earrings was published on the front page of the *Express* the following day alongside with the text of her speech and the headline *Unbowed*.

Later that year, as I was waiting for the Prime Minister to leave an event in North London, her driver recognised me. Leaning out of the car, he said, laughing, 'I thought you were going to come crashing through the back window that night in Brighton!' Kindly, he also let it be known that my picture had been, 'Well received'.

The photos I took that night were among several entered for the Press Photographer of the Year award the following year and I was delighted to win it again. My wife and family were understandably concerned for my safety with the kind of work I was doing, and I still felt very guilty about ploughing on selfishly.

Nor did I fully appreciate at the time that largely because of my obsession with my career, my relationship with Jeanette was coming to an end. That was really tough on Bryn, who felt caught in the middle, and he played up at school for a while. Jeanette realised that he was the most important member of our family and was brilliant at allowing me as much access as I wanted after we split up, letting me have him for weekends or for outings of his choice. Aside from the house, the biggest cost to me would once again be the years of his childhood that I missed.

Talking to Bryn one day about that and apologising for not always being around, he made me smile when he told me, 'Oh but Dad, I've told all my friends at school about you and they think you're really cool!' He added that they were always asking him, "Where's your dad, now? Which war is he in?" They were apparently dying to meet me. He said his mates were envious of the gifts I bought home for him, including military watches, an LAPD baseball hat, some foreign currency, my full Afghan dress including turban, a pin from a hand grenade and various shell casings. One thing that especially impressed them was my Cable & Wireless credit card with the logo of an aeroplane crossing the globe, which allowed me to buy a flight on any airline anywhere in the world at the expense of the *Express*. And apparently they fought each other to spend time in the downstairs loo, which was plastered with photographs, awards and the souvenirs and spoils of my adventures, including some shrapnel, the Sudanese arrows, various flak jackets, military hats, an African carved wooden head, and my framed fountain pen gun from Afghanistan.

'They all think their dads are really boring by comparison,' Bryn told me proudly. It never occurred to me that the mere fact of being my son would earn him bragging rights.

TEN

IN THE MID 80s, after I had split up with Jeanette and was single and living in Kingston-upon-Thames, I relished the opportunities to travel more than ever. Apart from anything else, it was a welcome distraction from my personal life. On one job I flew to the Middle East with Margaret Thatcher where I took a historic photo of her sitting at a table with the Saudi royal family (the first time a woman unrelated to them had ever done so), and in September 1985 I flew to Mexico City to cover a devastating earthquake that had killed five thousand people.

The city was in ruins when I arrived in the evening so I quickly found one of the hotels still standing. As usual I checked in, grabbed my camera bag, and went straight out. I worked all that night, photographing the rescue crews as they searched for survivors, often in vain. Hushed crowds watched and prayed for the estimated two thousand people trapped in the debris, obeying instructions to remain quiet as the rescuers listened for a human cry. When a baby was rescued alive fifty hours after the quake razed her home, there were tears and cries of joy. Then everyone fell silent again as the body of the child's mother was pulled clear.

At some of the collapsed high-rise buildings possessions recovered from the rubble were neatly bagged up for owners unlikely ever to claim them. Piles of shoes lying nearby summoned up images of the men, women and children who would never wear them again. I scrounged a lift in a helicopter to get an overview of the ruined city and heard that a specialist rescue team of firemen had arrived from the UK to assist a group of Royal Engineers already there, so I eventually found them and joined them for the rest of the day, along with teams of Swiss and French search dogs, sniffing for any signs of life.

At one factory we came to, the building had collapsed like a pack of cards. It had manufactured textiles and there were huge bales of material thrown around like cotton reels. One of these bales was holding up a collapsed floor by about two feet and the rescuers' heat-seeking devices indicated that someone was still alive but trapped deep inside. Everyone started digging madly and scraping away the rubble with whatever they could, even their bare hands. They needed to create a space wide enough for someone to squeeze through the gap. When it was finally big enough and they prepared to crawl in with lights and water, I asked, 'Can I come too?' They looked at me as if I was stark raving mad but they nodded so in we crawled on our tummies, swallowing floating particles of brick and concrete and choking on the thick dust.

It was unbelievably clammy and claustrophobic down there but I hoped to get a photo of the person they were rescuing. This was my first earthquake and I had no understanding then that there might well be aftershocks that could bring the building down on top of us, squashing us flat. Sadly, despite all our efforts, the shape of a human body that their devices had spotted turned out to be warm oil leaked from a crushed machine.

Covered in dust and extremely tired, I returned to my hotel to get my films away on the next plane out. Collapsing on my bed after I'd despatched the films, I was more than ready for a hot shower, a rest, and something to eat. After a few minutes dozing, though, I heard a commotion outside and wearily rose to my feet to look out. To my surprise, a large crowd had gathered outside my hotel and were pointing up at the wall close to my window. Grabbing my camera, I went downstairs to see what they were all gawking at and realised that a giant crack had appeared in the exterior wall of my hotel, running alongside my window and threatening to split the building in two.

As engineers and experts argued animatedly about the risks of the hotel collapsing at any minute, I shrugged my shoulders, returned to my room and fell into a deep, deep sleep.

That job lasted a few days longer than one I went on around the same time, which began – as they often do – with the telephone ringing to jolt me from a deep sleep. I opened a bleary eye and peered at the clock to see that it was just after 2am. It had to be the office. No one else would call at such an hour. Fumbling for the receiver, I put it to my ear and croaked a hello.

'Can you make the 7am flight from Heathrow to Delhi?' came a disembodied voice (no doubt some hapless night shifter). I knew exactly what this was about.

'Probably,' I replied, wearily, 'But, as I already told the desk, I'll need a visa for India.'

'Never mind that,' the voice added, with a flippancy that annoyed me.

If only the desk had listened to me about getting a visa two days earlier, when I'd pushed to be sent to cover the Bhopal gas tragedy that killed thousands. On December 2, 1984, a huge cloud of mesothyl isocyanate had leaked from the Union Carbide pesticide factory there. Hearing the news and knowing we had to react quickly, I'd asked for permission to apply for an Indian visa. Frustratingly, the Editor was away on holiday and no one else would accept the responsibility of sending me. Too tired to argue on the morning they finally decided I should go, I rose reluctantly from my bed, dressed quickly and rummaged around in the semi-darkness, topping up a small suitcase that was permanently packed. I was almost done when the office called again to tell me that the only ticket left was a first class return. 'Oh, shame,' I replied, without an iota of conviction and smiling to myself. It was just after 5am local time when, after a ten-hour flight in abject luxury, I joined the chaotic jumble of passengers in New Delhi's Palam airport pushing and heaving their way towards passport control.

'Good morning,' I said when I arrived at the desk. 'It's great to be back.' My ingratiating smile didn't work.

'Mr Downing, your visa is out of date,' the officer said flatly.

'Really?' I replied, playing the innocent. 'I thought it was a multi-entry one? Okay. Never mind. I'll buy one here.'

'No, Mr Downing, this is not possible. It is against the rules. Please go with this gentleman.' The 'gentleman' in question was a soldier in khaki, carrying a .303 rifle. Despite my protests, I was taken upstairs where the soldier produced a plastic chair in a hallway and indicated that I should sit. He then took up a position beside me, weapon at the ready. Passing passengers took a wide berth as they stared into my villainous face. The hours wore on interminably. The chair was getting the better of my backside so I decamped to the marble floor but the cold stone chilled my sitting bones so I found some cardboard and slept on that. I was allowed to phone London who promised to help. After several more hours an official from the High Commission appeared but his offhand manner echoed that of every British diplomatic official that I have ever met, bar the teams in Kabul and Tripoli. There was nothing he could do, he told me. A visa wouldn't be issued and I'd have to go home empty handed.

At the end of what my family call 'John's day trip to India', I flew back to learn more about the Bhopal disaster. The final death toll may never be known, but conservative estimates put it at sixteen thousand dead and more than half a million people affected. Subsequent litigation took decades to resolve and it was twenty-six years before anyone was held personally accountable for the shocking lack of maintenance and servicing at the plant. Even then, those in charge – who were found guilty of death by negligence – got off with a small fine. More shocking than that to me was the news that several reporters in the area had refused point blank to cover the story and that when one group of them arrived in Bhopal, they stepped gingerly onto the runway, claimed they could 'smell something funny' and flew straight back to Delhi. I couldn't believe my ears.

The Iron Curtain was still firmly in place across Europe when Danny McGrory and I flew into the dusk of Tempelhof Airport, West Berlin in February 1988.

Strictly speaking it was my day off but that was ruined just after I'd made arrangements to have lunch with an old pal. Until the phone rang the two of us were planning a reunion with an even older friend – a pint of the Welsh nectar that is Felinfoel IPA.

'We want you to go to East Germany,' the voice from the picture desk said. 'You'll have to leave this afternoon as the job starts horribly early tomorrow.' *Iechyd da* (Cheers).

In an unexpected flash of openness under the Reagan-Gorbachev arms limitation agreement, the East German government had decided to send home all the Russian soldiers stationed there along with the SS-12 intermediate range nuclear missiles they were trained to fire. Unusually, they allowed British journalists to witness this, giving us a rare peep under a corner of that immovable drape. This was a deeply political manoeuvre, which the authorities correctly assumed might give them some favourable publicity. As it was also unprecedented it would make for an excellent story.

The withdrawal was to take place deep inside communist Germany at the railway station of a small village called Bischofswerda. Due to the distance involved we were to make ourselves available for departure by coach at some nondescript government ministry in East Berlin at 5am the following morning. Knowing from experience the problems that can occur crossing any border, and particularly the unpredictability of the one in Berlin, we decided to go over that night.

Danny and I were decamping from a large black Mercedes near Checkpoint Charlie in the driving snow when out of the darkness came two lonesome figures, weighed down with what seemed like an excessive amount of heavy luggage for a two-day assignment. It was David Crump and Frank Thompson of the *Daily Mail* team, the only other newspaper invited. We greeted each other as the old friends we were. 'Welcome to new technology,' David said, pointing to the heavy metal suitcase he was lugging. 'If they put bigger wheels on it and an engine in the back we might get somewhere.' Frank, who was carrying a darkroom kit, piped up, 'Shame the expenses didn't run to a Sherpa.' Our pals were trialling one of the expensive new Nikon negative wire machines – (laughingly referred to as a 'mobile' unit) – a piece of electronic machinery about the size of two large suitcases and weighing twice as much that was attached to a telephone line to send pictures back to the newspaper. By contrast, I would have to rely on the good offices of AP (Associated Press), a worldwide news agency with offices in every capital in the world, West Berlin being no exception. This meant that if we were stranded only the *Mail* could wire their words and pictures, beating us hands down. Try explaining that logic to the office accountants. Mind you, having listened to David grumble about how we photographers had to carry more than half our bodyweight in equipment these days, I was no longer sure it was an advantage. To lift the mood, I decided that a photograph in front of the infamous border post was in order.

Checkpoint Charlie was all that we'd expected it to be and more with its officious form-filling and noisy stamping of papers. In a harshly-lit cabin we were passed through with relatively little bureaucracy until the wire machine was produced, which they treated as if it were a nuclear bomb. In the age-old tradition of Fleet Street few of those sent abroad spoke a foreign language, so our conversation with the East German guards was a nil-nil draw. With the help of a guard who had a smattering of English, questions were barked at us accusingly: 'Why are you here? What is your business? How long?' Informing them we were there at the invitation of the East German government afforded us no preferential treatment whatsoever.

After all the fuss and formalities, we were finally allowed through and stepped from the cabin into the dark street beyond as soldiers in drab grey uniforms watched suspiciously. There wasn't a soul in sight and no vehicles either – least of all a taxi to take us to the only open hotel we'd been given the name of. The Communist side of the city looked like a half-finished building site and was the total antithesis to the buzzy, bustling West Berlin a few hundred yards behind us. Standing in the falling snow, we were unable to shake off the creeping sense of gloom brought on by the austere surroundings and the feeling of being totally alone.

Eventually someone broke the silence by pointing out a street some distance away that appeared to be marginally better lit than the others. Hoping we'd be more likely to find a taxi there, we shared the cases out between us and dragged our burdens in the direction of the illumination – it was either that or leave Crump to die in the snow. Tired and hungry, we made slow progress. To no one in particular, I commented, 'Only a week ago I was being driven around Hollywood by Jackie Collins. Where did it all go wrong?' Some twenty minutes later we were trudging past yet another darkened doorway when – without warning – an armed policeman stepped from the shadows, giving us a nasty turn as he threw his half-smoked cigarette into the snow. Our request for a taxi involved some terrible miming and over-acting, but the offer of Western cigarettes appeared to clarify the situation. Once he realised what we were asking, he fell about in hysterics, which didn't much amuse Dan. 'Now I know why so many people escape from East Berlin in lorries,' he commented, drily. 'It's because they can't get a bloody taxi.'

We tried the policeman with the address of our hotel and he enacted what seemed to be a three-day route march whilst pointing in the general direction of the Ural Mountains. Whether it was the menace he saw in our eyes or just that he took pity on us, we will never know but he suddenly straightened up, pointed to the next road on the left and announced – 'Hotel!' We turned the corner and there, much to our surprise, we found the brightly lit Grand Hotel, incongruous in the darkened street.

Mightily relieved, we pushed our way through the glass doors and shook the snow from our shoulders. We straggled across the dazzlingly lit marble foyer to greet the only human beings in sight, two uniformed members of staff standing to attention behind the reception desk. It was nearing midnight when we asked if they had four rooms available. The manager glanced over his shoulder at hundreds of keys on hooks and, after a long pause, replied, 'I think we can manage that.'

'Can we get something to eat?' Danny asked. We were directed to the sixth floor restaurant where we were told they took Western currency only. Same old same old. Dumping our cases, we met at the door of the restaurant on the dot of midnight. An immaculately dressed barmaid asked, 'You will drink at the bar first?'

'No thank you,' we replied politely, 'We have a very early start so we'll go straight in to dinner.'

'No,' she said, her smile fixed. 'You will drink at the bar first.'

'Could be worse,' quipped 'McGrory the Story', as he was to become known. That later became his trademark catchphrase.

Having complied with her orders and discussed the merits of being compromised by such a delightful temptress (undoubtedly a honey trap set by the secret police), we were finally invited into an elegant restaurant the size of a school hall and immaculately laid out with tables and chairs, pristine table linen and gleaming silver. We were the only diners. In fact we were the only guests in the whole hotel. A small group of lethargic looking staff immediately sprang to life on our arrival, scuttling off at speed through a creaking service door. We ordered we knew not what from the menu, and enquired about the price of a good Scotch whisky. We were told it was a staggering £30 a glass so we opted for the inevitable bottle (or three) of wine.

As we waited for our dinner, a ten-piece orchestra in full dinner jackets suddenly appeared from nowhere and stepped up onto a podium at the far end of the vast room.

'Hello, hello, it's the Berlin Philharmonic on a night out,' quipped Dan, which was entirely possible, as we couldn't see any other reason for them to play to a near-empty restaurant. A male crooner and a female singer in a circa 1950s full-length off-the-shoulder evening dress struck up some passable renditions of American show tunes. At the end of the first number we applauded politely as the entire orchestra stood and took a bow. Feeling guilty, we gently suggested to the head waiter that we wouldn't be the least offended if they wanted an early night. That wasn't the way things worked in East Berlin, however. They were paid, so they stayed. Having realised this we applauded every song.

As we were about to tuck into our fatty grey meat of unknown origin served with white cabbage and potatoes, they played 'Puppy Love'. Dan, stabbing suspiciously at his 'steak' with a fork remarked, 'That's probably what we're eating.' The wine was brought and Crump tasted it before suggesting we shouldn't put our glasses too close to the candle. Needless to say we were out of there in record time, and hardly a drop was drunk. We retired to the strains of 'Some Enchanted Evening'.

At dawn the next morning, we boarded an unheated 1950s military coach with uncompromising seats and windows dripping with condensation. We were then driven for two hours through deep snow to the railway station in a town of thirteen thousand souls where the photo call was about to take place. The locals, who'd been marshalled into place to wave East German and Soviet flags in what was fast turning into a blizzard, seemed bemused and curious about the arrival of men from the West. Rosy-cheeked toddlers ran about in the slanting snow and a brass band played on as local media and TV crews were corralled into position on the railway platform. On the track sat a half-mile long snake of thirty-four wagons strained under the weight of eight rockets, five launchers, and four training missiles. At the front of the locomotive a Red Army major peeled back a tarpaulin like a striptease artist to reveal the nose cone of a 30ft-long nuclear missile as Russian soldiers scooped up local children in a stage-managed display of *glasnost*.

When the carefully rehearsed speeches began, I managed to slip away from our minders and walk to the far end of the platform. There I found a group of fresh-faced Russian soldiers, clearly delighted to be going home, singing 'Back in the USSR' – the only Western song they knew. They were fooling around in the snow, overshadowed by the cone of another deadly missile. Just as my shutter clicked, one of them playfully pushed a colleague off the carriage and another raised his arms and grinned. It was a winning shot in more ways than one – providing a human face to soldiers that Western eyes rarely saw and helped to scoop me my fourth Photographer of the Year award later that year.

Then, just as the whistle blew and the train started to move off, one of the soldiers looked directly into my lens and, clasping his hands together above his head in a gesture of victory, he smiled. It was so unexpected and a one chance shot that I was very happy to get. As the train pulled out of the station in the blizzard, I realised that the young man would probably spend the entire journey back to the Soviet Union in the open on the back of that flat back carriage. I shuddered at the thought.

There was an ironic postscript to this story as we humped that damn wire machine all the way down to the missile trains and back again. Having trundled it back through Checkpoint Charlie and into Reuters in West Berlin, Crump dismantled the fax machine and connected it up, but the damn thing didn't work. If he'd had any hair left he would have pulled it out. Instead, we simply sat back and let the cool efficiency of Reuters ping our pictures to London before heading to the airport. As we reached the kerb, I slipped on the ice and fell head long into the slush.

Just as I pulled myself to my feet, a large Mercedes pulled up and I heard a voice say, 'Taxi, *mein Herr?*'

In the summer of 1988 Mum and Dad were going to celebrate their golden wedding anniversary so we boys all got together to discuss how to mark it. We had asked them if they fancied going on a cruise but they were quite adamant – 'No, thank you. We just want to be with our family.' I can't remember which one of us came up with the final plan, but it was a good one.

We knew that Mum would definitely expect us to do something special but we wanted to surprise her so, the closer it got to the big day the more each of us began to complain how busy we all were and how we weren't sure we'd be able to celebrate it with them until later in the year. I explained that – although I was very sorry and deeply disappointed – it was highly likely that I would be abroad as world events were ever more demanding with the ongoing Cold War, terrorists hijacking planes and blowing up ships, an earthquake in Chile and an avalanche that nearly killed Prince Charles. David was working on the show *This is Your Life* for ITN and claimed that he couldn't take more than a few days off, and brother Ron said he couldn't make it home from Mexico. Only Andrew was free so he suggested the three of them go on a mini-break to a B&B in Wales.

Unbeknownst to either of my parents, we'd secretly booked a converted farmhouse and restaurant at Castle Howell near Carmarthen – not far from where my mother grew up – and agreed to meet there ahead of Mum and Dad with all the grandkids and several other close relatives as well. Few of us had mobile phones back then so we stopped en route to call in and check on progress. Needless to say, some were delayed so poor Andrew – who was driving – had to pretend to get lost or take the long way round as my seventy-five-year old mother sat in the passenger seat asking, 'Where are you going, son? This isn't the way!'

By the time they arrived we were all there waiting as a surprise. The room we'd set aside was full of chairs in true *This is Your Life* style as we three boys ran the whole event, complete with a big red book. Using a projector and screen, we showed Mum and Dad an emotional video clip of Ron, his wife and daughter wishing them well from Mexico sitting in front of a Spanish backdrop with some Spanish music playing softly in the background. Then, out of the blue, David turned to Mum and Dad and spoke those immortal lines: 'You haven't seen them in [however many] years...' and then Ron and his family burst in. There were hugs and tears all round as my Mum looked from one to the other in wonder and said, 'But we just saw you in Mexico!'

'No, Mum, that was filmed in John's house in front of an old blanket. It was John's girlfriend who was playing the guitar.'

A great weekend was had by all with a big family feast and lots of happy photographs, which I had printed up and put into a photo album. My parents loved every minute, and so did we. We arranged some after dinner entertainment around a campfire and a singsong with some of the men dressed as boy scouts and Hannah, David's daughter, dressed in full Welsh costume as we tackled songs popular from their wedding year like 'It's a Long Way to Tipperary'. My anniversary gift was a doctored copy of their black and white wedding photo, which had always taken pride of place on the mantelpiece. In it, Dad stood proudly to attention in his uniform, clasping the hand of my mother, looking so young and pretty in a cream suit and semi-veil. Standing around them were their sixteen or so guests, their bridesmaid and the vicar. Throughout our early childhood, each of us boys had asked my parents why we weren't in the photo (not understanding why this would be impossible), so I 'beheaded' some minor guests and glued in our four heads instead so that – at last – we were part of the picture. I printed a copy for every guest and – best of all – when I sent a copy to the *Carmarthen Journal*, they ran a story about it in their paper. Mum was dead chuffed.

From the familial warmth of Wales I was sent to the warmth of Sicily later the same year. There I found myself pointing my lens into the bloodstained face of a corpse in a neon-lit bar, the whine of my motordrive an eerie lament to yet another Mafia slaying.

This was another one of those long shot stories, gambled in London and paid off handsomely in Palermo – despite the most unlikely of prospects. It had started with the usual morning editorial conference, which had been dominated by one topic of conversation – the violent vendettas being played out on the streets of Sicily. 'There've been a hell of a lot of murders going on,' announced the foreign editor, David Richardson. 'Sixteen killings in the past ten days alone.'

'Good story,' everyone agreed, in that rather insensitive way newspapermen speak of other people's misfortunes.

'Send McGrory and Downing,' ordered the Editor, delegating John Ellison the London foreign editor to brief us.

'We'd like you to get the full story and pictures for next week's Sunday for Monday,' he said using an expression universally employed in newspapers to pinpoint the day a story is required and the day it will appear.

'Sure,' we replied in unison, daring not to catch each other's eye. Once we were safely out of earshot, however, we launched into a familiar comedy routine. 'Nip down to Palermo,' I said.

'Have a quick chat with Don Corleone,' Danny chipped in.

'Knock off a few smudges of the killings for Monday,' I added.

'No problem at all,' said Danny, heavy with sarcasm. 'After all we have a full *three days* to do it in.' Amazingly, though, that's pretty much what happened. Well, with the exception of the Godfather interview. But none of it would have been possible without the help of a pint-sized Sicilian journalist I'll call Sandro.

Danny and I flew to Palermo and waited patiently at the airport as three taxi drivers fought a noisy battle over who would have the dubious distinction of driving us to our hotel. We ended up being the losers because the winner, wearing *eau de garlic* and in urgent need of a bath, careered us off down the darkened road with the expertise of a blind assassin. After our car hit the kerb with a thump for the second time, Danny commented, 'We have nothing to fear from the Mafia, mate. At this rate we won't even make it to our hotel!' Incredibly we survived and next day, bright and early, we started our inquiries, building up background, collecting photographs, collating information, and making contacts – the nuts and bolts of the journalists' trade. That is when we found our little gem – Sandro – a journalist on the local newspaper and a specialist in Mafia affairs.

Sandro was a wisp of a man in his mid-thirties with thinning dark hair, a haunted look (perhaps not surprisingly), and an encyclopaedic knowledge of the *Cosa Nostra*. He had an inability to sleep more than three hours a night and a stunningly beautiful girlfriend with the unlikely but entirely accurate name of Juicy. Her boyfriend had suicidally set his heart on exposing the Mafia and – just in case that wasn't dangerous enough – he drove the worst little car it's ever been my misfortune to ride in. Danny ruminated that with this combination no one could be sure which would get him first.

The motor was hardly bigger than a bubble car with every wing crumpled, no back bumper, spider's web cracks obscuring the view through the tiny windscreen, hardly any brakes to speak of and treadless tyres polished to a high gloss. As for seatbelts, it would be churlish to ask. Oddly, I came to appreciate the joy of such a tiny car because on our second day Sandro offered a lift to three attractive female reporters from his office. Defying any natural law that Isaac Newton could devise, all of them somehow climbed into the back seat with me. I think it must have been a record of some kind – not so much in people per car but more in personal self-control as I was torn between the ecstasy of my position and the agony of an old back problem. Danny, from the relative comfort of his broken front seat, said we resembled a Henry Moore bronze. As the car spluttered off down the road, back tyres rubbing on the wheel arches, the car filled with a nauseous smell of burning rubber. It did occur to me then that if our little transport of delight hit anything we in the back would become a hermaphroditical mass and a supreme challenge to any rescue service.

Later that evening we joined up with Sandro on his lonely beat, cruising the bars, cafés and clubs. He made a few telephone calls and had several whispered conversations. The evening wore on through a haze of cigarette smoke and blood red wine and in another little seedy backstreet bar Sandro took a phone call that put us both on edge. Slapping the phone back into its cradle, he said, 'We go now.'

Quickly, we drove off down a myriad of narrow back streets, flanked by what had once been elegant houses, all sadly dilapidated by the etching of time. We made the final turn into a cobbled dead-end alley where a small group had gathered around a policeman who was blocking the entrance to a bar. Above and around us were high-rise apartments whose occupants were crowding their balconies to see what was going on.

'How close can we go?' I whispered to Sandro, acutely aware that I was already probably half a mile closer than any British cop would conceivably allow.

'As close as you like,' he replied, brightly. 'Follow me.' After brushing aside the officer with the words, '*giornalisti, inglesi!*' he led us into a small dimly lit room where we came face-to-face with the body of a man slumped over a table. His name, we were told, was Cosimo, and he was forty years old.

In front of his bloody face stood a half-drunk glass of beer, some playing cards and a pack of local cigarettes. On the chair next to him was a carrier bag of soft drinks that Cosimo was taking home to his children. Scrawled on the wall behind him was a notice inviting customers to: *Drink and forget your problems*. The bar's harsh neon light reflected in the pool of waxy blood that slowly oozed from Cosimo's head and congealed on the table that was covered in a cheap paper tablecloth featuring a hundred ship's wheels. 'Is this close enough?' Sandro asked. 'You can touch him if you like.' I politely declined.

The Sicilian policeman who up until then had taken little interest in the proceedings, ambled over to where I was gazing into the dead man's eyes – forever focused on infinity – and tugging at my sleeve said in broken English,

'Here, *Inglesi*, see his teeth.'

Teeth? See his teeth? I was bewildered by this seeming triviality compared with the loss of his life. Then I realised what had caused his fascination, for on the table in front of the cadaver lay three nicotine-stained incisors. Poking a grubby finger into his own mouth, his thumb cocked, the officer demonstrated with relish exactly how the gun had been thrust violently into the victim's mouth, shattering teeth, before dispatching its single leaden messenger of death. Sandro, with a nod of his head, assured us that this was the visiting card of the *Cosa Nostra*. It was a neat, professional job and, apart from the blood, the victim looked as though he'd fallen asleep next to his unfinished drink. Witnesses said that when his job was done, the hit man – known as a friend of the victim – kissed Cosimo on the forehead, slipped his Magnum pistol inside his leather jacket and walked out.

Sudden voices from the doorway caught my attention. A weary-looking police surgeon had arrived flanked by two detectives. We were told that this was his seventeenth victim that week. As he walked towards the table he drew on a pair of rubber gloves. Leaning over the body, he grabbed a fistful of its bloodied grey hair and, wrenching the head upwards, peered into the face through eyes half-closed against the cigarette smoke curling up from his mouth. He mumbled something to the detective about it being 'just another night' and casually let go of the bloody mane. Danny and I winced in unison as the head hit the table with a sickening thud and droplets of blood flicked across the table cloth.

Behind him the undertaker impatiently tapped his foot on the lid of a crude pine coffin that had just been carried in. The detectives barely bothered to interview anyone in the bar, as they knew of old that few would dare speak out. When the police surgeon was finished examining the body the undertaker stepped forward, picked up the victim's cigarettes, lit one and after taking a deep drag he pocketed the packet. Now this master of ethics was ready to work.

Sandro grinned at our grim expressions and said brightly, 'We go for dinner now.'

It was some time later before we two could face any food. Sandro had escorted us to a café on a pretty tree-lined square where, sitting at a pavement table, we were trying instead to clear the taste of death from our mouths with an ice-cold beer. Our brave little crusader then casually mentioned that he'd received death threats a month ago and that the police had taken it so seriously that they'd provided him with a bodyguard.

'Where is he now then?' I asked, suddenly nervous.

'Oh, this is my first night out without him.' The balmy evening suddenly took on a chill.

Three steaming bowls of pasta had hardly been placed on the table when Sandro was called to the telephone. After a hurried conversation and apologies to the restaurateur we were off again, this time into the countryside, heading to one of those secretive hillside villages where outsiders – and nosy local journalists – were definitely not welcome. Arriving in the dead of night we cruised the steep, deserted streets with their windows shuttered tight against the ghosts of the past. There wasn't a sign of life save for a scurrying rat, its eyes briefly reflected in the headlights before slinking into the gutter. Finally, we came across a small police station where we managed to rouse the occupants. One by one they tipped out onto the street and surrounded us, tense and suspicious, their pistols in their hands until Sandro repeated, '*Giornalisti!*' These trigger-happy officers of the law confirmed that there had been a reported shooting but admitted they hadn't found a body yet. They refused to go looking for it at that time of night, despite our cajoling. Disappointed, we trailed wearily back to town and crashed out on our beds for what was left of the night.

For the next two days we trawled the bars and hangouts gleaning whatever information we could from a mix of unsavoury characters worthy of Hollywood. Then, one evening, as I was idly looking out of the hotel window watching the last light of day melt into dusk, the telephone rang. Dan dropped the notes he'd been working on and grabbed the receiver. It was one of Sandro's contacts. I leaned over his shoulder to listen. The voice was sharp and to the point.

'Go to this address,' he instructed, as Dan scribbled. 'It's at the back of the station. Now!' There was a click and the phone went dead. Minutes

Top Kenneth and Glenys Downing, and their first son, John.
Bottom Drumming with the skiffle group, The Renegades. John's friend Bob Hay is on the tea chest bass.

The Downing family: Back, Kenneth, David, Glenys, Andrew;

John at school

Daily Express photographer John Downing, 29th June 1968

(Credit: Ballard/Daily Express/Getty Images)

Afghanistan. Photographing from shelter with Ross Benson. And posing in local costume with Danny McGrory

With rebel militiamen in Sudan, *top*. And with Ross Benson once more, in Nicaragua, *bottom*.

Checkpoint Charlie, West Berlin, in a snowy February 1988, with Danny McGrory and the *Daily Mail*

Reflecting in the shelter of a doorway, Sarajevo, 1992

With a UN convoy in the mountains of Bosnia

Photographing in a Chernobyl orphanage. The images, and Kim Wilsher's stories, were the foundations of the *Daily Express* 'Children of Chernobyl' appeal
(Credit: Kim Willsher)

The famously doctored family photograph, created for the golden wedding celebration for Kenneth and Glenys

At Buckingham Palace, Spring 1992, for his MBE investiture, with
sons Bryn and Gareth

John and his wife, Anita
(Credit: Hazel Thompson)

later we jumped into a taxi and on reaching the station elbowed our way through a gathering crowd, drawn by the sound of a woman ululating. Night had fallen and the crowd parted as we found ourselves staring down at a man's body, his white shirt speckled crimson as his life drained away into the gutter. His eyes were closed and in his hand he still clutched a set of car keys. His wailing widow was eventually drawn away and swallowed up by the crowd, her agonising requiem hanging in the air. The remaining throng comprised young and old and included scruffy kids, mothers with babies and old men with knowing eyes, all rubbernecking for a better view. People on balconies looked down, pointed, and exchanged confidences with their neighbours across the divides. They all seemed strangely untouched. Their only questions: 'Who was it? Which family? How many bullets?'

Our story was given a great show by the paper and we returned home triumphant. As the months passed and more and more people were killed in the Mafia vendetta, though, Danny and I became increasingly concerned about Sandro's safety. Dan tried to contact him several times but the numbers he had given us rang out. When he finally spoke to someone from his newspaper, the news wasn't good. 'Sandro disappeared several months ago,' they said. 'He's either dead or in police protection, but – knowing Sandro – the former seems more likely.'

Unlucky Sandro we thought, and then – rather shamefully – I couldn't help but wonder if I still had a number for Juicy.

ELEVEN

QUICK, JOHN, get yourself down to Gatwick, catch the flight to Belize and tie up with Ross Benson who's flying in from LA. Your tickets and money will be waiting for you at Thomas Cook.' It was September 1989.

What more could an enthusiastic photographer ask for than a bundle of money, an airline ticket to a romantic sounding place, and the chance to join my old pal, the sanguine Mr Benson. I didn't need telling twice. Jumping up from where I'd been lounging in the photographer's room, I pulled on my jacket and threw my camera case over my shoulder, asking, 'What's the story?'

The answer not only stopped me in my tracks, but swept away any excitement: 'Princess Anne's doing one of her charity romps around the poorer countries of South America for Save the Children, so we want you to get alongside her.'

Like many journalists, I hated this kind of assignment. The pattern was usually the same each time – an immaculately turned out VIP would arrive in a warzone, Third World country, or the aftermath of a disaster accompanied by an uncompromising PR and any number of fawning officials we dubbed the 'Gucci warriors'. A few appealing children would be cuddled along the way, a penetrating question or two asked and a well-rehearsed quote dropped, before the entire circus would adjourn to the nearest five-star hotel for cocktails and dinner, leaving the beleaguered and bewildered locals to their misery.

Princess Anne did at least have a reputation for supporting her charities with commitment and not much attendant publicity, but I still wondered what was so special about this trip. Then, almost as an aside, the picture editor added, 'Oh, as she flew out of the country, there was an official announcement from Buckingham Palace. She's divorcing Captain Mark Phillips after sixteen years of marriage.' My disappointment deepened for this was the type of story I loathed and believed passionately that the 'Avon ladies' should handle exclusively.

Reluctantly accepting that it was too late to try to wheedle out of the job by suddenly 'remembering' that I had a funeral, wedding or family reunion to attend, I was stuck with it. Racing home, I threw a bundle of clothes, some film and charging leads into a suitcase and set off towards the M25. I hadn't been going for more than half an hour when I ran into solid traffic. It was pre-satnav so I consulted a map and tried an alternative route. As it turned out, so did everyone else.

My mobile phone rang. It was the *Express*'s genial travel manager Derek Stark wanting to update me with flight numbers, ticket references and other relevant information. Staring at the gridlock, I warned him of my predicament. 'When's the next flight if I miss this one?'

There was a brief rustling of paper, then: 'Two days time.'

With rising panic, I asked him if he could help. 'Don't worry, he said. 'I'll get someone from Thomas Cook to do a meet and greet and see if anything can be done about the departure time.' I thanked him but doubted that even he could change that.

When I finally broke free of the jam I put my foot down and raced on. My phone rang and it was Derek again, cool as a cucumber. 'Go straight to the main entrance where someone will be waiting to rush you through.' Then he added softly, 'And don't worry, John. You'll make it!' His reassurance did little to allay my rising panic.

As I screamed into the car park I glanced at my watch – 5.25pm – five minutes before departure time. I didn't stand a cat in hell's chance of making the flight but – as I had done a hundred times before I went for it – running as fast as I could, laden with equipment and dripping with sweat. Airline staff refer to people like me in that situation as 'Have a go's'. Charging up to a surprisingly relaxed-looking young woman from Thomas Cook, I cried, 'Okay, let's go!'

'Take it easy,' she replied with a smile. 'The flight's been delayed by an hour. There's been a bomb scare.' I took a breath and counted my lucky stars. Then Derek's words flashed into my mind – 'Don't worry, John. You'll make it.' No, he couldn't have. Could he?

Two days later I found myself sitting in a beaten up, gas-guzzling old American taxi in the company of Mike Forster from the *Daily Mail* and the amiable Dougie Doig of the *Daily Star*. Each of us were lost in our own thoughts as the cab rumbled along what in Belize purported to be a road. My mind was still mulling over a conversation we'd had earlier with a snotty army captain who assured us, in his best clipped Sandhurst, that far from there being any facility to photograph Princess Anne he intended to make it impossible for us to do so. Normally that sort of remark would meet with a spirited response from such a resourceful troupe but, in the dripping humidity of that tropical island, none of us had the energy to argue.

A larger than usual crater in the road shook us out of our torpor and an idle conversation started up on which restaurant would have the dubious pleasure of our patronage later that night. 'Tell us,' Mike lethargically asked our driver, 'What's the local delicacy?'

'Gibnut, boss,' came the answer.

'What's gibnut when it's at home?' asked Dougie, absentmindedly staring out of the window.

'A big rat,' came the reply through a yellowing grin.

The three of us sat bolt upright, peeled our sweat-soaked shirts off the plastic seats and began to interrogate the driver. 'Will Princess Anne be offered any at the official reception tonight?'

'I dunno boss, but they sure do give it to all them kinda' important people.'

Bullseye. That was good enough for us. The reporters could corroborate the facts later. Although we knew that the story was relatively trivial (the hallmark of most royal trips) an edible giant rat would at least give us something to photograph. And I idly wondered if I might even get to try some too – after all I'd eaten parrot, monkey and bat in various hellholes, rich and poor – and all of it tasted like chicken.

Time was now of the essence as the afternoon was slipping away. It was urgent that we locate one of these gibnuts, photograph it, process the film and wire our pictures to London *toute de suite* so that – if the story stood up – our picture desks would be at the ready. Mike, a talented organiser, asked the driver, 'Where can we find one of these rats?'

'No problem, boss,' he replied with the easy confidence of a Belizean, adding more hesitatingly, 'Only I sure wouldn't put my hands on one! They're kinda fierce.' Making a violent U-turn, he steamed us up the road and drove us into Tesco's car park. 'In there, boss,' he said, almost jumping out of his seat when we bellowed, 'No, we want a live one!'

Shaking his head in puzzlement, he turned the car around and headed us off down an even more heavily rutted side road. As we lurched and bounced our way past shabby wooden houses built on stilts like crooked old legs, it felt like we were in a Tennessee Williams play. The houses were all bleached grey-white by the sun. A necklace of broken shutters hung from their timbered sides, and a single pendant of rotting stairs trailed from their front doors. Finally pulling off the raddled road and into a small compound, we found ourselves in a yard cluttered with boxes, used tyres, gas cylinders and an old 'sit up and beg' bicycle (minus its saddle). A leaking had turned the ground into a quagmire and the entire scene was liberally scattered with semi-naked children. In the centre stood an ageing caravan with a small, rundown DIY extension tacked on.

Our driver got out and introduced us to the owner, Mel – a diminutive and wiry fellow, unwashed, unshaven and undernourished. Much back slapping and local patois was exchanged until, with our patience running out, we demanded to see the pet gibnut our driver had promised us. With a regal flourish, Mel pointed in the direction of a two-foot gap beneath his home, a space fenced in with chicken wire, old oilcans and a few breeze-blocks. Cautiously, I got down on my haunches and peered into the darkness. A pungent smell of *eau de rat* met me or, to be more precise, *the* rat. As my sight adapted to the darkness I suddenly spotted an eye the size of a marble staring right back at me. 'Bloody hell,' I exclaimed, jumping up in one undignified move. 'It's the size of a pit pony!' Despite the obvious exaggeration, everyone took a discretionary step back.

We three then set about persuading Mel to crawl under the hut and produce 'Gilbert' – as we had christened him – for his photographic debut.

'Well, I don't know, boss. He's *real* mean,' Mel replied, stretching the word 'mean' like a piece of chewing gum, leaving us in no doubt of his character.

We protested, reminding him that only moments ago, he'd assured us that this was his pet. 'Yes man. He is, but I don't go near it!'

This was a problem that took all of ten seconds and a wad of Belizean dollars to remedy. Pressed into Mel's grubby hand with the suggestion that he rekindle a close relationship with his four-legged friend, we waited for him to leap into action. Surprisingly, he was still a little hesitant, complaining: 'Man, he could take your finger right off, no problem!'

This was a cue for a few more dollars to be added to his pile as we happily dubbed this gratuity 'grats for rats'. Lost digits were suddenly forgotten as the Great Gibnut Hunt swung into action. In fact it turned out to be less of a hunt and more a classic carrot-and-stick operation. Or should I say, banana-and-stick. Mel peeled back a piece of the chicken wire and, lying on his stomach, prodded the darkness with a banana, whilst his other hand defensively brandished a stick. Our quarry was unimpressed and simply backed further into his lair. Seeing this was getting us nowhere, drastic action was called for.

Everyone was duly issued with a weapon. Doug had an empty beer bottle, Mike fielded an ineffectual looking screwdriver, and I was given a coal hammer. The driver produced a long-bladed machete called a *panga* from the boot of his car, which we all regarded with envy. Acting far more courageously than we felt, we clustered around the entrance to Gilbert's den, weapons raised and watched as Mel, with a less than impressive broom handle, crawled into the stinky darkness. After a long silence, a sudden commotion broke out. Banging and crashing issued from the depths, followed by a series of angry growls and barks as we tightened our grip on the weapons. My overactive imagination pictured Mel retreating out on all fours and being laid out cold by a panicky stroke from my coal hammer.

'Did you hear that thing bark?' Dougie asked querulously.

'You'd bark too if you had a broom handle shoved up your backside,' Mike quipped.

By this time a goodly crowd had gathered, all of whom were pressed into service with anything they could find as a weapon. This included wooden sticks, iron bars and even a wire coat hanger. Then someone had the good sense to produce a cage. Thoroughly caught up in the excitement our driver ran to his taxi and – to our astonishment – pulled off one of his headlights. We watched bemused as he reached into the open window of Mel's caravan, produced a length of flex attached somewhere inside which terminated at his end in a bunch of exposed wiring. The scene that followed was worthy of a West End farce. As he attempted to connect the wires in order to shed more light on Gilbert's gloomy den, there was a brief flash of light followed by an impressive blue arc, delivering him a healthy dose of electricity. Yelping in pain, he dropped the cable onto one of the many inquisitive children who had congregated around him. The luckless boy let out a shriek and – leaping sideways – knocked a smaller child flying, right into the entrance of Gilbert's den. The rodent, inflamed by the rumpus, let out an almighty bark that scared us all. At this, the unfortunate kid panicked and – jumping to his feet and scattering people in all directions – tore out of the compound with the memory of a giant rat and his near-electrocution imprinted forever on his young mind.

Our driver, unfazed, suggested a second attempt. Fortunately for us all, Mrs Mel objected vociferously on the grounds that all the lights in her caravan had gone out. We readily concurred; standing as we were uncomfortably close to ten old canisters marked '*Butane gas – No naked flames*'.

After what seemed like a Titanic struggle, the driver hitched a noose round poor Gilbert's neck and, wriggling backwards out of the hole, dragged the hapless creature into public view, its back arched and legs locked on full brakes. I think he must have resigned himself to the inevitable then, for he suddenly gave up the struggle and slumped dejectedly. Seizing the moment, Mel grabbed the rodent by the scruff of the neck and held him triumphantly aloft as we took our snaps. I have to admit that we all felt rather sorry for Gilbert now that we'd so rudely disturbed him. He looked a sweet old thing really.

We never did find out if Princess Anne ate any gibnut at the banquet held in her honour at Government House that night, but we did discover later that the Queen was served it on her visit to the country where she is still the Head of State. Her Maj bravely declared afterwards that it tasted like rabbit. Thereafter gibnut became even more of a delicacy on the island and was dubbed 'Royal Rat' or 'Rat eaten by Her Majesty Queen Liz'. Hopefully Gilbert lived to tell the tale.

In 1990, I came close to being cooked myself, when I was sent with reporter Kim Willsher to the Chernobyl nuclear power station in the Ukraine; the first Western journalists given access to the scene of the world's worst nuclear disaster.

Four years earlier on Saturday, April 26 1986, the nuclear reactor went into meltdown and exploded during a routine safety test, spewing radioactive particles into the air and contaminating an area of several hundred thousand kilometres. The radioactive material released was four hundred times more than the combined fall out over Hiroshima and Nagasaki during the Second World War. It spread as far as the west coast of Ireland and the southern tip of Italy. Fewer than a hundred people died in the immediate aftermath but several thousand were affected long term and a World Health Organisation study found that it caused an estimated four thousand premature deaths. The total human cost may never be fully calculated but scientists say that Chernobyl will be unsafe for habitation for another 24,000 years.

At the time of our visit, the Soviet Union was gradually opening up but still remained a closed and repressive society. Kim Willsher, having sold the idea of an exclusive visit to our Editor, was then expected to come up with a story and photographs so she somehow persuaded the authorities in Moscow to reluctantly allow us access.

We flew to Kiev and were driven the twenty-five kilometres to the irradiated zone and the ghost city of Pripyat near the border with Belarus. Our transport was a black stretch Zil limousine provided by the Russians and we were accompanied by a minder and translator as well as an engineer and a scientist who'd both worked at the plant. When we reached the exclusion zone that covers more than one thousand square miles, we found it marked by high barbed wire fences and forbidding gates with rusting yellow nuclear danger signs plastered all over them. In a scene that could have come from a disaster movie and under the beady eyes of armed soldiers we had to swap our 'clean' vehicle for a 'dirty' black one to take us into the so-called 'dead zone' immediately around the nuclear plant. They also made us wear rubber wellington boots. It was at that point that we heeded their warning to wind up the windows.

The scientist reassured us constantly that everything had been cleaned and damaged trees taken away. They had scoured the earth and made the whole zone safe again, he insisted. They were desperate to assure us that everything was okay, but this belied the fact that there were miles and miles of forbidding fencing beyond which no members of the public were allowed to pass. Although the National Radiological Protection Board had given Kim some kind of device to carry that would test for levels of radiation on our return, we didn't carry a Geiger counter to check radiation levels so we had to rely on theirs. The trouble was none of their equipment seemed terribly reliable and their behaviour far from reassuring.

When we first arrived they scanned the car with a wailing radioactivity monitor and all seemed well. The dead zone was once home to more than 120,000 people but by then only a hundred or so staff lived there, constantly evaluating the risks. Spookily, outdoor speakers broadcast the doleful sound of a Russian male voice choir all day long – 'to cheer up the scientists', we were told. Wandering into homes that had been abandoned within minutes by order of the authorities, I found half-drunk mugs of coffee on kitchen tables, clothes still hung in cupboards and children's toys scattered across floors. Some of the flats had been looted, with drawers open and smashed photographs on the ground. Others had tables laid for lunch.

Returning to the car we drove towards the devastated nuclear plant where I asked the driver to stop so I could take an overview. 'Is it safe to take pictures here?' I asked our minder before getting out.

'Of course,' he said smiling. 'We have cleared the whole area and replaced the top surface so it is perfectly safe. I happily took him at his word and, stepping from the car, framed the scene through the viewfinder of my camera and took my first shot. Then, not quite satisfied with the angle, I walked forward into the knee-length grass. I was brought up short with an almost hysterical shriek from the car: 'Don't walk in the grass!'

I looked around stunned and started to say, 'But I thought you said it was safe…' when the look on his face told me a different tale. He quickly regained control and in an unconvincing tone added, 'Well, you know, we just like to be *absolutely* sure.' This was our introduction to Chernobyl.

All around us there wasn't a sign of wildlife, not even birds. At the nearby Research Station, Kim filled her notebook as scientists in white coats told us of terrifying mutants, including deformed mice. They showed us a tray of saplings grown from pine cones in the 'red forest', so named because in the hours after the disaster the trees glowed red. The entire forest had been uprooted and buried, but not before some cones were collected. The saplings were frighteningly bizarre: some grew tall and thin, others stunted, several had needles facing the wrong way.

At lunchtime we were led to a tin hut that served as a canteen for the scientific community. On arrival, we had to swish our wellies in a disinfectant footbath and press our hands up against a metal pad that was supposed to test our radiation levels. This odd machine, looking a bit like one of those old weighing machines they used to have in supermarkets, had a red and a green light and our minder explained that it would start off red and then go to green. When I placed my hands on it remained resolutely on red. Our minder babbled something and frowned. 'What did he say?' I asked our translator Vitaly.

'He says it's safe.'

'But it didn't go green.' The minder then claimed it wasn't plugged in – but if that were true then the light wouldn't have been on at all. Telling me to try again, the light stayed red until he gave it an almighty thump and – bingo – it went green.

'Well?' I asked.

Vitaly shrugged. 'He says it's safe. We should go now.' I wasn't convinced.

When we gained access to the plant itself, now encased in a vast concrete sarcophagus, we had to pass through a kind of metal turnstile that gave us a full body scan to confirm whether or not we had safe levels of radiation. Inside, we were astonished to learn that the other nuclear reactors at Chernobyl were still working, and that we could tour Reactor 3, immediately next to number 4, the one that had blown up. Inside the control room staff in white suits sat in complete silence in front of a bank of monitors and machines. The hush was broken only by the click of my camera and a brief shriek from Kim as I crouched to get a better angle and stepped back, my rear end getting dangerously close to a big red button. It was a rare light moment in what became an increasingly tense day.

Before we left, the scientists presented Kim with an armful of enormous red roses. She took them without thinking. It was only when we were back in the Zil that it dawned on us where they'd been grown. A few kilometres down the road, we threw them out of the car window.

Back in Kiev, people were eager to talk of all the death and sickness they attributed to Chernobyl. In nearly bare hospitals, desperate parents thrust their children at us begging us to take them to the UK for treatment or asking for money for medicines, diagnostic equipment or chemotherapy drugs. It was deeply upsetting to see so many sick children, although the government was keen to play down the situation so that we never knew whether we were seeing the worst cases or not. The hospital directors – who insisted we take a glass of 'champagnski,' cognac or vodka (even at 9am) – were clearly overwhelmed by the scale of the problem. It was too soon after the accident for there to be a recordable increase in cancer, but they had seen an increase in cases of leukaemia, heart and thyroid issues caused by radioactive iodine in children from the Chernobyl area. They showed us birth defects never seen before, like the babies born with what they called frogs' legs, their hip joints forcing legs outwards.

A scientist we spoke to retrieved a red notebook he was using at the plant on the night of the explosion and which had since been wrapped in foil and hidden away in a drawer. When he passed a Geiger counter over it, the clicking went off the scale. He told us that even those not directly affected by radioactive fall-out continued to eat contaminated food. Many were treated at the Institute of Specialised Radiation Protection on the outskirts of Kiev where they were kept for a few weeks to be given 'clean' food, before being sent back to their contaminated homes. The Soviet authorities advised families to avoid eating berries, mushrooms and milk, but many were poor and had no choice but to feed their children on whatever they could find. There were also several orphanages in and around Kiev, looking after children whose parents had either died or who simply couldn't afford to keep them.

One child among many we met, a girl called Viktoria, epitomised the human tragedy. Less than a week after the disaster, the teenager and her school friends were ordered out on to the streets of Kiev to take part in traditional parades. Viktoria's mother Galina wept as she and her husband Viktor spoke of their only child's unexplained sickness. In the next room of their small apartment, Viktoria lay dying, a skeletal figure staring blindly at the ceiling, hardly able to speak. She bore no resemblance to the healthy happy blonde girl in a mantelpiece photograph. With her parents' blessing, I went in to take her picture but after a few minutes I noticed that she didn't appear be breathing. Distressed, I went back to her parents and told them that I feared she might have died. They rushed in and cradled their daughter in their arms and the mother kissed her through the tears. Viktoria was still alive – just – but Kim heard some time later that she had died, along with so many others.

My photographs of Viktoria and others – including another mother cradling her dying son – appeared in the paper alongside Kim's excellent story as part of a *Daily Express* Children of Chernobyl campaign to raise funds to buy diagnostic equipment and drugs. It raised almost half a million pounds but our newspaper's generosity didn't quite match that of its reader-ship for they turned down our request for extra staff to handle the flood of mail received. In between our regular duties, Kim and I, with the help of a couple of secretaries set about opening, collating and totting up the monies from the thousands of letters. Cheques as large as £1,000 were always greeted with a frisson of excitement but the letters that touched us most were those from young children who'd write, 'I am sending you my pocket money for the sick children...' or from the elderly who, in a shaky hand, would pen phrases like, 'I am sorry but I can only afford £1 from my pension.' It was a moving lesson in Christian charity.

Our biggest donation, financially speaking, came from Cliff Richard who was having a sell-out season at Wembley Arena and promised that the profits from his final night's concert would be added to our campaign: a most magnanimous gift. The big night arrived and towards the end of the show Cliff stopped singing and gave a sensitive speech about how our story had touched him to the backdrop of a rolling slideshow of my images. He finished with an announcement that he was going to publicly thank those at the *Express* who had made the campaign possible so Kim and I, drinking gin and tonics at the back, puffed up with anticipation and pride.

'We would like to thank….' he began…then named our show business editor… 'for all the fine work he has done to raise this money'. To rapturous applause the 'hero of the hour' stepped forward and received a giant cardboard cheque. Kim and I were at first completely stunned but then we burst out laughing. The man everyone was applauding had never said a word to either of us about the campaign, let alone opened a single envelope or counted a cheque. I had a suspicion that he didn't even really know where Chernobyl was. Bemused, we headed to the bar set aside for the minor oiks like ourselves but inadvertently wandered into the adjoining VIP area stuffed full of *Express* executives and a sprinkling of stars. I saw that it was adorned with an exhibition of my framed and enlarged Chernobyl photographs but before we could take a closer look, we were promptly asked to leave.

By this time we were well into the spirit of the evening, and then Kim's mum joined us. She was still smarting from the fact that her daughter hadn't even been mentioned on stage, so when she heard of our ejection from the VIP lounge it became too much for Mrs Willsher's sense of fair play. Turning on her heel she marched straight into the VIP bar and collared our editor Nick Lloyd with a major tongue-lashing and finger wag. The moment we realised what was happening we scuttled off into a corner, burying our heads in our drinks, outwardly mortified but inwardly thrilled by her loyalty. It was some time before she returned, certainly long enough for us to consider our next career move, which we felt was imminent. Instead, she triumphantly announced, 'The Editor would like you both to join him.' Good old mum!

There was an addendum to that assignment, as some time after our story appeared a man, who didn't want to give his name, rang the *Express* claiming to work for a British company that supplied the machines that had tested us for radiation at the nuclear plant. He said the officials there had been instructed not to touch them, but kept turning the detection sensors up. 'They fiddle with them and they break down so we have to go out and fix them,' he said. 'Then they fiddle with them again, and the process is repeated.' The message was that you'd have to glow in the dark to set them off.

As if to confirm his words, we returned the device given to us by the

National Radiological Protection Board. This was subsequently tested and we were warned that the levels of radiation we'd received would have been high enough to spark an inquiry had they been found on a British nuclear worker. Great.

Still, it wasn't all bad news – Cliff Richard liked one of my photos so much that he asked to keep it as a memento. Congratulations?... I guess.

In the summer of 1990 Saddam Hussein invaded Kuwait and sparked the First Gulf War so every photographer and journalist worth his or her salt expected to be sent out on the next plane. It wasn't something anyone anticipated with great eagerness, however, as Saddam was known to use deadly gas on his enemies and the prospect of that caused many to falter.

I was no exception but I was still prepared to go. Annoyingly, my picture desk was a little late to act so, by the time I was finally despatched there wasn't a gas mask to be found in London. Minions were sent out to search everywhere but it was fruitless. Then some wise guy came up with an idea – 'There's a sex shop in Soho that sells all kinds of weird military kit,' he told the desk, with the air of a frequent visitor. 'Send John there. They're bound to have what he needs.' The order went out but I refused to darken the doors of such an establishment so a lackey was sent instead. He returned with a full gas mask and a hazmat suit, mercifully wrapped in cellophane, which I hoped indicated that they had never been used.

Despite being fully kitted out, I ended up having little to do with that war and – although I had a few trips out to Jordan and to the border where Kurdish refugees were fleeing *en masse* – I was kept busy elsewhere and managed to avoid much of it. One of the things I was asked to do was take part in a popular television programme called *In At the Deep End*. In it, the former *That's Life* presenter Chris Serle shadowed me for a week to try his hand as a Fleet Street photographer. But another assignment was probably my jammiest – a £1.5 million race from Victoria Station in London to Venice on the luxurious Orient Express train to raise money for the Royal Marsden Hospital.

A group of celebrities and wealthy passengers, among them the singer Cher and the actress Morgan Fairchild, were pitted against a group of eleven drivers and celebrities including racing driver Jackie Stewart who were driving supercars the 1,000 miles through six countries in over thirty hours. I've always loved trains and that really was five-star all the way, being served five-course meals by forty discreet staff in luxurious surroundings. Plus I got to spend some time with the supermodel Jasmin Le Bon, while her pop star husband Simon raced to the Veneto in a Lamborghini.

A few days later, it was down to earth with a bump and back in Amman, Jordan, with Danny and a large press contingent seeing if we could get into Baghdad for the First Gulf War. While I was there, I made a routine call home to check on Ian Jones, who was living in my house in Camberwell as my latest lodger. 'Everything all right, mate?' I asked. 'Any mail?'

As I waited, he opened all my letters and bills and let me know what was inside. Suddenly I heard him say, 'Bloody hell, John, you've got a letter from Buckingham Palace!'

'Really? What does it say?' I heard him slice the envelope open, then another, 'Bloody hell!'

'What?'

'Are you sitting down? You've been awarded an MBE for services to journalism!'

I could hardly believe my ears as Ian read out the full text of the letter, explaining that I had been nominated anonymously and that it was up to me if I accepted it or not. If I did, then I wasn't to tell anybody until it was formally announced in the Queen's New Year's Honours List on December 31, 1991. A ceremony would then take place in the Spring of 1992 at Buckingham Palace and I'd be allowed to bring two guests.

The temptation to call my parents and tell them immediately was enormous, but I did as I was told and surprised them with the news a month later, on New Year's Eve. They were over the moon. I longed to take them with me to the Palace, of course, but in my heart I knew that I'd take Gareth and Bryn instead. My dad, although naturally disappointed, told me, 'That's the right decision, son.' What was sad about that for me was that dear old Dad wasn't so well by then having had to take early retirement because of a leaky heart valve. He died at the age of seventy-nine later that year but not before my brothers and I sneaked in to see him in hospital out of visiting hours dressed up variously as (male) nurses and vicars.

I had no idea who'd nominated me for that award but I assumed that it must have been my Editor so I went to thank him once it was announced, but he only laughed and promised me it wasn't him. Someone then suggested that the Queen may have seen me on TV. Who knows? Whoever it was, I am eternally grateful.

On the morning of my investiture, suited and booted in a grey morning suit (which I don't think I'd ever worn before and have certainly never worn since), I took the boys in a taxi to the Palace and sat nervously with them waiting for my moment to stand before the Queen. When I thought back to the first time I'd seen her as a schoolboy in 1953 on Clapham Common, waving at the crowds, it seemed impossible that this acne-faced kid could be receiving a medal from her for doing the job I loved. By the time I was summoned up to the podium to bow my head before her, I was so nervous that I had to clamp my hands behind my back to stop them from shaking.

The Queen exchanged pleasantries with me although I can't now recall a word she said and then it was my turn to respond. I had a thousand things prepared to say about photographing her Mum or covering some of her royal tours in places like the South Pacific and Africa. I could have chatted about the races at the Derby, our time aboard the Royal Yacht *Britannia*, how I covered several State Openings of Parliament or about her son Charles's wedding. Instead I mumbled something foolish and stared into her face incredulously throughout.

Adorned with my stunning medal dangling from its lovely red ribbon, I posed happily with the boys for photos outside and then took them and it to show my Mum, Dad and brothers in a restaurant I'd booked for a celebratory lunch. It was one of the best days of my life.

Working in the news industry means accepting the fact that you never know what each day will bring. One moment you might be on a high because of a great assignment or an accolade, and the next moment you might be despatched to something that will bore you to tears.

Being on the election trail fell into the latter category and was almost as dreary a job as covering a party conference, but it was something I had to endure every now and again along with everyone else. The routine was always the same – each morning there'd be a press conference at the relevant Party HQ after which the travelling press would either jump in their cars or board a waiting coach for the day's campaign events.

For security reasons we were only informed of our destination at the last minute; a system that was instigated on Margaret Thatcher's first campaign leading to it being dubbed, 'Maggie's Mystery Tour'. For her second, I produced T-shirts for all the photographers bearing the logo 'Hilda's Personal Photographer,' (alluding to Mrs T's middle name and affectionate nickname by the press). I even had one made up for her that read, 'Tour Leader.' Sadly, she declined to wear it as pulling it over her head would have disturbed her perfectly coiffured hair, but she was sporting enough to hold one up in front of her for a photograph.

Once on the road we'd head to the next venue on the election trail, always arriving before the PM so that we could record the event before scuttling to the next. Our coach was usually very popular amongst the political minders due to the endless mischief we'd get up to in order to compensate for having to listen to oft-repeated speeches and photograph endless handshakes. As each day wore on, the election trail would become increasingly chaotic, due to a combination of our imminent deadlines and the influence of Bacchus.

There was an unwritten rule that on any election trail we'd try to help the representative of the only tabloid for the Opposition get one amusing picture a day that poked fun at our Tour Leader. On a Tory campaign, that would be the *Mirror*. This arrangement would be duplicated in reverse by all those following the Labour candidates, thereby creating a sort of photographic democracy. Wilting with exhaustion (and boredom) after weeks on the road, we were driven to Sheerness docks in Kent one bitterly cold morning to take photographs of John and Norma Major posing in front of a vessel built by British workers. This predictably dull visit went well enough until, right at the end, a small group of dockers on top of a crane started yelling abuse. Major, who was out of earshot and unaware of the language being hurled in his direction, smiled and waved back, which gave us our shot.

As we all ambled back to our bus our own pint-sized jester, the *Sun* photographer Nigel Cairns, commented casually, 'Did you see that docker drop his pants and moon at Major?'

'What? When?' everyone cried. For a moment I went cold. Had I bloody missed it? I could see my fellow photographers were equally surprised.

Suppressing a smile, Cairns went on: 'Yup. While you were all photographing Major waving and trying to control his hair in the wind, I put my long lens on the dockers and that's when one of them did the deed. I thought you'd all seen it.' There was a stunned silence. Seeing our disappointment, he added, 'It happened ever so quickly, and I took it on a 600 so it'll probably be out of focus.' It was then that we saw him wink. The only photographer who didn't see this was our sole Left wing representative, Roger Allen, known to all as 'Dodger.'

Rising to the challenge, everyone reached for their giant bricks of mobile phones and set about making fake calls to their offices about the photo that never was. 'Yes, that's right. Mr Major was mooned. No, I haven't got the picture, but the *Sun* has. We're hoping he might share it with us.' Our charade put Roger into a frenzy, as he'd be in for the roasting of all time if he'd missed a gem like this. In a state of panic, he went to a quiet corner of the coach to call his picture editor and warn of the storm about to break. As he did so, one of the chaps was dispatched to the front of the coach to quickly call the *Mirror* desk to tip them off that it was all a leg-pull and ask them to play along.

Cairns, meanwhile, carried on winding up Roger mercilessly. 'Look, I can't see you losing your job over this, Dodger. If I've got a spare neg, I'll give it to you.'

'You're a pal!' said Roger, relieved, before promptly calling his office to assure them that he could get his hands on the shot of the day. At this point I felt the joke had gone far enough and signalled Cairns to stop. He nodded, but he wasn't done yet. Lifting his camera onto his knee he made a play of fiddling with the catch on the back before it suddenly flew open, exposing the phantom film. Frantically, he slammed it shut again with a cry of, 'Oh shit. I've buggered it!'

I thought Roger was going to die. He went white, his mouth fell open and he stared at Cairns in disbelief. You could almost see him thinking, 'What am I to tell the office now? First I fail to get the photo, then I promise I can get it and now I've lost it again.' Cairns put on a faultless display of sympathy but still didn't put the poor bloke out of his misery.

Then Roger suddenly had a bright idea. 'Look, all we need is a picture of somebody's arse. If we all take it, then nobody will know the difference.' Everyone burst out laughing apart from Nigel who said, 'But who would agree to do that?'

It was like throwing a life belt to a drowning man. 'I will!' announced Roger eagerly, duly hooked line and sinker.

When we arrived at our next location, a traditional working hop farm where there was to be a falconry display, we merrily ignored the political caravan after telling the cronies that Major holding a hawk would be pointless to us photographically. Instead, we tripped off the bus in high spirits, desperately trying not to give the game away. Finding a large barn, we slipped around the back and split into two groups, one each end, cameras at the ready, while Roger stood centre stage next to some metal railings that might – on a bad day – be mistaken for part of a ship. Nervously, he called, 'All clear?'

'Yes, yes, get on with it!' came the chorus, as we struggled for control. He slipped his belt and had just started to lower his trousers when one of the farm workers suddenly appeared from a window directly above him. 'Oi! What are you lot doing here? Clear off!' I swear that as Roger zipped up his trousers, red-faced, some of the photographers almost wet themselves. Determined not to lose momentum, Roger quickly found a new location and, taking a deep sigh, said, 'Okay. Let's get on with it.'

A minute or so later, the trousers and boxer shorts had come down and, after a count to five, the deed was done. It wasn't until he turned around and saw grown men in hysterics, rolling on the ground that we finally confessed to the joke. To Roger's undying credit, he took it in good part. Realising what a fool he'd made of himself – he joined the raucous laughter so heartily that one of the press officers told us to be quiet as we were inter-rupting Mr Major. This, of course, only made us laugh harder still. Happy days.

Twelve

IT WAS EARLY one Sunday in 1992 on a crisp, clear Spring morning. The proud people of Sarajevo were out on the streets of their besieged city, heads up and defiant as ever. Many were on their way to church, others to the mosque. Some were merely promenading in the few remaining clothes they hadn't yet pawned for food. The men wore their shabby Sunday best and the women turned out in elegant finery, hair swept up and high heels clicking on broken pavements.

Danny and I were there as part of a huge press contingent covering the Bosnian civil war and what was to become the four-year long Siege of Sarajevo – the longest siege Europe would witness since the end of the Second World War and one that would claim more than ten thousand lives and injure more than fifty thousand. For 1,425 days thousands were held hostage in their own city by Bosnian Serbs who took up positions in the hills all around them. Their separatist leader Ratko Mladic famously told his men, 'Shoot at slow intervals until I tell you to stop. Shell them until they can't sleep. Don't stop until they are on the edge of madness.'

The men, women and children he was intent on eradicating were left without running water, electricity or medicine. Those trapped also had very little food. Of the thousands killed, more than 1,600 were innocent children, forty per cent of whom were targeted directly by snipers. This was my first of many trips with Danny since Ross Benson had moved to the *Mail* and Dan was made Chief Reporter, but our tours to this historic city during this bitterest of conflicts was the one that marked us for life and cemented our friendship forever.

That April morning, the sun's rays crept up the bullet-pitted walls and across the damaged rooftops of the oldest quarter, warming the spirit along with the ancient wooden structures. Shimmering in the light were the many blue plastic sheets provided by the UN to cover shattered windows. For now, all appeared at peace amongst the crippled buildings. Then, without warning, out of the blue sky a screaming whine followed by a crashing explosion broadcast the arrival of Sarajevo's regular but most unwelcome visitor, a Serbian mortar. That modern day Grim Reaper ripped its path through mortar and flesh with total disregard.

Tom Stoddart, a fellow photographer and close friend, was walking just ahead of me when the mortar exploded. Turning from the half-crouched position that we all instinctively adopted, he yelled, 'Shall we go?' For a moment, I wasn't sure of his meaning – go forward or retreat? Nervously, I glanced over my shoulder for guidance from Danny and the last of our little group, a young freelance photographer named Paul Lowe. I was in some quality company on what could well be my last day on this Earth.

Paul hesitated, and with good reason, for it was a well-known Serb ploy to delay before launching a second or third shell, hoping to reap further carnage as they caught rescuers rushing to aid the injured. Looking back at Tom, I nodded and he shouted, 'Let's go!' Still bent double, we ran forward as one and around the corner dreading the scene of slaughter we fully expected to find. Fortunately, this time there were only a few wrecked shops partially obscured by a fog of settling dust and accompanied by the usual broken glass and splintered wood. We quickly scanned the street. No one was injured. Turning to retrace our steps, we heard the instantly recognisable whine of another mortar. We ran like hell to a nearby doorway and, as the explosion rocked the ground, we barged our way into the hallway where other frightened souls, eyes wide with fear, were sheltering.

'I told you it was bloody dangerous here!' Tom scolded, reiterating his earlier warning. He was right and, furthermore, the attack turned into a sustained one. To take our minds off the continual danger, we engaged in that favourite Fleet Street pastime of insulting banter. Having repeatedly found ourselves on assignments together in the various armpits of the world Danny, Tom and I had become known as the 'Three Musketeers' and we became quite inseparable on jobs like this especially. As I was the oldest, Tom threw the first jibe at me: 'Didn't know an old fart like you could run so fast.'

'That's a bit rich,' I parried. 'Considering you were the first under cover.'

Danny waded in with: 'What do you expect from a fat Geordie?' We all laughed and the tension eased momentarily. Later that year the 'fat Geordie' we knew and loved was almost killed when, in precisely the same kind of situation, a mortar exploded outside Sarajevo's Parliament Building. The blast threw him over a wall, breaking his ankle in six places and badly fracturing his shoulder, which had to be pinned in place with metal. Thereafter he referred to himself as, 'fat Geordie with a limp.' Thanks to the exemplary conduct of the *Sunday Times* and their outstanding picture editor Aidan Sullivan, he was medevac'd out and hospitalised in a fancy London clinic. The newspaper took full responsibility for his wellbeing – something other journals were nowhere near so conscientious or caring about. Tom never lost his sense of humour even after his injury and when asked by a car salesman to choose a colour for the new Lotus he was purchasing, he opted for titanium, 'To match my shoulder.'

Within months of his recovery he hobbled back into ravaged Sarajevo to carry on recording the plight of this city and its brave people. To quote television journalist and MP Martin Bell in his introduction to Tom's exhibition of Sarajevo photographs launched a few years later: 'He went on to prove that a dodgy ankle and a titanium shoulder are no impediment to the practice of world class photography.'

What happened to Tom would be a salutary lesson for all of us, but for some even being there was almost a religious one, for had we ignored Danny's request to first nip into the Catholic church and say a quick prayer for a few life-saving minutes, we would have been placed at the very heart of the explosion – four more headstones for the city's overcrowded Groblje Lav, or Lion Cemetery.

Only thirty-six hours earlier and what seemed a lifetime away, Danny and I had breezed into a car hire office in Zagreb with the air of the innocent. This was my first of nine visits over three years to the Balkans, each one lasting about a month. In one pocket we carried our driving licences, in the other our newly issued UN Bosnian journalist passes. The first was to be passed over the counter; the second was most definitely not. To the inquiry, 'Where are you going?' we assured the young lady behind the counter that we were making our way down the coast. Not a lie, I hasten to add, just somewhat economical with the truth.

For the next seventeen hours Danny drove the little Peugeot she gave us at a furious lick towards Split and thence to Sarajevo. Our only hold-up came near an island where a bridge had been blown up, forcing us to take a circuitous route via an old ferry. The queue for the boat stretched from the quayside over a nearby hill and out of sight. We sat in it for the best part of four hours, our frustration mounting as we inched slowly forward. Deciding that I should go in search of food and drink, I left Danny with the car and took the long trek to the head of the queue where I joined a small gathering at a rundown coffee stall. Waiting to be served, I contrived a conversation in broken English with a scruffy, unshaven official leaning disconsolately on the counter. Over a few *pivos* (beer) I gleaned there were only two more ferries that night, and that we didn't stand a chance of making either of them. 'Too many cars you behind,' was his verdict. He then went into a rambling complaint of how the war heaped endless problems on him. As I affected deep compassion for the extra work, he finished by saying how sorry he was that he couldn't help us, casually adding that only the emergency services were permitted to jump the queue.

A glimmer of hope appeared. I poured him a couple more sympathetic pivos, threw in a packet of highly sought after American cigarettes and pursued our cause. After some alcohol-induced consideration, he draped an arm around my shoulder and declared words to the effect that the municipality's regulations on emergency services (sub-section B) *should* encompass journalists, and therefore we could come straight to the head of the queue. I shook his hand energetically and made the long journey back to our vehicle with the good news. Danny eased our little red car out of the line and, driving on the wrong side of the narrow country road we slipped past mile upon mile of vehicles, each one containing drivers freely expressing their opinions of us as we passed.

Leaving the ferry on the other shore we stopped briefly in the coastal town of Split – the main jumping off point for the conflict – to grab a couple of hours sleep. Once refreshed, we made contact with the other hacks in town to glean the latest information and pick up any helpful advice. They warned us to stock up with food and water, as basic provisions were practically non-existent in Sarajevo. Of these, petrol was the most important as this wasn't available anywhere *en route* and only at exorbitant prices via the black market in the city. Buying petrol wasn't a problem in Split, but finding suitable cans to carry it proved to be a nightmare. We scoured the town in vain but the international TV crews had been through the place like a swarm of locusts stripping it of everything useful and driving prices sky-high. There were even rumours that some of these organisations had bought up many more armoured vehicles than they needed simply to ensure their competitors went without. There were certainly a few white armoured cars emblazoned with the letters 'TV' in bold black writing that never seemed to move from the car park of the Split Hotel. This issue made little difference to most British journalists and photographers, as our offices wouldn't dream of laying out that sort of money for our safety.

After a fruitless search of stores, shops and garages for a petrol can we finally came across a large plastic container for storing homemade wine sitting on a shelf. About two-and-a-half feet square with a tap at the bottom and a screw cap at the top, it looked as if it could hold seven or eight gallons. Perfect. We snapped it up to add to the full tank we had in the car, and an old Army Jerry can we'd acquired from a mercenary taxi driver for the outrageous price of $100. With luck, that lot should just about see us to Sarajevo and back.

Ready for what lay ahead, we set off along the coast road in the direction of Dubrovnik and on reaching the village of Blace turned north towards Mostar. As we passed through this ancient town with its arched medieval bridge, still intact at this early stage of the war, the streets quickly emptied as a couple of shells fell close by. Dan pressed his foot down on the accelerator and we sped off, intent on getting clear before we'd be forced to take shelter. As we tore along the empty high street of this bombarded town, a policeman launched himself into the road from the shadow of a tree and waved a stop sign at us that looked just like a cartoon lollipop. Dan and I both went rigid in our seats and stamped on the brake – he on the real one, me on an imaginary equivalent. As we screamed past the officer kicking up dust from our locked tyres, his face changed from puce to white as he leaped out of the way.

We came to a shuddering halt some yards past him whereupon this diligent officer of the law straightened his cap and dusted down his uniform, before pulling his jacket and his dignity together and marching towards us. Stepping sheepishly from the car we waited for our roasting. Then without warning Dan grabbed the officer's hand, shook it vigorously with a broad grin and blocked the torrent of words coming our way. Just to make sure it didn't resume, he then warmly embraced him in a truly Irish way. Amazingly, it did the trick – well, that and another mortar shell that exploded nearby. Momentarily distracted, the policeman glanced over his shoulder in the direction of the 'crump' and waved us on.

As we left the hapless town behind us, everything grew uncomfortably quiet with only the occasional car passing in the other direction until even they petered out. There were no human beings to be seen anywhere at all. As we drove on into the scenic countryside, we began to spot pretty red-roofed houses in ruins, their whitewashed walls streaked with the sooty fingerprints of fire, a trademark of the insidious ethnic cleansing that came to define this war. Despite the complete lack of road signs we managed to reach a dam that we needed to cross. We'd been warned that this could be extremely dangerous so we approached gingerly, searching the blockhouses that stood guard at either end for signs of life. Nothing was moving but for the rippling water glinting in the sun. There was complete silence. Studying the road surface ahead, we knew we couldn't make a dash for it due to the extensive shell damage, some of which had been patched with old doors, lumps of wood and metal hoardings. We had no idea if these Heath Robinson repairs would bear the weight of our car, which meant that we'd have to slowly manoeuvre around them if we could – making us an easy target for anyone fancying a potshot.

With no other choice, I stepped out of the car and walked ahead as Dan slowly snaked it left and right on my directions to avoid the worst holes and navigate to what I hoped were safer areas. The temporary repairs creaked alarmingly as we crossed them but luck was with us, for not only did the patchwork hold up but also no one that day chose to target two sitting ducks in what became another deadly fairground shooting gallery.

Travelling further, we found ourselves in a steep-sided valley that ran alongside a series of perfect aquamarine lakes. We decided this would be a good spot to investigate our plastic container of fuel, as the smell of petrol had grown stronger and stronger and was starting to make us feel nauseous. We also wanted to use the white insulating tape we'd brought from home to plaster all four sides of the car with the letters TV (shorter and more instantly recognisable than PRESS). We cut the engine and got out of the car, stretching cramped limbs as the sun beat down. Once again, there was complete silence. Not the rustle of a tree, or the cry of a bird. We stood for a moment in the absolute stillness, taking in the beauty of the lake and the wooded valley that seemed to reach to the sky, each of us lost in our own thoughts – a heady combination of fear at what lay ahead, memories of home, and the cruel contradiction of such tranquillity in the middle of a vengeful war.

Danny was the first to break this magical moment when he suddenly cried, 'Oh, shit!' and pointed to the liquid dripping from the back of the car. Dragged back to reality, we whipped open the boot to discover that the large plastic container had sprung a leak and pooled much of its contents in the enclosed space, soaking our clothes and ruining our bread and cheese lunch. After much swearing and cursing, we affected a temporary repair with a plastic bag and the indispensable 'Gaffer' tape, lying the container on its back, leaky tap facing upwards. The silence, which in most warzones would be a warning of an impending attack, was starting to pick at our nerves, so we hurriedly finished our repairs and moved off.

We hadn't been going long before the narrow road wound its way into a long tunnel, the end of which was obscured from view. We had no option but to enter, driving into the blackness at a snail's pace, painfully aware that this would be an ideal place to launch an ambush or lay a mine. On tenterhooks, we rolled slowly on, eyes straining for any signs of danger while in our peripheral vision we seemed to see moving shapes that turned out to be a combination of our over-active imaginations and the car's headlights reflecting off the puddles and casting sinister images up the walls.

After what seemed like an age, we exited the tunnel and came blinking out into the light. The tension fell away almost immediately but our relief was short lived, for ahead was a second tunnel. Our confidence growing, we negotiated this one a little more quickly only to find a third tunnel lying in wait. Feeling more blasé and slipping into that dangerous syndrome of over-confidence, we went lickety-spit into the dark but, as we rounded the bend and accelerated towards the exit, we suddenly became aware of shadowy figures scattering left and right. Danny slammed on the brakes and a fresh wave of petrol fumes filled the car. I don't know who was more frightened then – us, or the soldiers who'd been lolling around idly in the shade of the tunnel. It took a moment or two to persuade them to lower their rifles and accept our apologies for nearly running them over. Equilibrium was restored with the handing over of that international war currency – Marlboro cigarettes – and our newfound friendship was sealed with a few cans of petrol-infected beer.

As soon as we opened the boot to locate their bribe, we smelled petrol and realised that our wine container had sprung a further leak along one of its seams. The soldiers, smoking heavily, were eager to see what other goodies they might be able to liberate from our car. Despite the language problem, we made a valiant attempt to explain the principals of combustion, pointing at the cigarettes then the petrol, waving our arms in an exaggerated mushroom cloud. We needn't have worried for, the moment they saw the fuel sloshing dangerously around, they backed away. As we decanted as much of the petrol as we could into the tank via a plastic bottle, Dan casually mentioned that one stray bullet would make us the first Bosnians to be launched into space.

Undaunted, we drove on through the sunny afternoon, enjoying the beautiful countryside with its profusion of wild flowers, our pleasure only tarnished by the ebb and flow of petrol fumes. 'This must have been what it felt like in Europe in 1939, at the outbreak of the Second World War,' Danny mused. 'Nothing much had happened that first warm autumn and then – boom!'

We came to an unmarked crossroad and knew that we were thoroughly lost. Poring over a rather ineffectual map spread out on the bonnet, we looked up as a beaten-up car came around the corner and screeched to a halt within inches of us. The driver and two passengers eyed us suspiciously as they got out and walked towards us, menacingly fingering their guns. They were heavily armed and their fatigues sported crucifixes – the badge that spelled out, loud and clear, that we had blundered into Serb territory.

Appreciating that we were in serious trouble, Danny smiled and repeated the word – '*Engleski*!' – as a few staccato sentences were spat at us in a language neither of us understood. To our surprise the tallest one demanded in English, 'Where you going?' As one, we replied 'Sarajevo' before realising that this was the capital of their mortal enemy.

Attempting to smooth things over Dan reiterated, 'We are English – journalists,' at which they seemed to relax noticeably. That is except for an older man with bad teeth, matching breath and an eye on the main chance, who made it very clear he wanted to see in the boot. We duly obliged and watched as he reeled back at the fumes, suddenly losing interest in the spoils of war. The men became fairly affable after the inevitable tobacco fix and a dose of our diminishing supply of 'petro-ale' but their statement, 'You follow us!' left us in no doubt it was not a request. To their credit they found us a garage and an obliging proprietor who not only sorted us out with a five-gallon petrol can but also – with a length of hosepipe – syphoned what remained of our fuel into it via his mouth.

Our chaperones then led us on into Ilidza, the Serb-held suburb of Sarajevo, where we were escorted to what was either the army or police HQ with a fully manned tank outside. Instructed to 'stay there and don't move', we waited as they went into the building to report our arrival and – we prayed – organise a pass for us to cross their front line. We lounged about the car in studied indifference, trying hard to avoid eye contact with the tank commander leaning out of his turret to glare at us. Our newfound 'friends' then left with the promise that someone would issue us with a permit shortly. A few hours dragged by and the afternoon light began to show the first purple tint of evening as the shadows crept up the walls.

Growing increasingly concerned, and knowing that no one in their right mind would attempt to cross *any* front line in the dark, we considered quietly slipping away. Just then a beanpole of a soldier with the largest crucifix we'd ever seen and strung around his neck like an anchor, sauntered up. In a pleasant enough way, he asked if we were English. Ignoring the complexities of our Irish and Welsh backgrounds we nodded. He seemed agreeable so we fell into conversation with him and discovered that he'd been studying at Luton Polytechnic when the war broke out, and had given it up to come home and 'do his duty,' as he saw it, fighting for the Bosnian Serbs. He finally got round to asking us what we were waiting for, and when we explained our need of passes, he offered to expedite them. Ten minutes later he reappeared shaking his head. 'These people are so slow. You'll be here all night,' he told us. It wasn't a prospect either of us relished.

Seeing our disappointment, he said abruptly: 'Come, I will take you.' He jumped into our car and directed us across town until we turned into a street of neat semi-detached houses. We could have been in Surbiton had it not been for the fact that the homes were all deserted and there was the heavy chatter of rifle and machine gun fire flying all around us. Occasionally heavier ordnance joined in. Assuring us we were safe, he directed us into a narrow alley between two of the houses, barely wide enough for our faithful old Peugeot. He then proceeded to give us final instructions: 'Drive to the bottom of this garden where you will meet the road,' he said, pointing. 'Turn sharp left, then take the first right into the airport.' We sat in stunned silence. Was this a trap? Could we be driving into a minefield, a tank trap or a hail of bullets? Was the garden even firm enough to drive over? What if we missed the turning?

The questions flew round and round in our minds until I broke the uneasy silence. 'Would you please point out exactly where we are to drive?' He not only agreed, but told us to follow him. Running into the open garden he calmly climbed to the top of a mound of earth and beckoned us to follow. Once in position, we could see exactly where he meant. We were back in the safety of the alley before you could say Radovan Karadzic.

As the last traces of purple evening light leached from the horizon we shook hands and thanked him profusely, before Dan revved the car and we roared off down the garden to the accompaniment of flying gravel and fizzing bullets. He negotiated what remained of the fence and hit the road with a thump that tested the suspension in a way never intended by the manufacturers. I held my camera tightly against my chest in readiness, though God knows what I was expecting to photograph other than our own demise. It seemed like ages before Dan was yanking the steering wheel hard right and we were screeching to a standstill at the entrance to the heavily protected airport, an area festooned with barbed wire.

Within seconds, eight fully armed French UN soldiers appeared, covering us with their automatic rifles as they surrounded our car in a well-rehearsed manoeuvre. We carefully produced our passes without making any sudden moves. Our luck was holding well, for just as we struggled to explain our dramatic arrival from a somewhat unconventional quarter in appalling schoolboy French, who should be leaving the airport but the doyen of Sarajevo journalists, Kurt Schork of Reuters. Having stuck his head out of his car window to ask if we needed any help, he cheerily told us to follow him into the city.

With his scruffy beard, John Lennon glasses and wiry physique, Kurt didn't easily fall into the image of guardian angel, or for that matter international war correspondent – he had in fact been a Rhodes Scholar at Oxford – but as we were soon to discover, he fitted both bills perfectly (tragically, he was killed some years later reporting from Sierra Leone). With his parting warning for us to: 'Drive like hell, particularly over the motorway bridge where you'll be totally exposed. Oh, and don't forget to stop at the checkpoint!' he took off ahead of us with an expression that belied what we were about to face – Sniper Alley.

His jaw set determinedly, Danny let in the clutch and stamped on the accelerator as the Peugeot lurched forward with a scream of objection, tyres scarring the tarmac. Our two cars raced down the road onto the empty motorway, long since abandoned by all except the occasional UN convoy and the odd crazy journalist. This concrete artery struck straight as an arrow into the very heart of Sarajevo and acted as a natural front line for the two warring sides. In those areas closest to the city it was flanked on either side by concrete high-rise apartment blocks that were to prove deadly for many who passed below.

The next few minutes were a blur of speed and fear as we thrashed on to a background of gunfire towards the hellishly exposed bridge. As we flew up onto the ramp I was suddenly vividly aware of the beauty of the rich red evening sky but there was no time to daydream as, with a smell of burning rubber (and leaking fuel) we dropped down the other side into the welcoming shadows. Once past the checkpoint where scruffy soldiers with dead eyes sat behind a battered kitchen table, we were ready once again for the last and even more dangerous race along the worst part of Sniper Alley. This deadly section was that flanked by the empty blocks of flats, mostly on the Serbian side, each of their glassless windows a perfect position for human hunters.

Only those who have driven along this stretch in an unprotected vehicle can fully understand the feeling of utter vulnerability and nakedness in the face of a hidden enemy. Your life hangs on the whim of an unseen, unknown killer. You try to mentally reassure yourself that they probably won't shoot you; that they must be able to see the big white 'TV' on the bonnet. But deep down you know that logic plays little part in war, particularly in this bitter Balkans conflict. Your life or death is in the hands of some scruffy young man lounging about in what was once someone's home but is now a burnt-out shell with a commanding view of the city. Bored and restless, he will put down his beer can, stub out his cigarette and say to himself or others, 'Let's take a shot at the next car.' And on that arbitrary decision, or the lethargy of his comrades, innocent people will die.

Revving up to punish the engine still further, we flew down the empty motorway in pursuit of the speeding Reuters' car like two beetles scuttling across open ground, making for the relative safety of our hotel. We were probably one of the last few to attempt to cross it alone in this way for later on it was only possible to do so in the lee of an armoured vehicle forming part of a UN convoy. Thank God, we made it.

In Beirut, the journalists' hotel of choice was The Commodore. In Jerusalem it was The American Colony. Baghdad had the Rashid, Belfast had the Europa, Salisbury had Meikles, and Kampala The International. But Sarajevo had the most inappropriately named of all – the Holiday Inn – the irony of whose logo: 'A better place to be,' was never lost on the visiting press corp. Every one of these hotels had their own distinct characters, yet each was the honeypot that journalists made a beeline for when arriving in that country. The main thing they had in common was that – despite the ravages of war, insurrection, riot, military coups and other calamities – they all managed to keep the lines of communications open. This was not just important for personal safety; it was the very lifeblood of our business, and these establishments acted as the conduits through which vital information flowed.

Within seconds a tip-off or the hint of a news story would spread like a virus through the waiting news gatherers, stirring them to fresh enthusiasm. Plans would be made, costs split and expeditions arranged. In the lobbies and bars one could witness day and night the constant ebb and flow of writers, photographers, TV crews, fixers, translators, drivers, soldiers, informants and spooks. Most of all, though, these hotels offered a unique kind of camaraderie built on mutual respect that grew ever stronger with the rising tide of danger, injury and death. Any time you returned, you could bump into a colleague you had left only hours before and half a world away, or run into an acquaintance from the last big story you'd been on. Together, you could share the exhilaration of leaving a war zone or the relief to still be in one piece. Always, we could spot those who had recently arrived, cloaking their anxiety with gallows humour whilst eagerly hoovering up information from everyone in sight. Local knowledge was passed on willingly, with advice like: 'Take care at the second checkpoint as they're always drunk... there's no petrol in sector five... don't go via so-and-so as the commander there collects cameras.' Old hands would recommend the best places to eat and fixers would write out a list of do's and don'ts in the coverage of this particular conflict.

The Holiday Inn, Sarajevo was unique in one other way – it sat slap bang on the front line of the war, with its front door opening out onto the deserted motorway that led directly to the airport. Not that anyone would dream of using the front door, for this was the end of the killing ground. There were almost certainly other, safer places to stay in the city but none would even consider it. This was where the first journalists covering the siege had settled and this was where we would remain. The stoicism of the people of that city served as an inspiration to us all.

As if to remind us of this, without fail every night that I was there a tiny act of defiance was played out in the hotel lobby. To a backdrop of thumping field guns, the cackle of small arms and the odd ricocheting bullet, someone would risk coming into our blacked-out building to play the grand piano. In the ghostly darkness the music floated its way up the atrium, from shattered ground floor to cracked glass ceiling. The soothing bars of Mozart or Brahms permeated the silent, dust-filled bedrooms where splintered window frames substituted for curtains and shards of glass were impaled in unusable mattresses. Like an invisible drift of sadness, it infiltrated every dark corner, cascaded down shrapnel-pitted staircases and swept happier memories aside. This heart-rending concert always finished with Chopin's rousing 'Revolutionary Etude', a defiant shout into the Serbian-controlled darkness.

Over time we developed a near-Pavlovian response to the nightly recital, wandering from whichever dark corner we'd been working or drinking or resting in, to partake of our evening meal in a windowless back room, the only place a light could safely burn. A grand dinner it was not – usually cold pasta shells and limp cabbage with the occasional treat of an egg. And yet we were the lucky ones compared to those poor souls beyond our walls in cold, windowless homes, whose staple diet were shells of a very different kind. Every now and again we high-paying guests would be offered some acceptable (if exorbitantly priced) wine, and on one unforgettable evening we had some cheese. One never queried where such treasures came from; we just coughed up a wad of the favoured currency (German Deutschmarks) and smiled gratefully. This was the only war I ever experienced where any currency was more desirable than the faithful US Dollar, a hangover I assumed from the days when holidaying Germans thronged the city's cosmopolitan streets.

One evening we were stunned to see a local military commander and a group of his acolytes stride into our 'dining room' and noisily plonk themselves down at an adjacent table. More surprising still was what followed – the presentation of a silver platter full of freshly cooked vegetables and other delights all beautifully arranged around a large pink lobster. This naturally caused serious rumblings of discontent in our ranks, not least because we were being charged the full five-star rack rate of a peacetime hotel. The manager was duly summoned and in the time it took to say 'We're leaving!' a tray of pizzas miraculously appeared, accompanied by some very quaffable wine.

A favourite pastime after dinner was to climb the stairs to the tenth floor (nobody used the lift for fear of getting stuck in it during a power cut, as I once did) and then grope our way along the corridor to room 1036. There we would crawl to the window on our hands and knees, avoiding broken glass, to peep over the sill and watch the endless arcing of coloured tracers writing their morse code of death across the night sky. It was in this room one night when a group of journos spotted something moving across the ceiling.

'What's that red dot up there?' one asked, seconds before the window came in. The sniper's infrared target light that could easily have killed them was designed to spook them instead. It worked. After that, the American

TV crews would always wear helmets and some even donned flak jackets for our nightly vigil. We Brits, needless to say, scorned such precautionary measures – not least because in the early days we hadn't been allowed to purchase such protective items. Doughty we called it. Daft said everyone else. Mind you, when Danny and I were later authorised to buy bulletproof vests we soon discarded them for they weighed us down so much that it felt like we were walking around in suits of armour. We swapped them for green flak jackets that we hoped would offer some protection against the ballistic firepower of the Serbs. As advised by those already there, we pinned badges to them stating our blood type in case we were injured. Mine was perfect for a photographer – A negative.

Wherever we went in the world, the wealthy TV crews always had the best of everything and that was especially true in Bosnia where what we envied most was their seemingly endless supply of armoured vehicles. These were usually fairly basic Land Rovers with toughened glass, Kevlar sides and solid steel doors. To their credit, some of the television crews were very helpful and would always squeeze us in if they had space. Two of the most generous were the BBC's indefatigable Kate Adie and the lovable and loyal Malcolm Brabant, both true colleagues and fine journalists. There was always a wonderful feeling of relief when, having managed to cadge a lift, we climbed into the dark almost windowless interior of these vehicles and slammed the heavy doors shut, taking care not to crush our fingers. Whether it was the womb-like interior that gave us a psychological lift or just the knowledge of having something so solid around us for a change I can't say, but everyone became chattier as the tension seemed to roll away – that is, until we had to get out again.

Most of the time, though, Danny and I had to make do with ordinary cars, which the army tellingly referred to as 'soft-skinned' vehicles, offering no protection at all. Askold Krushelnycky, a friend and journalist with the now defunct *European* newspaper, drove into our little billet on the outskirts of the city of Vitez during one trip and announced indignantly: 'I've just been shot at from the Serb lines!' A bullet had pierced the driver's door, passed straight through his seat and out the passenger side. His surprise at being shot must have been a result of the shock, as not only were we close to the front line but – as he admitted, somewhat sheepishly – the car had been borrowed from the local Bosnian army commander.

In these conditions, we always jumped at the chance when friends like Kate or Malcolm offered us a lift in something a bit more substantial than our flimsy Peugeot. I had first met Kate many years before, hanging off the back of a crowded lorry in Bombay where we were covering the Queen's visit to India. She was always a pleasure to work with as she was not only good company but also a wealth of useful information, much of which she garnered from the senior ranks of the British forces who courted her company with the undisguised satisfaction of having a star in their midst. Unselfishly, she shared much of this with Danny and I.

What surprised us whenever we accepted a ride in one of the 'Beeb's' armoured Land Rovers was that Kate preferred to drive these heavy, demanding vehicles herself. She did this with a great deal of skill, which was more than could be said for dear Malcolm Brabant about whom some felt it might be safer walking than being his passenger. Holding the record for the most damaged vehicles of any correspondent in Bosnia, he would hunch over the steering wheel as though expecting a direct hit at any moment, twisting his head from side to side like one of those nodding dogs in the back of a family saloon. He made up for his driving by being smashing company with a raft of jokes and a very passable Stan Laurel impersonation, blinking his eyes and pulling at his wispy hair. His dress sense also afforded us some ribaldry, with his colourful shirts and knee-length shorts more appropriate for a Florida beach than a war zone and doing little to enhance his fuller figure. But he was a good five-a-side football player, and surprisingly fast – as we found out when we challenged the British Army cooks to a game in Vitez's requisitioned school hall. We tactfully lost, or so the excuse goes, as the soldiers were laying on a barbecue and a few beers for us afterwards.

Not that Bosnia was all football and barbecues. Far from it. In one two-car convoy in Sarajevo, Danny and I were in the front vehicle with David Williams, the *Daily Mail*'s chief reporter and among the finest in our profession. We were approaching the Old Town Square, one of the most dangerous parts of town as it lay open to the Serb guns on the hillside and was constantly under fire. It had become too dangerous to go all the way around the square according to the layout so everyone raced across the top corner. Preparing to do so, Danny dropped a gear and roared out into the open space, pulling hard on the steering wheel to round a building into the relative safety of a side street. Unfortunately, coming the other way at a similar breakneck speed was a red Volkswagen that missed us by inches. 'Oh no!' I cried, correctly foreseeing that as the car following us came racing around the blind corner behind us, the two vehicles would collide.

With a horrendous crunch, they did.

Jumping out and racing back to the scene, we dragged everyone out of the wreckage as quickly as we could and were surprised to find that no one was injured. Shaken, the VW driver and his passenger went off in one direction and we headed on foot to a small café to settle our nerves. When we returned half an hour later, though, both of our cars had completely disappeared. These were the spoils of war for some happy Bosnian, although for us unhappy souls their disappearance would somehow have to be explained to the accountants back home.

On another occasion Danny and I were bouncing around in the back of Malcolm's Land Rover somewhere deep in the Bosnian countryside when we came across one of those heartbreaking clusters of refugees that we were to witness so many times. An old woman was wearing a white blouse that fluttered like a flag of surrender against the distant greenery of the mountains. As Malcolm said later, 'This family was insignificantly small and could have been dismissed as just a passing glance yet there was something insistent and compelling about them.' They were walking along a railway track that had sprouted weeds through lack of use. The grand-mother sat exhausted by a hedgerow, her head in her hands. She was surrounded with worn old bags stuffed with clothes. Well ahead, a skinny woman who didn't look much younger but who was wearing incongruously pink trousers and a headscarf, was still struggling on. She was bent at a ninety-degree angle by the weight of blankets and bedrolls that were tied to her back with string in two huge hessian sacks. She carried a red bucket for washing clothes and pushed a rickety wheelbarrow loaded with cheap household goods. Trailing in her wake was a boy and a girl of about six and seven, wearing grubby vests and shorts, their bodies streaked with sweat and dirt. As with all the children of war I was to witness in my life, their sunburnt faces were etched with an uncomprehending expression beneath dead eyes. Between them they dragged a bulging shopping bag of inconsequential bits and pieces – their pitiful legacy.

We pulled over and the three of us walked back with some water to see if we could help. The women seemed grateful of the chance to stop, rest and drink something although the daughter – who we suddenly realised was probably only thirty – remained bent double throughout. They had been walking for days, she said, sleeping out in fields overnight, and were making their way towards relatives they hoped were still alive in another part of the country. Before Serb soldiers torched their house and bullied them into fleeing during the ethnic cleansing of their village, their few valuables had been taken from them, including the mother's wedding ring and the daughter's cheap gold earrings. The father had been taken away months before and not been heard of since. At each new Serbian checkpoint the little family's few possessions had been further picked over and looted. I wasn't surprised as we had driven through a similar checkpoint earlier and I had sneaked a couple of photos of mounds of confiscated belongings stashed alongside the makeshift barricade.

They were tired, hungry and thirsty so we gave them clean drinking water and what scraps of food we had in our vehicle including a few biscuits that had gone soft which the children gobbled up without any sign of pleasure. After this meagre lunch we bundled them and all their kit including the wheelbarrow into the Land Rover, piling in after them and slamming the door shut. In the semi-darkness, the two women spilled silent tears of gratitude that embarrassed and humbled us as we had done so very little. Thankfully, their story was one of the few with a happy ending for several hours later – with the help of the old lady's pointed directions – we drove them into a small courtyard where we witnessed a tearful reunion with their relatives.

In Vitez we were able to facilitate another reunion of sorts when we begged a room from a family who were happy to make a few Deutschmarks for the rent of a bed. They were sweet and kind and extremely resourceful. Proudly they showed us to how they had created hydroelectricity from a local river using the drum of a washing machine. Generously, they shared what little food they had with us. Over what we laughingly called dinner, the father told us that he did not know if his parents were still alive as they had no means of contacting them in a distant part of the country. Danny and I immediately offered them the use of our satellite phone to try to call them, but at first they were reluctant as they knew it was expensive. Once we assured them that the newspaper would pay, the father placed the call and couldn't believe it when he got through. There were tears and hugs and lots of laughter and he quickly passed the phone to the next family member, fearing the cost, until we encouraged them to speak a little longer as it was obviously so important to them.

These moments of joy were few and far between in that conflict and, in the winter of 1992, we came across a vast new tide of human misery as towns close to the British forces who were desperately trying to provide aid became choked with refugees. Hundreds of women and children, their

men taken and missing, were left without blankets until a team of British
soldiers tore into the town of Travnik in the middle of an artillery barrage
to deliver them, along with some of their own combat rations. In April 1993
we witnessed the British airlift of injured and terrified women and children
from the hell of Srebrenica where eight thousand Muslim men and boys
had been slaughtered and the remainder of the population forced to leave,
crammed into the backs of lorries – among more than two million who
were displaced.

Danny and I hired a young female translator that we had inherited from
Tom and befriended on our first trip to Bosnia. Her name was Aida Cadvar,
aged nineteen, and as brave as a lion. An English student, she agreed to
work as our translator and guide with no thought for her own safety. Every
day she would cross enemy front lines and drive past Sniper Alley. She
didn't do it for the money. Aida truly wanted the rest of the world to know
how her city was suffering and dying. Her family comprised her father
Enes, her mother Lila, and her younger sister Anela, all of whose lives were
ruined. They had little food or drinking water and no power or telephones.
They couldn't flush their toilet. They were scared to light a candle after
dark in case the snipers saw them. They felt abandoned and alone. Even
though they had so little they'd insist on sharing their meagre humanitarian
aid rations and their precious coffee, which by then cost nearly $200 a kilo
on the black market. Most of all, they shared their conviction that decency
would one day prevail. They didn't even seem to have hatred for those
devastating all that they held dear; simply regret for the friends they'd lost
and the Sarajevo they remembered.

Danny and I tried to give Aida one of our flak jackets but she flatly
refused. When she told us that she was taking her final English exams but
didn't know if she could get to the examination centre, we accompanied
her and waited outside as bullets ricocheted off the walls. Despite all this,
she passed with flying colours and decided to study journalism so that she
could tell the world what was happening in her country. Then the university
closed and most of her male friends became soldiers, so she had no choice
but to stay home with her beleaguered family and wait out the siege.

In a letter Aida managed to smuggle out of the country to us after we
had escaped home for some respite, she wrote,

> I have a feeling that people are gambling with our lives and that every
> day I pull out the lucky number that brings me another day…. Our
> savings ran out ages ago so we can't buy anything on the black market.

We live like beggars. I know it upsets my parents because we should not have to stand in queues for food handouts or collect water in plastic buckets. We just want to be normal again… we want to taste an apple again…. The future looks pretty hopeless. Very often, I think about you and about how we would go to the hospitals, to the mortuary, to the children's home to see what new horrors had happened. Every day we thought the West would do something to end all this. I was full of hope that this war would stop and that you would be guests with my family. That we could laugh again. I wonder if we ever will….

It was in Bosnia that I really honed up on my survival skills and tried to imprint them into the excitable brains of newcomers in the hope that this might save their lives. 'Pick a good driver and always take two cars, in case one is shot up,' I'd tell them. 'Never step off a tarmac road unless someone or something has gone ahead to check for mines or booby traps. Most importantly of all, never, ever, ever carry a weapon. If you get caught with a weapon you discredit every journalist here and put yourself and others at huge risk.' My surprise tip was, 'Stay away from flagpoles.' I learned that one in Vietnam where the VC tied hand grenades to the poles because they knew that government troops would immediately take down their flags once they retook an area. It might make a great pic as the flag is lowered but I've known men killed and photographers badly injured by shrapnel as the grenade exploded.

Back in Vitez the following year, I decided to try and get a picture of the British contingent of the United Nations Protection Forces (UNPROFOR) on patrol in the most battle-scarred districts of the region around Mount Igman. Along with two other photographers – Colin Davey of *Today* and Darryn Lyons of the *Mail* – we set off to an area destroyed by the warring factions where the most notable feature was a mass graveyard of white crosses.

There, we found an old burned out building from which to take photos and waited for a patrol to pass. After an hour or so with no sign of anyone, we decided to head back and got into our car but suddenly two civilian cars pulled up, including a white Russian Lada. Before we could drive our vehicle back to the safety of the British base in Vitez, five men leapt out and started shouting at us very aggressively. They were dressed casually in jeans and trainers but carried bullet-filled bandoliers across their chests and wore bandanas around their necks. We had no idea who they were but we immediately sensed we were in trouble, especially as by this time there was the equivalent of a £100 bounty on the head of any journalist covering the conflict.

The shortest of the men, a man in camouflage combats (whom we dubbed 'Psycho') seemed especially angry and pulled a large silver-handled pistol from his belt before pointing it directly at us. The .44 weapon was quite beautiful with a carved bone handle. Pyscho was trembling as he held it and his eyes were glazed, so we immediately assumed he was drunk or on drugs, as so many of the combatants were. It was like Kampala all over again.

He was screaming and shouting at us in Croatian at the same time waving his gun inches from our noses. We had no idea why but that hardly mattered if the outcome was the same. Colin muttered, 'Jesus, John, this doesn't look fucking good!' but I stared out the gunman and said as loudly and as calmly as I could, 'He is *not* going to shoot us.' Secretly, I wasn't so sure. Darryn held out his press card but that only served to anger them more and they tore it from his neck. Suddenly, the men became very worked up and started throwing punches. Grabbing our arms, they bundled us back into our car at gunpoint. Desperate, I too lifted my UN press card and waved it at them as confidently as I could but received an extra blow to the jaw for my audacity. The men then frenziedly reached in and tried to grab the camera that was also around my neck but I resisted which only resulted in the flash being snapped off.

The men then manoeuvred their cars so that one was in front and one behind, virtually touching our bumpers. With Psycho hanging out of the window of his Lada still waving his pistol at us and the other car hooting and pushing us forward, we had no choice but to follow.

'What do you think they want?' Darryn asked quietly.

'And who the hell are they?' Colin said, his eyes wide.

We all knew of armed gangs roaming around the area that randomly robbed and killed people, never to be found, but we had no idea if that was now going to happen to us. Life had no value in this war but between us we were carrying a lot of expensive kit us that would be worth a great deal on the black market. Not to mention the £300 for our three scalps. The situation seemed hopeless.

Suddenly, coming the other way along the road we spotted a convoy of UN military peacekeepers in their ubiquitous white and blue vehicles. Frantically, I started waving at them out of the car window as my colleagues similarly shouted for help and also attempted to flag them down. To our horror, the peacekeepers just smiled and waved back as they flashed past.

Turning to the others, I said, 'OK, boys, what's Plan B?' In any other circumstances, that might have raised a laugh.

Instead of being forced to a remote spot to be robbed, stripped and shot in the head as we half-expected, we were somewhat relieved to find ourselves escorted to a sort of military camp. Psycho fetched one of the few men in full uniform, who was accompanied by a personable young man in his late teens or early twenties who spoke perfect English. He informed us that we were at the HQ of one of the local Croatian brigades. The man in uniform was the commander and Psycho was his bodyguard. They then began to interrogate us as to what we were doing in the area.

In a voice deliberately stripped of all emotion, I calmly explained who we were and what we were trying to do, but all the while Psycho stood caressing his pistol with the weirdest of smirks on his face. In the end, it got to me and I foolishly lost my temper, jabbing at him with my finger and angrily telling him to stop.

Just as I was making a formal complaint to the commander about how badly we had been treated, the translator hastily interrupted my rant, grabbed my arm and pulled me away. Pushing us towards the gate, saying, 'You must go, NOW!' adding about Psycho under his breath, 'He is a little man with a very big gun.' We didn't need to be told twice, so we jumped back in our car and got the hell out of there as fast as we could, heading straight to the bar for the stiffest of drinks.

We heard some time later from others that the man we knew as Psycho had been charged with war crimes. Near to where they had grabbed us was the scene of a massacre in which many Muslim women and children were murdered. Psycho was directly involved and thought we were trying to gather evidence of the crime. It was another lucky escape.

Sarajevo's beleaguered Emergency Hospital was one of the most damaged buildings in the city with every pane of glass shattered and only rainwater for washing, drinking or cleaning wounds. In this hellhole, I photographed doctors wild-eyed with exhaustion and splattered with blood as they continued to provide emergency treatment night and day and under near-constant bombardment to those whose broken bodies could be rescued from the city.

Such was the inhumanity of this war that the Serb gunmen who squatted in hillside apartment blocks knew that if they paralysed the hospital then those brought there would be denied even the faintest chance of life. The

Red Cross symbol of international aid had become a prime target and one round of shelling destroyed twenty-six of the thirty ambulances, crippling the rescue operation. Often the gunmen waited until they saw an ambulance screech to the halt at the entrance before opening fire, hoping to hit as many doctors, nurses and drivers as they could. It was outside the hospital that I picked up a piece of jagged shrapnel that I still have, as a reminder of what flying hot metal can do to human flesh.

Vladimir Burina, one of the courageous doctors, chain-smoked by candlelight while wearing a blood-smeared T-shirt that warned: *Smoking Can Seriously Damage Your Health*. Looking up at us, almost too tired to speak, he added, 'Not half as much as working in this place.'

Beneath the casualty clearing station the basement was full of the injured, shell-shocked, dead and dying, many of them children. As I walked around I spotted one sad little boy aged about eight who was sitting fully clothed on the edge of a hospital bed leaning on wooden crutches that were far too big for him. His right leg was missing below the knee and his jeans had been rolled up to flap emptily on that side. I asked a nurse what had happened and was told that he'd been playing football with his friends when the ball was kicked into a field and he ran after it. A Serb landmine went off, taking his leg with it. As I lifted my camera the boy tilted his head shyly to one side and rested on his arm as he stared at me with sad brown eyes, before dropping his head to cry. It was a very touching picture and, as with so many of my photographs of the children of war, I often wonder what happened to him.

Further along the corridor, we came upon the crowded mortuary where the corpse of a little girl was laid out with as much dignity as staff could muster. She was reaching out with her left hand to where her mother was. Both had been shot once through the head. Nobody even knew their names. On an adjacent slab were the bodies of two little orphans who were among many that were permitted to escape from Sarajevo, after long negotiations with Serb troops. As they were leaving, snipers fired on their bus, killing these two and injuring many more. This picture was, without doubt, one of the most harrowing photographs I ever took and still reduces me to tears when I think of their tiny broken bodies lying there.

An estimated 100,000 people were killed in the civil war in the Balkans, eighty per cent of whom were Bosniaks. In an alarmingly short space of time, neighbour turned against neighbour right in the heart of Europe. It's hellish hard to forget what we witnessed there.

THIRTEEN

IN BETWEEN my many tours of Bosnia, I was sent to Afghanistan with Danny for a series of articles about the plight of women and children there and to Brazil with him to cover a story about the drugs gangs that reminded us of Sicily. Then in 1992 I was sent to Somalia with one of the *Express*'s foreign correspondents Peter Hitchens. The latter was to cover 'Operation Restore Hope' in which President George W. Bush had authorised the dispatch of US troops to assist with famine relief as part of a larger UN effort. Unfortunately the lawless Somalian rebels regarded this as a full scale US invasion.

Although Peter was an accomplished journalist who'd been posted all around the world, he had never been sent to a warzone before and I think he was keen to see what it was like. I could have tried to explain, which would almost certainly have dissuaded him, but sometimes you just have to let people do what they think they want to do.

I met up with him in Kenya where he had flown in last minute from an assignment in Jerusalem and we started to look for a ride into Mogadishu. At the edge of Nairobi airport we came across a small Soviet cargo plane on which the world's press appeared to be trying to cadge a lift. The back of the plane had been lowered to load crates of aid but several international TV crews, aided by teenage locals, were desperately trying to pile on all their kit as the Russian pilot ran around tearing his hair out and pulling it off. He knew that plane would crash if it was too heavily laden with the extra sat phones, wire machines and camera gear, but nobody was paying him much attention.

I knew that Peter had worked in Moscow and spoke fluent Russian so I suggested he take the pilot to one side and ask if he could allow us on, as we had minimal luggage. Peter looked very dapper dressed in a blue city suit with polished black shoes and his charm and command of the language worked. We were allowed on board while dozens were left behind. Sitting on a cargo of food in the back, we soon discovered that they were supplies destined not for the starving thousands but for one of the international news agencies.

From the moment we arrived in Mogadishu I could tell that Peter was having second thoughts. So was I. The Union Jack I'd packed and rolled up in my camera case for an emergency seemed suddenly ridiculous. It was a beautiful afternoon with the sun slowly sinking in the west but there was no time to appreciate it because as soon as we clambered out, a group of young men armed to the teeth crowded around us vociferously demanding that we take them on as bodyguards.

Faltering and rather overwhelmed, we looked at this ragged crew – some of whom were only teenagers – and doubted our need for such youthful renegades. 'Maybe we should get someone older and more experienced in town?' I suggested. Then a Westerner approached the plane who turned out to be from the news agency, collecting his cargo from our plane. Peter asked him if we should hire these kids and he replied flatly, 'If you don't have guards, you will be dead and naked by the morning.' Fair enough. After pocketing the wad of American dollars we peeled off for them, these frightening-looking young men carrying Kalashnikovs jumped onto the back of a waiting battered Toyota pick-up, and gestured us to sit up front with their driver. Together, we headed into the capital of troubled Somalia along wide avenues made entirely of mud.

It was immediately evident that this assignment was going to be extremely dangerous and almost impossible to assess. In a place that had once been an example of Italian elegance in Africa, there was now no law enforcement, no electricity, no telephones and no diplomatic staff. There were also no windows in any of the buildings. The place had a level of wild madness I had rarely seen, with heavily armed militia driving around shooting anything they liked. As we turned into one avenue we came across an entire convoy of dreadlocked cowboys, dead-eyed and armed to the teeth with every imaginable kind of weapon including machine guns. I had to be extremely surreptitious with my cameras so that they didn't see they were being photographed or believe that we were threatening them in any way.

Having been advised to find somewhere to stay that night as a matter of priority, especially as darkness was about to descend, we discovered that there was nowhere available because all the white-painted hotels were either boarded up or squatted in by the kind of men you didn't want to share a country with, let alone a room. Any journalists already there had negotiated in advance to sleep in aid houses owned by some of the many charities trying to save lives affected by war, anarchy and famine in that hell on earth. Our teenage guards could offer us no help as we drove down street after street looking for sanctuary. Peter wrote later, 'Were it not for John's reassuring presence, I should now be gibbering with fear. I am numb and desperate and unable to see how we are going to survive the night. There is no way out. Night in Mogadishu, in which we will be at the mercy of anyone who cares to threaten us, is fast approaching.'

What happened next was what Peter described as a 'miracle' and I guess it was. As we rounded a corner, I happened to spot the familiar figure of a photographer I'd worked alongside in Sarajevo and I called out his name. As he turned and smiled, I knew we were saved. Even though we spent what was probably the most uncomfortable night of our lives sleeping on a bare concrete floor in a compound alongside a German TV crew and several other photographers as we listened to the rat-tat-tat of gunfire and the cries of humans in distress beyond our walls, we survived the night.

We remained in Mogadishu for two or three days and were right there on the Indian Ocean beaches in the early hours of that December morning when the American and UN forces arrived to bring 'hope, peace and food.' Peter and I lay waiting on the cool sand facing the sea and, to begin with, we weren't sure if they were coming. Behind us on a low wall were about one hundred Somalians, waiting for the show. After a while, someone said, 'Hey, what's that grey thing out there?' as we all squinted into the gloom. 'Shit! It's a bloody boat!' someone cried and all of a sudden the entire US forces seemed to be roaring up onto the sand in landing craft. It felt like the D-Day landings all over again.

With no rule of law and the invasion time announced in advance, the heavily armed US Marines and Navy Seals, their faces blackened behind their night vision goggles, found themselves quickly mobbed by hundreds of waiting Somalians as well as being blinded by the lights from TV crews, reporters and cameramen. Pointing their guns at everyone, there was then a near farcical scene in which people cried, 'Welcome to Somalia!' as they told them to 'Fuck off!' and then ran off into the dunes to take up defensive positions (or perhaps to hide). The situation was out of control until helicopter gunships flew in to cover the arriving tanks and a burst of tracer bullets was fired three feet above our heads. Then commando ground forces moved in to disperse the locals and force the rest of us to lie face down in the sand.

The Americans were understandably nervous but they needn't have been. Despite their bravado, the militia had left town the night before, biding their time to hide away in the countryside until they decided it was safe to return and start thieving and killing again. Without any resistance, the US task force quickly secured the port and harbour before seizing their derelict embassy. They would then begin their attempt to restore the wretched country to some sort of order, even though few had any hope that they would succeed. In Mogadishu, we witnessed a nation on its knees. By the time we hitched a ride back out on an empty cargo plane (having madly waved my Union Jack at a US Army helicopter pilot who seemed about to gun us down on the runway), Peter and I were both convinced of one thing. It was somewhere we never wanted to visit again.

Back at home I'd had a rather bad break-up with the girlfriend who liked to hurl things at me, even though we'd been together for four years and bought a house together.

Her least violent but perhaps most vengeful attack was one of her last before we split. Sitting outside on the terrace one day after another row, I heard my camera motor drives going off one by one in the house. Unable to pinpoint the noise, I wandered into the bathroom to find an entire case of expensive photographic equipment dumped in a bathful of water. These belonged to the *Express* and, if I'd been younger, it would have cost me my job. Instead I somehow got away with it after coming up with some cock and bull story about the case slipping off my shoulder. Not very believable but, by then, I was too senior to challenge.

The drama with this girlfriend finally ended when I returned home from another foreign late one afternoon to find our house stripped of much of its furniture, apart from the curtains. She'd even taken a potato peeler that my Mum had given to me. This unnecessary cruelty reminded me of Soapy Watson and the missing lino. Danny kindly went out and bought me a new one, which was never used but took pride of place in my downstairs loo – a stark reminder of my latest war. Kim Willsher bought me some cutlery and new pans and my neighbour, the reporter Lois Rogers and her husband bought me a brand new fridge.

Before too long I met a young single parent who moved in with me, along with her one-year-old daughter whom I adored. In the four years that we lived together as a family, I wanted to adopt the child but I wasn't married to her mother and when we went to see a solicitor about it he advised us that it would be simpler and far cheaper to simply change her surname to Downing, which made me proud and happy.

Despite my new relationship and its incumbent responsibilities, I was still travelling and doing what I wanted to do, of course, which was fly around the world covering the main news stories. In the early 1990s Danny and I spent a lot of time in Africa and were sent to cover the tragedy of the Rwandan Civil War, involving Tutsi, Twa and Hutu tribespeople that took place between April and July 1994 in what became known as the Rwanda Genocide.

In just one hundred days as many as 800,000 men, women and children were slaughtered, many of them hacked to death with machetes as neighbour turned against neighbour and families against relatives. After Bosnia I had hoped never to see such wholesale slaughter again. Hundreds of thousands of Rwandan survivors, refugees and orphans had fled to Goma, Zaire, so Danny and I flew there. In searing temperatures in a place coated in thick volcanic ash from the nearby volatile Mount Nyiragongo, we arrived at an airport that was little more than a landing strip and a small breezeblock building. As soon as we entered, we heard a familiar voice say, 'You took your bloody time!' It was Tom Stoddart. Luckily for us, he had a van and drove us straight to the refugee camps in Ndosho and Munigi, along a road lined with refugees heading in the same direction. Beside the route we saw hundreds of piles of rush matting lined up on the ground and I asked what they were.

'Bodies,' came the reply. 'They truss them in matting and bind them with the fronds from sugar cane. The black volcanic rock of this area is too hard to bury them so they lie there until a truck comes along and picks them up, forty at a time. More than five thousand are already in an open grave near the airport.' I held up my camera and took pictures of the dead and the ever-lengthening procession of misery shuffling past. Several grieving parents sat rocking beside pathetically small bundles waiting at least until their dead children were carted away. It would be the closest to a funeral they would get.

We could smell the camps long before we saw them, lying in the lee of a small mountain range two miles south of the airport and just seven miles from the Rwandan border. A haze of putrid air hung over the camp, which not even the smoke from burning piles of medical dressings could obliterate. The refugee camps were, as Danny later wrote, places where all hope was lost. Everywhere we looked we saw bloodstained, emaciated, traumatised people including many of the four thousand orphans and other children. Cholera was rife so we had to wear protective gloves and not touch anything unless we were appropriately protected. Wandering around, I found a recently arrived Israeli medical team operating in a makeshift tent and I stayed with them as they treated horrific machete wounds. The pictures I took that day were ones that I hoped would shame the world into action.

Lying on a plastic sheet in what was called Ndosho Children's Village, we came across a group of lifeless emaciated toddlers who I initially assumed were dead – until one of them moved. We found out that they'd been lain together in the sun by the women looking after them – refugees themselves – who had no training and could do little else without medicines, blankets or clean water. These toddlers and infants – the youngest of whom was two – their bodies ravaged by cholera, lay huddled in a knot of limbs, naked and entwined as they sought comfort from each other. Not one of them made a sound. We were told that by morning some of them could be dead.

A little boy with a bloated stomach and his eyes wide open didn't speak and stared at us as if he didn't want to see anything ever again. It was a blank, dead-eyed expression we'd seen countless times in a place where people were resigned to their fate. The children of war especially cannot understand what they have seen or continue to witness – death, violence, blood and destruction. The incomprehension on their faces and in their eyes especially really touches your heart and tells the reader much more of a story about war than any photograph of a bombed building or a broken bridge. Another boy struggled to his feet, took a few faltering steps and fell down, not moving again. As we watched, two Israeli medics walked over and began to step carefully between the bodies, checking for a pulse, for any flicker of life. One little girl was dead and couldn't be resuscitated. Giving up, they wiped the ash and filth from her face and carried her to a tent with as much tenderness as urgency would allow.

Elsewhere, the sick and injured were also too weak to cry. Many of the victims simply died where they fell. Exhausted relatives tried to pick them up but their limbs could no longer support them and they slithered to the ground in a grotesque dance. Few had access to clean water and people were dying in the thousands with precious little being done to stop it. As Danny wrote: '*Apathy is finishing what Rwanda's death squad set out to do – the extermination of a country.*' In the nearby Munigi cholera camp we found a scrawny newborn baby still clamped to her mother's breast.

The mother was so sick she hadn't realised that her baby was dead. The hand-woven straw mat she lay on would soon become her shroud.

Just like I'd seen in East Bangladesh, I came across children sitting next to the bodies of their loved ones. This time it was two little girls – one in pink pyjamas, the other in a torn grubby yellow dress – gently prodding the prone figure of their mother and pleading with her to open her eyes. Two men wearing red plastic kitchen gloves intervened and sprayed disinfectant over the corpse, splashing the girls who were suddenly mute with loss. One father Danny spoke to lost all but one member of his family to the machete gangs and carried his eleven-year-old son for miles to what he hoped would be sanctuary. The boy died the previous day for want of a single sterile bag of clean water mixed with a little sugar and salt, the saline drip that costs only a few pence but which can save a life.

The shocking photographs that appeared in the *Express* later that week along with Danny's moving story included a front-page splash of the knot of orphans lying in the sun. It sparked such outrage in Britain that a campaign was launched to raise funds for what was most badly needed – fresh water and saline drips. More than £170,000 was raised in a single day, which hopefully did some good. Encouragingly, when Danny and I went back later on, we were able to reconnect with the Israeli medics we'd encountered in the children's camp and they proudly introduced us to one of the children I'd photographed lying on the plastic sheet. His name was Ruzabarande and he was still very weak but they told us that, after several days of care, he was going to live.

'When he started to cry and holler, we were delighted,' one of them told us. 'We thought it was a most beautiful sound.' With their help, little Ruzabarande would survive, although we had doubts whether the spirit of his people ever would.

A few years later I went back to Africa on a much happier story, joining two Liverpool housewives on a mission to transform the welfare of an entire community. Accompanied by reporter Heather O'Connor, I travelled to the landlocked West African republic of Mali, the world's fourth poorest country, to meet up with Ann Entwistle and Rita Ryan.

These two indomitable middle-aged women had hardly been further afield than a holiday to the Canary Islands when they found themselves in the Sahara Desert, invited to witness what their years of fundraising for Christian Aid had achieved. For almost two decades the pair sold secondhand clothes and knick-knacks from their charity shop in Huyton, Liverpool to raise money for water projects in Mali. When Christian Aid realised that they'd managed to raise more than £100,000, funding almost three hundred wells in one of the most arid and hostile regions of the country, they invited the women to fly out for two weeks to see the fruits of their labours.

'I've only ever spent one weekend away from home in thirty-three years of marriage,' said Rita, excitedly. For her and for Ann, it would be the start of an adventure that would change them forever.

Everywhere we went the villagers treated these two friends as if they were royalty. Their arrival in one camp where the women of the village had previously had to walk five kilometres and back every day to fill a bucket from a well was greeted with a volley of gunfire from ancient muskets. Men in terrifying wooden masks surrounded us in a traditional tribal dance and the women and children fled in genuine fear. Once they'd recovered themselves, the women told their Mersey saviours how much more freedom and independence their new well had given them.

In another village reached along heavily potholed tracks in a bone-shaking minibus, the British aid had provided not only running water and a vital watering hole for livestock but a washing pool that children played happily in as I laughingly took their photographs. One mother, who lost seven of her twelve children to disease caused by a lack of clean water, wept in gratitude as she kissed the hands of the visiting Brits.

Rita, who collapsed with dehydration during our visit and had to be treated in an appallingly under-resourced hospital, was moved to tears by her 'trip of a lifetime'. She said afterwards, 'I'll never grumble again if I have to walk to the shops in the rain.' Ann, equally overwhelmed, said, 'They have told us that we have given them life, but they have given us so much too.' As with all my assignments in places where people have so little but give so much, I had to agree.

Before we parted Rita was kind enough to donate a new souvenir to my collection – a heavy wooden walking stick, beautifully carved with a snake's head top and intricate patterning all down the shaft. It was purely ornamental until recently and now I use it every day and think fondly of that trip and of those two doughty women.

The assignments just kept coming, and I was soon back in Africa – this time to cover the first ever multi-racial elections in South Africa that triggered high emotion and a lot of inter-tribal violence. Sent to Johannesburg in 1994, we tied up with photographers Tom Stoddart and Keith Bernstein with plans to share a car to Durban where there were reports that the Zulus were 'necklacing' people – a ghastly practice where a heavy rubber tyre was wedged around a victim's arms and neck in a twisted parody of a necklace before being doused with petrol and set alight. Victims burned alive and could take up to twenty minutes to die, suffering terribly.

Before we set off for that grisly assignment, we decided to first cover a colourful protest by Zulus in tribal dress taking place in Library Gardens in the heart of the financial district. It was a chaotic but peaceful gathering until someone opened fire and began to gun down people right in front of us. There was immediate pandemonium as everyone scattered and Danny and I hit the deck. It was impossible to tell where the shooting was coming from as bullets were flying all around us. In their panic the police and secret service started firing wildly back and mayhem ensued. One old lady dropped to her knees wailing over the body of her son who'd been shot in the back trying to shield her. With so many shots being fired, there was no hiding place and we ran in any direction we could, seeking sanctuary.

Having experience of previous war zones doesn't make you any less scared when the unexpected happens, but it does rather focus the mind. Rather than be affected by fear you think, 'Something's happened, act like a photographer.' Your first instinct is still to save your life but the second – to take a picture – is surprisingly strong. So, when I spotted police shooting at the fourth floor window of an office block, shattering the glass to screams from within, I followed them into the building, hoping to photograph them catching one of the gunmen. It was a mistake on my part for all we found were terrified workers and I'd missed escalating events outside.

Running back down the stairs, I was momentarily overwhelmed by the chaos and the carnage I saw outside. Women in vibrant dresses who, moments earlier, had been dancing and singing with half-naked Zulus carrying traditional spears, shields and axes were screaming in panic and confusion. Members of the Red Cross, police and volunteers were desperately trying to stem the bleeding of the thirty or so fallen. Passers-by were tearing off scarves as makeshift tourniquets or simply covering the faces of the dead with newspapers. Incensed by the shooting, many of the protestors were pressing forward in a solid angry mass while firing off their own weapons into the air. It was only when police reinforcements arrived with helicopters that the situation eventually calmed and a tally was made. The final toll across the city that day was at least thirty dead and as many injured and, of course, each side blamed the other.

Grateful to have somehow survived what very nearly turned into a massacre, we ran to a nearby photographic shop and asked them to process our pictures. Still shaken, we adjourned to a nearby café in the same building to steady our nerves while they were being developed. As we were sitting at a table reliving our experience, all the lights suddenly went out and our initial reaction was to laugh at each other in the dark. 'What next?' someone cried. Then, with sudden horror, we simultaneously realised what the power cut could mean for our precious photographs which would be halfway through the developing process. Running back to the shop, we burst in to find a stalwart employee with a coat draped over him to protect our negs as he worked the machine by hand in order to keep the process going. Bless him. A few photos were lost but not all and, thanks to him, the day was saved.

With that dramatic news story in the bag, all thoughts of Durban were abandoned and we travelled instead to Soweto to cover the first political rally by the ANC leader Nelson Mandela, recently released from twenty-seven years in prison. Soccer City, the sprawling football stadium on the city's outskirts, was full to bursting with jubilant South Africans chanting Mandela's name. It was a mass gathering like no other, a stampede waiting to happen as the thousands of followers pressed in to celebrate not only Mandela and the historic elections but 'the beautiful game' that had been such an important weapon in the war against apartheid.

We were allowed to shadow Mandela as he walked through the crowds on the pitch and that was crazy enough but then the excitement was too much for those kept behind barriers and they broke through and absolutely swamped him. I feared for his safety and for my own as we were swept along with the vast tidal wave of chanting, screaming, crying people waving flags and calling out his name. Every time I raised my camera to try to get a shot, I was thwarted by someone getting in the way or Mandela being led further through the throng, and all the other photographers were having the same difficulty. It was impossible to get a clear view. Then all of a sudden, like a biblical parting of the waves, there was an unexpected gap between him and me. At precisely that moment, Mandela turned my way, looked directly into my camera, raised a victorious clenched fist and gave me an award-winning smile. It was a split second only and I took just one shot before he was swept away moments later. It was my lucky day.

Covering that election was one of those occasions when I really felt that I was part of world history. After all those years of apartheid and open racism, black people were finally being allowed to vote. The photos I took of snaking lines of people queuing for hours in order to vote at polling stations, the lines stretching back as far as the eye could see, were surprisingly moving. In the queue were old (white) ladies accompanying their black maids and white families queuing with their black nannies to vote. The photos that made the paper that day include the silhouette of a line and a smiling black 'Mama' sitting with a white child on her lap. Times were changing.

In 1995 Danny and I joined TV presenter Anneka Rice on her attempt to break the world record for travelling around the world on scheduled flights as part of her TV show *Challenge Anneka*. This involved more than forty hours of bum-numbing punishment to get into the record books as we flew 23,000 miles from London to Singapore to Tokyo to Los Angeles to New York to London. We almost didn't make it for want of a minute when we missed our connection in Los Angeles, but Anneka bullied a flight crew, air traffic controllers and airline supervisors to get us home in time. We shaved twenty-three minutes off the previous best and beat the world record at forty-three hours, forty-three minutes.

After yet more foreign trips the following year, my latest relationship finally came to an end. My long and frequent absences were once again mostly to blame. This time I was truly devastated because my girlfriend's departure meant the loss of my surrogate daughter, who was by then aged five. Once again, as I had with my first wife, I found myself not only alone but childless. Although I saw the child I considered a daughter a few times to begin with, when her mother married it became increasingly difficult to gain access. I fought hard in the courts for the right to see her and it cost me thousands of pounds and caused me a great deal of grief, but in the end I had to stop trying. It wasn't until she reached the age of twenty-one that we were finally able to reconnect and are now happily reunited. I am now a surrogate grandfather to her new baby.

Perhaps partly because of the loss I felt about my children through the years but also because of my early determination to mentor the next generation of photographers, I was surrounded much of the time by some wonderful young people, several of whom moved in with me at various points, seeking shelter and advice when times were tough. The ones that I became especially close to were Jonathan Evans, Paul Massey, Ian Jones, Jonathan Buckmaster and Hazel Thompson – each of whom showed incredible early talent and would have made a success of their lives without any assistance from yours truly.

Jonathan Evans was a student of one of my Llanelli friends, who was teaching photography and asked me if I could give the lad some work experience. The young man who turned up on my doorstep soon afterwards was enthusiastic and bright and he loved taking pictures with every bone in his body. When he first came to London I took him in and treated him like another son, pouring hours of advice into him – photographic and other-wise. Jonathan loved his craft, he loved life and he wasn't afraid of hard work. He reminded me a bit of me when I was younger. He also had great raw talent and did some remarkable work. But life has a habit of interrupt-ing dreams and when his father became ill he returned to Wales to take over the family boating business, a great loss to the art of photojournalism.

Paul Massey, who was just sixteen when he joined the *Evening Standard* in the 1980s (the youngest ever to join the staff) was another young photog-rapher I tried to help. The *Express* shared their darkroom so I'd stand next to him when his prints came out of 'the hole in the wall' (through which the printers would pass our finished prints) and offer some suggestions of how he might improve his framing, timing and lighting. I took him to a local café one day and talked about how to use a flash in a different way from the usual 'point and blast.' I explained how in a dark space you could leave the shutter open, then use a small flash gun, fired multiple times to 'paint' the room. He was mesmerised.

The next day I dropped a small brown parcel into his pigeonhole in the photographers' room. Inside was a Mecablitz flashgun with a note from me: 'Now show me what you can do with this... Good luck. JD.' Paul claims that, after this, he walked six inches taller for a week. Kindly, he said in later years that he learned more from me than any other photogra-pher before, during, or since. As he went on to have an amazing career of his own that flattered me enormously, as you can imagine. After seven years with the *Standard*, Paul moved to the *Daily Mirror* and later the *European*, having been chosen personally by Robert Maxwell. Multi award winning, he went on to the *Times* and *Sunday Times* before carving himself a hugely successful freelance career in fashion and portraiture.

Jonathan Buckmaster had come to Fleet Street from the South London

Press in 1986 aged twenty-three and then freelanced for all the main London papers, settling at the *Express* where – like all of us who started – he had to pick up all the last minute and late night jobs. I took him under my wing and especially loved that he was so interested in the developing and printing side of things, watching as I took care to over-expose and under-develop my prints before giving them to Larry Bartlett to work his magic. Being a junior member of staff, Jonathan and I rarely went on jobs together – as he was in what Smiff jokingly referred to as 'the chorus line' – but I did try to teach him to ignore the general rule of thumb in Fleet Street of a photo needing to be 'upright, bright and tight' (to which some wryly added, 'shite') and that he should always strive for something different.

He was not only keen but dedicated to our profession and I persuaded him to join the PPA as a new recruit when he was eventually offered the staff job he deserved. Aside from repaying me a thousand times over later when I needed all the help I could get with new technology, I am delighted that he is now on the board of the BPPA so the baton has truly been passed on.

Ian Jones was working for a London-based sports picture agency but happened to be in the right place at the right time for the bombing of the London Stock Exchange in the summer of 1990 and brought his exclusive photos to the *Express*. I was sitting on the desk that day and when we got talking I was flattered to discover that this fresh-faced twenty-year-old had studied my work. Two weeks later he happened to be on the same Moscow flight as me and Kim Willsher when we flew there to write about Chernobyl and a few other Eastern Bloc stories. Bizarrely, we all then ended up on the same overnight train to St Petersburg a few days later and, after sharing a couchette and staying up talking all night, became friends. When he told me he was looking to move from his flat in Waterloo, I offered him my spare room in Camberwell. This move gave him an immediate entrée to my friends and fellow photographers which eventually persuaded him to go freelance in 1991. Then the first Gulf War started, filling the paper with news of the conflict, and there were suddenly very few shifts going. With no work forthcoming, he applied for a job as a trainee insurance broker to make ends meet, but after Tom Stoddart and I drove him down to the interview and heard what kind of work he'd be doing, Tom made an announcement: 'There is no way you're doing that job,' he told Ian. 'We'll help you out and get you some work.'

For this and other reasons, Ian ended up living with me for almost four years and I took him on a few jobs to give him some work experience, in between boring him with my usual droning on about light and honesty, integrity and the importance of stepping away from the pack. When Ian asked me one day, 'What makes a good photograph?' I told him, 'Simple. It's good if I look at it and wish I'd taken it myself.' He says the best piece of advice I ever gave him, however, was, 'Shut up and listen!' He must have heeded it and he was a fast learner as he sat with me and mates like Tom Stoddart and Danny McGrory in pubs and restaurants soaking up our stories and reaping the benefit of our combined experience.

I think Ian – of all people – saw firsthand what a toll my passion for photography took on my personal life as I was dealing with the fallout from my relationship breakdown. He once said of me, 'When a big story happens it is like a switch goes off inside John, triggering 100% focus. Everything else is put to one side, including relationships. He is determined to be the best, and that drive and determination comes at a price.' I guess he was right.

I was delighted when Ian was taken on by the *Daily Telegraph* in 1992, a job he kept for fifteen years, covering everything from wars to royal stories. Six years later he was justifiably voted the Royal Photographer of the Decade and in 2000 he was chosen by the Palace to take Prince William's official eighteenth birthday photographs. Since then he has become an renowned cameraman of everything from sport to corporate events. I couldn't be more proud.

Hazel Thompson was nineteen when I first met her in 1998 and came from the *Croydon Advertiser* to Fleet Street for some work experience. A Christian teetotaller with a quiet faith, I gave her the nickname 'Archangel' and took her under my (far from angelic) wing, showing her the ropes and taking her on many of my UK-based jobs. In what was always an entirely platonic father/daughter relationship I invited her to cover the dawn of the new millennium with me in London and the wedding of Prince Edward and his bride Sophie. I called her 'Kid' and gave her the first £100 towards the pension that she now enjoys, and loaned her equipment and cameras, on top of whatever advice I could offer because I believed in her.

Everyone loves Hazel, who always lights up a room. She quickly became part of the family, joining me and my brothers for our traditional Sunday roast, Welsh dinners, and singalongs with Mum and Dad. She was the willing chauffeur of my silver Saab convertible so that I could have a drink, which was extra handy once I joined my brothers as a bass in the

London Welsh Male Voice Choir, because we always went for a pint or three after each concert. As with all my protégées, she knew that she could crash in my spare room whenever she wanted and that pretty much what was mine was hers. At the age of fifty-eight, I became her surrogate father – especially as her relationship with her own father was not at all close. I was even on standby to walk her down the aisle at her wedding, and I stepped in for the traditional 'Dad's dance' with her.

Tom Stoddart was also a great mentor to her and it was he who encouraged her to start entering competitions, many of which she won, including one with a winning portfolio about the biker gangs of America. Her career finally broke in 2005 when she went undercover in the Philippines to expose the horror of children in its prisons. This won her the prestigious Hodge Award for the *Observer* and threw her onto the international circuit. The *New York Times* offered her a contract and she spent the next decade travelling back and forth to India doing extraordinary reportage on the trafficking there, using her camera to gather evidence, and reporting on rape in the Congo and Sudan. I couldn't be more proud, and am happy that the little multi-tool penknife, complete with a compass, that I gave her years ago is now her talisman, carried on every assignment. Of me, Hazel says, 'John is my home,' and she wrote me a very touching poem, 'Penknife (An Ode to my Mentor)' for my 70th birthday with the same theme. In it, she ended with:

> Unknown places my adventures lead
> Giving me direction
> When I feel lost
> Pointing to the man
> That this compass once led to
> My inspiration
> To move forward
> A gauntlet to carry
> To run with
> Till it's my time
> To pass the penknife on.

When I look back on these youngsters now I am so grateful that I was able to help them. I still carry a lot of guilt about my personal life, so the fact that I offered the hand of friendship to those following in my footsteps redeems me somewhat – I hope.

FOURTEEN

A S I APPROACHED my sixtieth birthday I became disillusioned with the technological side of photography even though I accepted that it was an important and necessary breakthrough in newsgathering. That and the advent of colour was the biggest change in my career and completely new to those of us who grew up in the age of hot press black and white printing. We had a whole new set of skills to acquire and it felt like starting all over again.

I switched to digital Canon cameras along with everyone else but I missed my old Nikons and the challenge of getting the focus and the light right. It is fair to say that I never quite grasped the new technology, which only gave me a massive headache. In fact, I was hopeless, and I was ill-prepared for the changes. The picture desk sent me out with a sat phone that I couldn't work and a computer for which I had no training. They trained just one person on the desk, Neil McCarthy, and he would talk me through all my problems. I also relied heavily on the youngsters to show me what to do and my colleague Jonathan Buckmaster was my saviour, a young man who fully embraced new technology. In sheer frustration, I would phone him from some godforsaken place at some ungodly hour and cry, 'It's jammed again, Jonathan!'. Ignoring the complaints of his partner whose evening had also been disturbed, he would talk me down.

If I still couldn't get it right and was trying to wire photos from my home, he'd get dressed and come to Camberwell or I'd put the infernal machinery in my car and drive to him in East Dulwich. I would often be close to tears with frustration at myself for not being able to understand what he was telling me, but he was always incredibly patient and kind. It was he who taught me to carry a paperclip wherever I went to stick in the side of a machine and release the disk. I will forever be grateful to him for that valuable tip. Cheeky bugger that he is, though, he bought me a mug with a logo that read: *My Computer Hates Me*. I had to laugh.

Far more than the technical problems I had, though, was the fact that I just didn't love colour photography as much as black and white. Someone once said that when you take a photo in colour you can see the colour of people's clothes but when you take a photo in black and white, you can see the colour of their souls. I agreed wholeheartedly with that. Digital photography also took away all the excitement of running back to the darkroom. Instead I had to upload my photos (if I could) and go straight to the next job. I missed the atmosphere of the office with everyone rushing around, the noise and the buzz and the tension. You really felt you were at the heart of something.

The other issue with the advances in technology was that it put an end to the kind of foreign travel I had always enjoyed. In the old days we'd always be sent off to cover a news story in a distant land but with the speed of technology, including emails and social media, the first photos would arrive from overseas before we'd even made it to the airport. This meant staying home much more and covering stories that rarely excited me and with reporters I wasn't used to since my dear friend and colleague Danny McGrory had left the *Express* to join the *Times* in 1997. The time was looming for this old dinosaur to finally accept a change in climate.

All my life, I'd worried about how I would cope in retirement when I no longer had to go out and take photographs. With my feelings about digital and colour, though, I had already distanced myself from it in many ways and had finally done something I'd been meaning to do for years – join the London Welsh Male Voice Choir, which was first established in 1902. My brothers Andrew and David had been members for years along with my nephew Paul and I often took the photos for their monthly concerts all over the country. I have to admit to being envious as they stood proudly alongside their fellow singers in their scarlet jackets, black trousers, white shirts and black bow ties, but now I was a part of the respected 'Red Jackets' too. Singing with them took me straight back to my childhood in Llanelli and the joys of the rich Welsh voice. Several cheeky friends couldn't resist commenting that, when up on stage amongst those one hundred proud men, I had never been so smartly dressed.

Having realised that there really was a life beyond newspapers, I began to think more and more about retiring. It helped that the *Express* was unrecognisable from the newspaper I had joined as a kid in the fifties. It had gone from a respected Fleet Street black and white broadsheet renowned for its photographic coverage to a colour tabloid full of paparazzi shots. In 2000, it was bought by Richard Desmond, the publisher of *OK!* magazine as well as numerous soft-core porn mags, which affected me enormously as he seemed to me to stand for everything I hated and had stood against. Not surprisingly, the then Editor Rosie Boycott quit along with columnist Peter Hitchens and many others. Printer extraordinaire Larry Bartlett was long gone and the darkroom was a foreign country to me. It was time to think about getting out. When the paper started to make a series of redundancies as its circulation plummeted, I decided in 2001 to accept voluntary 'redundo' and cut my losses.

As if to endorse my decision, my final job for the paper was taking a photo of six bottles of shampoo for the women's page. Although my career hadn't all been about jumping on a plane and running off to the next adventure and there were plenty of routine jobs and a lot of standing about in the rain, this felt to me like the last straw – a pointless job for a newspaper I was no longer as proud of. The sad thing is that, after all those years there I didn't even have a retirement party, something Danny thought was a disgrace. Lots of people were being made redundant at the same time then so nobody made much fuss. Previous colleagues of mine had been 'banged out' of the building, when all the printers and every member of staff bangs something metal and makes a terrible racket as the person leaves, usually in tears. I was deeply envious of that. On my final day I simply emptied my desk into a black bin liner and walked down to the car park.

Not having to get up and go to work every day was a huge adjustment but I was very lucky because Nigel Skelsey, the picture editor of the *Sunday Telegraph*, immediately offered me one day a week so that I could keep my hand in. It was a position I kept for four years. The jobs he sent me on were much simpler and far less stressful as I didn't have to wire my photos, I could just bring them back to the office. One of the first he sent me on was to cover the World Cup play-off in Tehran in 2001, a game which was noteworthy because they were playing Ireland and – for the first time in history – the mullahs had agreed that forty female Irish fans were to be given special dispensation and allowed into the Azadi Stadium with the nine hundred Irish fans.

The rules governing their behaviour were extremely strict – they all had to wear long coats and hijab veils that covered any flesh or hair – and even though they complied, it was clear from the moment they took their seats that the 120,000 men in the venue strongly objected. Descending like a biblical swarm, their chants of 'Iran! Iran!' thundered around the terraces until the *adhan* called the faithful to prayer just before kick-off. The presence of the women had already sparked demonstrations and angry reactions from the clerics, but as it became clear that Ireland was going through to the next round on aggregate, things turned uglier still as the men started throwing missiles and making obscene gestures. As the game finished, the baying Iranians set fire to their programmes, tore down banners and vandalised the seats until the riot police were called. There was a tense stand-off until the women could be put on an Aer Lingus plane the following morning, where they could finally remove their veils.

I didn't miss the work but I was still addicted to the news and whenever a big story broke I'd wait for the phone call that never came. I also couldn't kick the habits of a lifetime that included always sleeping with the curtains open a few inches so that I'd know what room – and which country – I was in if I woke in the night. Or sitting in neither the front or rear carriages on a train (too many crashes covered) and within five rows of the exits on a plane (ditto). I also took to carrying the 'Mary Poppins' bag I had so wished I'd had in Sudan and elsewhere everywhere I went, filling a man bag with everything from a first aid kit to a screwdriver. This became a running joke amongst my friends and family who teased me that they'd never likely need a tool to remove a stone from a horse's hoof and that malaria tablets weren't a requirement in the Home Counties. They were nevertheless grateful whenever they needed a pair of scissors, a sticking plaster, a battery, or a needle and thread and I rummaged around in my bag to find them just the thing.

Most of all, though, I missed all the wonderful people I had worked with, although Danny and I remained very close even after he left the *Express*. Tragically, he and Ross Benson died two years apart not long after I retired completely. Ross, who'd become a diary editor for the *Mail* but still traded on his languid persona of a Peter Pan character who never wanted to grow up, died of a heart attack aged fifty-six. A keen supporter of Chelsea football club he had just returned from watching his team beat Barcelona at Stamford Bridge and died in his own bed. Married three times, he left a widow the royal biographer Ingrid Seward and three children. As usual, of course, there was some gallows humour involved at his funeral in a church in West London, when Tom Stoddart and I couldn't help but notice that amongst the mourners there was a higher than usual percentage of pretty women with dyed blonde hair, almost as well groomed as his had always been.

Dear Danny died in 2007 aged fifty-four from a brain haemorrhage shortly after returning from an assignment for *The Times* about a forthcoming terrorist trial in Pakistan. He had recently been reporting on the death of Russian dissident Alexander Litvinenko and had written a book about Islamic extremism. The post mortem found that the haemorrhage was exacerbated by the fact that he had 'an unusually big heart,' which came as no surprise to those of us who knew and loved him. Danny, who had survived so many war zones and was almost killed in Iraq in 2003 when ambushed by militia, left behind his wife, the reporter Liz Gill, and two children, Anna and James. The loss of Danny especially felt hard to me, and I was enormously privileged to be asked to give a reading at his funeral held in a church in Hampstead. He also had a splendid memorial service at the journalists' church, St Bride's.

Luckily for me, I wasn't alone at both funerals for in 2004 I met a wonderful young woman and a marvellous pianist by the name of Anita D'Attellis, in a rather unusual way. Anita was the accompanist to the London Welsh Male Voice Choir for about a year. She also worked in a small but posh private school called Trevor-Roberts in Hampstead, whose students included the children of Jude Law, Lesley Garratt and Anish Kapoor to name a few. Wanting a change, she applied for the Head of Keyboard at Sherborne Girls School in Dorset and was immediately offered the job. This meant leaving London – and the choir.

I have to admit that I'd hardly noticed her in the rehearsals at first even though she was the only woman in a room of a hundred men (can you believe that of me?) But on the night of Anita's last concert with us at the Hawth Theatre in Crawley, Sussex, everyone congregated in the theatre bar for a send-off drink. I was late arriving after taking some photos and doing my usual last minute check of the changing room for anything we might have left behind. As luck would have it, my two brothers were chatting with Anita and I joined them just at the point in the conversation when David explained that it was his birthday the following day. Kindly, he invited Anita to join our Sunday family lunch at a nearby Italian restaurant. After some persuasion she agreed, so I entered her name and number into my phone, and gave her my business card telling her to ring me in the morning and I'd pick her up.

After a lovely evening with the rest of the choir, I eventually drove back to my new home in Shad Thames in the early hours of the morning when my car phone rang. The name Anita D'Attellis flashed up on the screen and I have to say my hopes took a leap. Who knew, maybe it would be my lucky night. Answering the call, her warm voice filled the car: 'Is that John? John Downing? The chap I met earlier with the choir?'

'Yes,' I replied, eagerly.

'I've tried phoning everyone I know and no one else is answering,' she said, and for the first time I could hear panic in her voice. She added, 'There is only you left.' The plane that had been flying high took a sudden downward spiral.

'Well, it is half past one in the morning,' I reasoned, trying to cover my disappointment. 'What's the matter?' It soon transpired that she'd arrived home from the bar to discover that her flat had been broken into. She had called the police but they weren't intending to visit until the following morning and she was frightened the burglars might return.

'Do you want me to come over?' I asked, gallantly. When she said yes, I asked, 'Where do you live?' It was Wembley. Bloody Wembley. That was right the other side of London from where I was, a good hour's drive. Still, a promise is a promise, so I turned up on her doorstep some considerable time later.

Had I carried any hope that there may be a few embers of passion left knocking around that was quickly dissipated when a tousled apparition opened the door in grey, passion-killer pyjamas with a little girl lost expression. I did stay the night in the end – but on the settee. Despite the fact that I was twice her age it was the start of a wonderful relationship. And if the burglar happens to be reading this, I'm offering him a reward for the introduction.

The year after I met Anita, I gave up freelancing for the *Sunday Telegraph* and never took any more news pictures. I rarely took photographs again and quite enjoyed having nothing to do, apart from the choir and my music and her. Anita was very pleased to have met me when she did, as she says she wouldn't have appreciated me disappearing to dangerous places all the time. Not that anyone ever did.

We were married in Weybridge Registry Office on July 4, 2007 – which was Independence Day in the US, ironically. When she recited her wedding vows and promised to take me as her husband 'for better for worse, richer or poorer, in sickness and in health,' the poor girl had no idea what she was letting herself in for. We had a lovely reception in the Orangery of Foxhills Golf Club near Ottershaw in Surrey before I took her on honeymoon to South Africa. By chance this happened to be courtesy of a British Airways competition I'd won seven years earlier. My winning photo was of the London Eye in the morning mist at sunrise and my prize was two first class tickets to anywhere in the world, but I was travelling so much then that it took me years to use them. Generously, BA agreed to honour them even after all that time.

Anita, who grew up in Essex and had not travelled as widely as I had, always wanted to go on safari so I suggested South Africa. As luck would have it – a good friend and freelance journalist Paula Kerr had just landed a job with an exclusive South African travel company so she kindly arranged everything. We flew to Cape Town and hired a car before doing the 'Garden Route,' five-star all the way. We stayed in the Shamwari Game Reserve outside Port Elizabeth on the Eastern Cape, where we saw lions and leopards and white rhino. When they discovered that we were on honeymoon they kindly upgraded us to a premier lodge at the Eagles Crag, where all sorts of Hollywood stars had stayed. It was very romantic.

After I'd made an honest woman of her, Anita gave up her job in Dorset and found work as a piano teacher at Eton College so we both sold our respective homes and resolved to move to the Thames Valley, settling on a lovely apartment in the centre of Henley. The joke was that we needed a place big enough for her grand piano (I bought her a Bösendorfer) and she needed a handbag big enough for my camera when I finally gave up the Mary Poppins bag. We took up kayaking on the Thames and had lovely holidays around the UK and all over the world with longtime friends Bob Hay and his wife Pauline, and Malcolm and Julia Lockwood.

For five years I also worked as a volunteer keeper one day a week at Shiplake lock alongside lock keeper Andy Feak, who operated out of a picturesque rose covered cabin and was a joy to be with. I also joined a local choral society as well as joyfully keeping all my singing commitments with the Male Voice Choir. It was with great pride that I wore my MBE on my red jacket at several of our concerts, including at the Cenotaph in London for Remembrance Sunday in 2008, in Ypres, Belgium with the Royal British Legion to mark the end of World War I and at Buckingham Palace for Prince Charles's seventieth birthday in 2018.

Even though I'd retired, I continued to receive further honours and was granted an Honorary Fellowship to the Royal Society of Photographers in 2011, and became a life member of The British Press Photographers' Association, two glorious accolades for doing a job I loved doing. Perhaps the greatest award though was receiving the Lifetime Achievement Award from the Picture Editors Guild, which was only the second time it had ever been awarded. For that ceremony, they sprang a surprise on me when I suddenly heard singing and thought, 'What's that?' Then my choir was brought on singing. That award was undoubtedly the most emotional and finally reduced me to tears, as it was the highest compliment to be so highly judged by my peers.

My third – and final – marriage coupled with retirement has been very good for me. After a high-octane lifetime of running to catch planes or to meet deadlines, I can finally take my time. I have mellowed and relaxed. Since the day Anita came into my life, she has been my saviour in every possible way. She organises my entire life, she is my friend and my companion and my lover and I love her very much. She was also able to help me through some of the saddest times of my life – losing Danny and Ross to begin with – and then my son Gareth who died of lung cancer in 2007, leaving a wife and two children, Oliver and Ellie. I had told Gareth time and again to stop smoking but he wouldn't, so it was even harder to watch him suffer and go into a hospice when it was self-inflicted.

Happily, I was reconciled with him by the end, especially after he was diagnosed. We had a lovely relationship from the outset and we never lost that, in spite of our bad start, and we were close. We loved being together and I have such fond memories of him despite our forced separation when he was younger. My first wife Barbara was still alive when he died (she died not long after) and she organised his funeral. I went with Anita, Bryn and a few close relatives and friends and was very hurt by the fact that nothing in the service or eulogies even mentioned me. It was if I didn't exist.

Then in 2010 my dear old Mum died, at the age of ninety-seven. She'd been charging about everywhere up until the point when she broke her hip at the age of ninety-two. But even then she wouldn't give in and still enjoyed life and loved seeing her boys and her grandchildren and catching up on all our news. She'd jump at the chance to be taken out anywhere and only three weeks before she died she went for a family curry. Glenys Downing had been a nurse and a Navy wife, a mother and a teacher. She'd lived through a world war, was widowed, lost a grandson and no doubt suffered all kinds of anxieties from the days when I went missing in Llanelli right up until my latest war exploits. She deserved a rest.

It wasn't all bad news, though. In 2016 Bryn, now running his own film production company, decided to make a documentary about me, entitled

Behind the Lens. As Bryn said, he'd heard so many of my stories over the years that he wanted to record them for his children and anyone else who might be interested. We spent a day filming in a freezing cold warehouse in London, a day that provoked a mixture of laughter and tears, and then we spent a few weeks editing it with my photographs until we had a 35-minute film we were happy with. Bryn was so pleased with it that he secretly entered it in a couple of film festivals and – to my amazement – it received an outstanding achievement award at the Berlin Flash Film Festival and then won the Crystal Palace International Film Festival. That was a wonderful moment in my life when Bryn and I stepped up to collect our award, with his fantastic team from INP Media. It is really something to be recognised alongside your son. I have made my mark on the world and he had made his, but sharing that success together was very special.

My cancer diagnosis in January 2019 came as a horrible shock after a lifetime of good health. When the consultant came in, sat down, and told me, 'I'm afraid it's bad news, John. It's the disease we thought it might be and it's incurable.'

Anita was understandably devastated but – although disappointed with the word 'incurable' – I took it all on board and didn't break down at all. I just couldn't feel down. It brought home to me that I have had a long and happy life and lived to a good age. This is the natural order of things. It was Anita I felt for more, as she'd had every reason to believe that we would have longer together. It was only when we were driving home that it struck me that this was it, but even then I remained very philosophical about it and the first thing I did when we got home was open a bottle of champagne.

In one of the umpteen hospital appointments that followed I remember that Anita and I were sitting in a stark and sterile hospital waiting room for the latest results when I noticed how the sun's rays were shining through the slatted blinds of the window to make an interesting pattern on the floor. On auto-pilot, I pulled out my camera and took a photo of it. Minutes later, after hearing the bad news, I looked back down at the floor and noticing that the geometric pattern of sunlight was still there, just as before, and I found some strength and beauty in that.

Thinking of Anita, I agreed to have surgery to remove most of the tumour from the lining of my lung but they couldn't get it all out because it was too close to my aorta. My brothers and my darling niece Hannah (who always cheers me up) came to see me in hospital after the surgery and I was very poorly. I still made them laugh, though, when Andrew – having commented how dreadful I looked – added, 'I bet you don't have your camera with you now, John!' Pointing to a drawer, I made him open it and there it was, just in case.

When I declined any further treatment or chemotherapy and decided to carry on for as long as I could, my specialist Dr Brown agreed. He told me, 'It's time to start ticking things off your bucket list.'

'I don't have one,' I told him. 'I've done pretty much most of the things I always wanted to do.' Thinking about what he said afterwards, though, I realised that I'd always wanted to ride on a zip wire I'd seen in North Wales so others quickly arranged it and we went with friends and family to Zip World in the former Penrhyn slate quarry near Snowdon; the longest and fastest zip wire in Europe. Hazel Thompson came, along with our friend Paula Kerr and Hannah, my niece, so we all had a go while my brothers watched from afar. It was fun, but I found it a bit too tame for me.

Paula then suggested I try a parachute jump and Hazel and Hannah thought that was a great idea and said they'd do it too, so in August 2019, we all went to the Chiltern Aerodrome near Woodcote in Oxon and prepared ourselves to jump while Anita and a handful of supporters waited excitedly with cameras on the periphery of the airstrip. I had been told by the doctors that going to any sort of altitude could exacerbate my illness, and the instructors at the airfield asked me to take a breath capacity test before the jump. In light of the results it was agreed that I would jump out of a light aeroplane strapped to my instructor at eight thousand feet while the others went up to the normal ten thousand feet to do their jumps. It was so exhilarating and quite scary but I was happy to do it and – on a word from my instructor – we leapt out together to fall freely through the air while being filmed for posterity by someone who jumped ahead of us. It was a brilliant four minutes and fifty-five seconds. The weather was lovely and sunny so I could see the whole Thames Valley in all its beauty.

Far too soon, it felt, the instructor pulled the cord, our parachute opened and we prepared to touch down but unfortunately I got unlucky with the landing. I stretched out my legs as instructed but my heel clipped an uneven patch of turf, which badly snapped my left thighbone. I heard my leg crack right up near my hip, so I knew immediately that something was wrong. I've never broken anything before but I've worked in some pretty hairy places so I kept calm and knew to lie still and wait for help.

Anita and friends were all watching and cheering from the sidelines but they weren't allowed onto a 'live' airfield, so you can imagine her alarm when not only didn't I stand up and do a victory wave but there were suddenly loads of people crowding around me on the ground. Someone took her to the office where they could radio the instructor and it was there that she heard I'd landed badly and had probably broken my leg but she didn't know much more than that. She had to watch, helplessly, as an ambulance arrived and – having assessed me – summoned the air ambulance, which wasn't far behind. I was in agony if I tried to move so they gave me an injection and the next thing I remember was being in the air on my way to the hospital. I thought this somewhat ironic because I took the pictures of London's first air ambulance after the *Express* raised the money for it and now there I was as a patient, something I never thought I'd end up being.

I was finally reunited with a frantic Anita in hospital before I was taken to theatre to have my leg pinned back together with titanium screws. As I was seventy-nine years old, they kept me under observation for a week before discharging me. It was a pretty nasty break but I was delighted to be told by the doctors that I had the bones of a man twenty years younger. I'm still very glad I completed the jump and I don't regret it at all. You've got to try these things. In fact, try everything. I did.

The next thing on my short bucket list was to produce a book of my photographs after fifty years in Fleet Street. I have always been so full of gratitude that I was the man behind the camera and privileged enough to witness some of the most dramatic world events of our time and I wanted to share some of those experiences with others. Sadly, the *Express* sold its picture library so a lot of my photos were lost forever and I never had the time to make up much of a personal collection. I'd kept a few prints when I was entering competitions, but I didn't have the matching dates times or captions. Luckily the picture agency Getty Images had some of the photos and generously let me have them. They were also helpful at digging out shots I never thought I'd see again. And I had my old dad's scrapbooks of my cuttings, ten large books of them all lovingly clipped from the paper with pride, which were a great help.

Some friends set up a crowd-funding campaign for me, which I doubted would work but it raised more than £30,000 for the book in weeks. I was amazed and touched. The launch of my huge hardback book *Legacy*, beautifully published by Bluecoat in November 2019, and featuring 150 photographs, was at the London Welsh Centre. Dozens of friends and family came and the thing that finally reduced me to tears after an evening of speeches and high emotion was the arrival of the London Welsh Male Voice Choir as they sang some of my favourite songs and Anita played the piano. It was truly a night to remember. Many a tear was shed that evening.

The thing about knowing you are going to die is that you get a unique chance to reflect back on your life and look at it almost from afar. I know that I have been extremely lucky. My career has spanned many years and every continent and I've met some wonderful people and covered some great stories as well as some harrowing ones. The children with the dead eyes still haunt me but even then I had to keep going. I was the eyes of my reader and it was my job to get the pictures back. Now the only photographs I take are of Bryn's two girls Olivia and Madeleine and Anita's lovely nieces, whom I all love equally.

My greatest ambition – which I think should be the ambition of every photographer worth his or her salt – was to create pictures that would outlast my lifetime; and hopefully to create one or two that would be so good that they would be famous long after I stopped taking pictures. A general rule of thumb is that a good pro takes ten or so high-grade photographs a year but even then it would be hard to choose outstanding ones from those. My dear departed father told me right from the start to focus on the quality; that quality would always stand out. I heeded his advice and I hope that with a few of my pictures at least, I might have actually achieved that. How many people can say that they have done what they set out to do? Not bad for a boy who was branded as: 'thoroughly idle; the only thing in which he is thorough' or a man with the 'face of a truck driver, soul of a poet.' Now, that wouldn't be a bad epitaph.

Talking of which, when I finally shuffle off this mortal coil, I know exactly what my funeral will be like and where I want my ashes to be scattered. For the service I have chosen the piece of music I'd like to be played at my funeral – the beautiful 'Nocturne in C Sharp Minor' by Chopin – to be played by Anita if she can manage it. Then, after my crema-tion, I want her and the family to take my ashes to a beautiful hidden cove called Mwnt on the rugged Ceredigion coast near Cardigan Bay. Dolphins splash in the waves and there is something serene and lonely and rather wild and wonderful about the place. A single-track road leads over a cattle grid and then there are steep steps down to the secluded sandy beach, now owned by the National Trust.

I first took Anita there after my diagnosis and together we wandered to the little white chapel at the top of the cliff, which is thought to date back to the thirteenth century. Inside the Church of the Holy Cross, all is simple and peaceful with whitewashed walls and a few wooden pews, some arched oak beams, and a few small, unadorned windows. It smelt of the sea.

At the back of the tiny chapel, Anita found a little wooden organ of the kind that had to be pumped up with pedals. Sitting on the organist's threadbare seat, she managed to prime the rickety old instrument as I took my place in the pew. Gradually, she coaxed a few notes out of it and began to play a hymn that I must have sung with my brothers and fellow choir members a hundred times – 'Blaenwern', perhaps better known as 'Love Divine, All Loves Excelling'. It had never sounded more beautiful to me than in that peaceful place.

Sitting there filled with gratitude and love, I softly sang along in Welsh: '*Anadlwch, O anadlwch eich ysbryd cariadus*'… 'Breathe, O breathe thy loving spirit, into every troubled breast. Let us all in thee inherit, Let us find thy promised rest…'

Amen to that.

THE END

ACKNOWLEDGEMENTS

I've laid great store in friendship all my life and have been lucky enough to work alongside some outstanding colleagues over the years. There are far too many to name here, but special mention must go to my comrades-in-arms and friends Ross Benson, Danny McGrory, Hazel Thompson, Tom Smith and the internationally renowned photographer Tom Stoddart.

Ross and Danny were brilliant reporters who worked with me hand in glove. Sadly both passed away far too young. Danny and I were especially close and I miss him still. My son Bryn has been a source of great pride and joy to me over the years and I am proud and happy to be a grandfather to his two lovely girls, Olivia and Madeleine.

This book couldn't have been completed without the help of Wendy Holden, a former journalist and war correspondent turned bestselling author (and a friend for thirty years) who dropped everything to meet my somewhat pressing deadline. Wendy is grateful to all those who helped her with her background research including Paul Massey, Jonathan Evans, Roger Allan, John Rogers, Colin Davey, Malcolm Brabant and especially my loyal brothers Andrew and David, who have come to mean so much to me. We are all of us grateful to Getty Images for allowing the use of seven of the news images published in this book and, in particular, Matthew Butson, Vice President of the Hulton Archive, and Stephen Kirkby. The London Welsh Male Voice Choir has given me twenty years of undiluted pleasure as a member (now an audience member) and I thank them all very much.

When I met and married Anita, my wife of fourteen years, nobody thought our marriage would last. She may be half my age but she has twice my compassion and patience, and has fulfilled her vow of 'in sickness and health' a thousand times over. She is young enough and musically talented enough to have a full and rewarding life long after her time with me and I wish her nothing but blue skies and easy chords.

John Downing

WENDY HOLDEN was a respected journalist and war correspondent for the *Daily Telegraph*, covering news stories around the world. She is also the author of more than thirty non-fiction titles featuring inspirational men and women, many of which are international bestsellers and several of which are being adapted for film. They include the No.1 bestseller *Tomorrow Will Be A Good Day, the memoir of Captain Sir Tom Moore*, the 100-year-old war veteran who raised £40m for the NHS, and *Born Survivors* the story of three mothers who hid their pregnancies from the Nazis, now published in 22 countries.

Index